J.D. MOYER

THE LAST CRUCIBLE

This is a **FLAME TREE PRESS** book

Text copyright © 2021 J.D. Moyer

FLAME TREE PRESS
6 Melbray Mews, London, SW6 3NS, UK
flametreepress.com

US sales, distribution and warehouse:
Simon & Schuster
simonandschuster.biz

UK distribution and warehouse:
Marston Book Services Ltd
marston.co.uk

Publisher's Note: This is a work of fiction. Names, characters, places, and incidents are a product of the author's imagination. Locales and public names are sometimes used for atmospheric purposes. Any resemblance to actual people, living or dead, or to businesses, companies, events, institutions, or locales is completely coincidental.

Thanks to the Flame Tree Press team, including:
Taylor Bentley, Frances Bodiam, Federica Ciaravella, Don D'Auria,
Chris Herbert, Josie Karani, Molly Rosevear, Mike Spender,
Cat Taylor, Maria Tissot, Nick Wells, Gillian Whitaker.

The cover is created by Flame Tree Studio with
thanks to Nik Keevil and Shutterstock.com.
The font families used are Avenir and Bembo.

Flame Tree Press is an imprint of Flame Tree Publishing Ltd
flametreepublishing.com

A copy of the CIP data for this book is available from the British Library
and the Library of Congress.

HB ISBN: 978-1-78758-588-1
US PB ISBN: 978-1-78758-586-7
UK PB ISBN: 978-1-78758-587-4
UK PB ISBN: 978-1-78758-587-4
ebook ISBN: 978-1-78758-589-8

Printed and bound in Great Britain by Clays Ltd, Elcograf S.p.A.

J.D. MOYER

THE LAST
CRUCIBLE

FLAME TREE PRESS
London & New York

For my parents

PROLOGUE

Director Balasubramanian sipped his tea while reviewing the reports from the *Stanford*'s Repopulation Council. The ringstations were repopulating Earth at a rate much faster than anticipated. It had started with the *Stanford*'s own research station declaring independence. The *Liu Hui* had responded by building an even larger settlement on the island that had once been Taiwan, and more recently the *Alhazen* and *Hedonark* had founded their own towns.

The Ringstation Coalition was a tenuous alliance. Its members shared a joint Human Rights Charter and Ecological Charter, but there were no provisions for enforcement. If one of the communities started torturing and executing people, or strip mining and clear-cutting, all Bala could do was wag his finger.

There were existing communities on Earth to consider as well, those that had survived civilization's fall and the great eruption of Campi Flegrei. Repop, for many years, had observed a strict policy of Non-Interventionism. But that had broken down when a *Stanford* anthropologist had fallen in love with one of her subjects, and then had a child with him.

"Director, I'm sorry to bother you."

He looked up to see Zinthia, a bright young woman who worked as a liaison between Repop and the Security Council.

"No bother at all, Zin. How can I help you?"

"Security wanted you to know that the *Michelangelo* is approaching. It looks as if they'll be moving into a geosynchronous orbit within a few days."

"Around Earth?" he asked. Zinthia nodded. It was a stupid question, but Bala was dumbfounded. The *Michelangelo* had resided in the outer solar system for decades, powered by a fusion core. "Have they responded to hails?"

"Not so far."

The *Michelangelo* had started off as a museum ship, hosting and protecting many of Earth's great historical artworks. But gradually the *Michelangelo* had slid into isolationism, cutting off communications with the *Stanford* and the other ringstations. There were rumors that its inhabitants had gone mad, becoming paranoid and investing their resources into deadly weapons systems.

"Well, I look forward to welcoming them. Maybe we can be reunited with some of Earth's long-lost artistic treasures."

Zinthia nodded and excused herself, handing him a viewing tablet on her way out. The tablet displayed a visual recording of the *Michelangelo*, which was now close enough for detailed telescopic observations.

The habitat ship, a black, rotating cylinder dotted with blue and violet lights, was vast in scale, dwarfing even the *Liu Hui*. What if the rumors were true, that its inhabitants had gone mad? And why were they returning to Earth orbit?

Bala tossed the tablet onto his desk, accidentally knocking over his tea. The hot liquid spilled and dripped onto his pant leg, burning painfully.

PART ONE
THE MAGHIARJA
CHAPTER ONE

Sardinia, 2757

Jana struggled to guide the plow behind Pinna, a hulking red ox. Where the blade cut the earth, it revealed rich, black volcanic soil, but it kept getting caught on rocks. And now Pinna had stopped entirely.

"What is it?" She patted the huge beast, which she had seen birthed by its mother when she was just a child, and looked to see why it had stopped. A half-buried boulder blocked their progress. She squatted and tried to lift it, but her lanky arms strained uselessly against the big rock. She considered just going around the obstacle, but she knew Papà would be displeased. He wouldn't scold her – he was a gentle, quiet man by nature – but his own fields were always plowed in perfectly straight lines. Not only that, but he arranged his tools carefully, kept their house neat and tidy, and generally abhorred disorderliness of any kind. Jana didn't mind a little chaos herself, but if she went around the boulder it would drive Papà crazy, like an itch he couldn't scratch.

"Antonio! Cristo! Come help me!"

The young men were lounging beneath an oak tree, passing a pipe back and forth, most likely gossiping about women. Probably about Filumena in particular, even though Cristo was engaged to Sabina.

"We're still eating lunch!" Cristo yelled back. They'd finished lunch – barley bread with olives, cheese, and fresh tomatoes – nearly an hour ago. Jana was already starting to get hungry again.

"Wait here, Pinna." She patted the ox again and jogged over to where Cristo and Antonio were lounging. Searching the ground, she found what she was looking for: a sturdy oak branch. Cristo flinched when she picked it up.

"Come help me move this rock, if you think you're strong enough."

She dug away at the loose earth beneath the boulder and drove the branch in as far underneath as she could. Using the branch for leverage, she was able to budge the rock, just barely.

"Here, let me try," Cristo said, handing his corkwood pipe to Antonio. As she'd predicted, posing the task as a test of strength had snapped the boys out of their slothful stupor. Cristo grabbed the oak branch and heaved, grunting loudly. The boulder moved a few centimeters.

"That's not going to work," Antonio observed.

Cristo heaved and grunted again, with similar results. "Do you have a better idea?"

"We could harness the ox to the rock. Pinna is strong enough to drag it."

Jana frowned. "That was my first thought, but we'd have to go back to town for rope. And tying the plow to the boulder might be difficult."

Antonio nodded. He was more reasonable and thoughtful than Cristo. "What do you think, Jana? Any ideas?"

"Just leave it there and go around it," Cristo said.

"My father wouldn't like that."

"Well, then have *him* come move it." Cristo didn't like Papà, but Cristo's father and her own father had been friends since childhood. Cristo was obligated to help when asked.

"We could ask Sperancia to move it," Antonio suggested.

Jana hated to ask Sperancia to do manual labor; the old woman had enough on her plate with doctoring and teaching. But it would probably be the fastest way to move the boulder.

"*You* can ask her," said Cristo. "I'm scared of her." There was no shame in being afraid of the village *maghiarja*, as she was sometimes called. A word from the old language: a sorceress. It wasn't that Sperancia would curse you or give you the evil eye, but it was easy to feel judged when she looked at you. She was old – at least a century and maybe two – and had strict notions of how people should behave. Those she disapproved of heard about it at length. And one didn't interrupt Sperancia or treat her with anything other than the utmost respect. Not only because of her venerable age, but because she was strong enough to kill a pig with a single punch to its forehead. Or to move a heavy boulder with her bare hands.

"I suppose I can go to town and get some rope," Jana said. "Will one of you unharness Pinna and lead him to the shade?"

Jana tried to stay in the shade herself on the path back to town, walking on the edge of the packed earth road. Evergreen and cork oak forests covered most of the island of Sardinia, or at least the parts Jana had seen, with the exception of the coastal areas where some gardeners grew artichokes. Sperancia said she could remember a time when the forests hadn't been so thick and oppressive, a time when people had cut down so many trees that the sea had eroded the soil and made the land barren. The volcanic eruptions on the mainland had fixed that problem, depositing huge amounts of mineral-rich ash all around the Mediterranean. Unfortunately those same eruptions had killed nearly everyone in Europe, but winds had sheltered the people on the western coast of Sardinia. Those survivors were Jana's ancestors.

The island had gotten bigger over the centuries, not just from the ash fall, but because the oceans had receded. Sperancia said that the water had been sucked up and away into the ice fields, far to the north and south, great expanses of glaciers that flattened forests and the remains of once-great cities, pulverizing metal and stone alike. It was hard for Jana to imagine such things; she'd only seen ice in thin, clear crusts over still water on the coldest winter mornings. But Sperancia insisted on the existence of entire mountains made of ice, kilometers high.

Jana wasn't exactly clear on how Sperancia could know or remember all this. If Sperancia was as old as she claimed, she'd been born in the 2600s, or the mid-2500s at the earliest. If Jana remembered her history correctly, the Campi Flegrei cauldron had erupted in 2387. Sperancia claimed that she talked to her ancestors directly, that they lived inside of her somehow. Did she mean that literally, or did the old sorceress just have a colorful way of describing her internal dialogues? Jana sometimes imagined conversations with Nonna Ànghela, her father's mother, who had died a few years ago, the day after Jana's eighteenth birthday. But Nonna Ànghela didn't live inside of Jana, not really. She was dead and buried in the cemetery.

She supposed she would find out the truth soon enough. The Crucible ceremony was in midsummer, only a few months away.

She arrived home, entering through the side gate into the garden, where she guessed she would find her father, Leandro, tending his tomato vines, greens, potatoes, carrots, and mirto berries. Like most people in town he spent much of his time growing and preparing food. Those who didn't garden or tend orchards spent their days in fishing boats, hauling in huge amberjacks or giant black grouper that could feed a family for a week. Those who lived upriver in the hills that fed the Temo herded sheep and goats or grew grapes and olives. Plowing fields and planting grain – barley and farro – was a relatively new tradition pioneered by Sperancia, who had gathered wild variants descended from ancient island crops gone to seed. Though the soil was rich, it was difficult to find open fields, and preparing an area for planting meant clearing trees and burning out the stumps. Jana's father was one of the few willing to put in the work. The rewards – dense bread and rich, nutty grain dishes – were delicious, but Jana wasn't sure it was all worth it. Her arms were sore from guiding the plow, and the winter barley wouldn't be ready to harvest for months. Other sources of food produced results more quickly: goats gave milk every day; a fisherman could eat his catch the same day; tomatoes could ripen overnight. But Sperancia was always pushing for new ways of doing things, while at the same time keeping the old ways alive. The old woman seemed to know everything, either from reading ancient books or from the direct experiences of her long life.

"Papà!" She called for her father several times but no one answered. She checked inside the house to make sure he wasn't napping, and again in the garden, but he was nowhere to be found. Maybe he'd joined Cristo's father at the bar for a glass of wine. Though it would be unusual for him to stop working so early in the day.

She found a length of oak-bark rope in the toolshed, closed the side gate, and started back up the road to the field.

"Jana Manca – come here!" It was Filumena, beckoning her from down the road.

Jana's heart sped up, as it always did when she saw her best friend. She knew she wasn't unique in that regard. Filumena, with her long, brown hair, olive-gold skin, and strong, supple body, set many hearts aflutter. Not only because of her beauty, but because she was big-hearted and gracious, loving others as much as she was loved. Filumena was kind to children, to grandparents, to nearly everyone.

"What is it?"

"Jisepu said he saw something while fishing. He's telling everyone about it at Micheli's."

"What did he see? A whale? A turtle as big as a house? A kingfish longer than his boat?"

"No, not another one of his fishing tales. He's seen visitors. And they want to meet with us."

"Visitors from where? From the mainland? I didn't think anyone lived there."

"C'mon! Leave that rope and come with me."

"Antonio and Cristo are waiting for me up at the new field."

Filumena scowled at hearing Cristo's name. "Let them wait."

Jana hung the loops of rope on a nearby branch and took Filumena's extended hand. Filumena started to skip, not daintily but taking huge leaps with each step, just as they'd done as children. Jana had to do the same to keep up. For a moment she actually felt good in her own body. What came naturally for Filumena, to feel and act physically comfortable, was a struggle for Jana. She didn't hate her body – it functioned well enough. But nor did she feel connected to her lanky frame. Nor did she enjoy looking at her pale skin and big nose and wide, awkward mouth in the mirror. Filumena could look at her own reflection, brushing or arranging her hair, and seem satisfied, even absorbed in her own image. But Jana passed mirrors as quickly as possible.

Minutes later, they'd reached the town square. While most of Bosa was in ruins, surrendered to time, much of the old town was still intact. Stonework from as far back as Roman times, though chipped and cracked and crooked, remained standing. The town masons did as much as they could to preserve and repair the oldest buildings.

Dozens were crowded into Micheli's restaurant-bar, listening to Jisepu's tale. She saw her father in the front row. He nodded solemnly when she caught his eye, then returned his attention to Jisepu.

"How did their boat fly?" someone asked. "Did it have wings?"

"I don't know," Jisepu answered, twirling his mustache. "It hovered above the water like a gull catching the wind, but it had no wings."

"What language did they speak?"

"Italian. Only the red-haired woman spoke. Her accent was strange, but I understood her. But she also addressed me in the old language."

"In Sardo?" Jana's father asked.

"Yes. I recognized a few words."

"How could she have learned the old language?" someone asked.

"Nobody here is fluent except for Sperancia." Jana scanned the crowd but didn't see the old woman.

"I don't know."

"What do they want?"

"They said they want to meet with us, to talk and share knowledge. They're coming to the docks tomorrow morning."

"Did they have weapons?" her father asked.

"None that I saw. They seemed friendly."

"Maybe too friendly?" asked Iginu, Cristo's father. He was a good man, kinder than his son, but careful and suspicious.

"Maybe."

"What questions did they ask you?" Filumena asked. It was an insightful question, Jana thought.

"They didn't ask me anything!" Jisepu answered, surprised by the realization. "They knew about Bosa, about the docks, that we are many."

"They've been spying on us!" Iginu shouted, banging on the bar.

"Calm down." Sperancia had not shouted, but the room went silent as if she had. People made way for the maghiarja as she approached Jisepu. She was tall for a woman, and stood perfectly straight, her spine unbent by age. Her face was lean and craggy but had few wrinkles. Where her skin was thinnest, around her eyes and temples, a fine latticework of black threads was visible beneath her deep tan.

"Tell me everything, from the beginning," she said. Jisepu nodded and complied.

Jisepu and Zorzi had been out fishing as usual. They'd gotten a late start – Zorzi had been drinking the night before – but had still managed to net a good haul. They were about to head back to shore for lunch when Jisepu had spotted another boat on the horizon. They'd waved, thinking it was Nevio or another fisherman, but the vessel had approached them rapidly, faster than any boat. Zorzi had wanted to flee (at least according to Jisepu – Zorzi was now napping and could not say differently), but Jisepu had readied his oar as a club, ready to bash in the brains of whatever Corsican savage or other pirate dared threaten them.

But the vessel had slowed as it neared them. It had hovered like a bird over the water, and was made of materials other than wood. Maybe metal, but how could something heavy float like that?

An older, red-haired woman had hailed them. She'd introduced herself as Ingrid, speaking Italian, and then repeating herself in the old language. She'd introduced her companions: Tem, a strong-looking young man with long, dark hair and light brown skin, and Lydia, a woman about the same age as Ingrid, with pale skin.

"Did they resemble each other?" Sperancia interrupted to ask. "Were they of the same family, or kin group?"

Jisepu shook his head definitively. "Not at all. They looked as unlike each other in features as they looked unlike us."

"And only the red-haired woman – Ingrid – only she spoke to you?"

"Yes. Though the others appeared to understand, and they conversed with each other in another language."

"Did the other language sound like this?" Sperancia said something in an unfamiliar tongue.

"Maybe. I couldn't say for sure. They were speaking quietly to each other."

"Go on."

Jisepu continued his story, enjoying the attention. The old fisherman was happy to talk forever, but Jana had heard enough. If Jisepu was telling the truth, the visitors would be back the next day. She would be there, at the docks, to speak with them herself.

Outside on the street, she felt a little better. There had been too many people inside Micheli's, and too many smells: garlic and wine and mirto, fish and unwashed bodies. To her surprise, Sperancia joined her on the cobblestone street only a few minutes later. "What do you think, Jana?"

"I think Jisepu enjoys the sound of his own voice. But I don't think he's lying."

Sperancia nodded. "Nor do I."

"Who do you think they are?"

"Not Corsicans. They could have travelled a long way. From Jisepu's description their vehicle sounds like a hovercraft – a type of flying machine."

If the visitors could build complex machines – and some machines could perform what seemed like miracles, from Sperancia's descriptions – then they were powerful. "Are we in danger?"

"I don't think so. But we shouldn't let them get too close. They might carry diseases for which we have no protection."

Sperancia was the village healer, and had taught Jana many of her remedies: garlic and sage for flu, eucalyptus honey for skin infections, chamomile and fennel seed tea for menstrual cramps. But there were many conditions and diseases the maghiarja could not treat. Like Pietro, a sweet, charming boy whose muscles wasted away for no apparent reason, and who had lost the ability to walk. Sperancia said the condition was the result of heredity, though neither of Pietro's parents was sick. Whatever the reason, Jana knew that Sperancia was frustrated and upset at her inability to help the boy, even though no one in the town blamed her or expected a cure.

"Are they from the mainland?" Jana asked. "Jisepu said they spoke Italian. Maybe they're descendants of people who lived in Rome or Naples."

Sperancia's face changed suddenly, as it sometimes did. She looked older, and angry. "Everyone died on the mainland. The air was hot enough to cook flesh. And if you didn't burn alive, you suffocated. The volcanoes sucked all the oxygen out of the air."

It frightened Jana when Sperancia spoke like that, as if she were someone else. Someone who had lived through the destruction of the world. She wondered if she would be the same way after the Crucible ceremony.

But now Sperancia seemed herself again. "There's something I want to show you." She looked up at the sky. "If it stays clear, come to my house after dinner."

Sperancia bid her goodbye and re-entered Micheli's. Jana considered following her to say goodbye to Filumena, but her friend knew that she couldn't stand bodies packed close together, and would understand. Instead she retrieved the rope from where she'd left it and headed back up to the field.

Antonio and Cristo were gone. Pinna the ox was wandering loose. The idiots had tied him to a thin branch that Pinna had easily snapped off to graze at his pleasure.

"Thank you, Pinna, for not wandering far. But now we have work to do."

She tried several configurations of ox, plow, and rope, and finally found one that looked promising. But the oak-bark rope snapped as soon as Pinna pulled. She retied the rope and tried again, with the same result. Tired, frustrated, and running out of light, she led Pinna back to town, wondering what kind of material would make a stronger rope. Not wool – it would pull apart too easily. You could weave cord and rope from long grass, but that wasn't even as strong as rope woven from twisted bark strips. She would discuss the problem with her father, and maybe ask Sperancia later that night.

* * *

Papà was unusually talkative – almost agitated – as they prepared dinner together.

"I wish your mother could be here to meet them."

"You always say that, Papà, whenever anything happens."

"Well it's true. I still miss her."

Jana's mother was a huge presence in Papà's life, but to Jana she was just a hazy memory. She'd drowned when Jana was just a baby. Papà had never remarried, despite interest from several women in town. Not only widows, but also from unmarried women just a few years older than Jana. But Papà insisted to everyone that he had already remarried – to his tomato vines and mirto berry bushes. Jana had been relieved at first, but now she worried what would happen after the Crucible ceremony. According to Sperancia, Jana wouldn't be the same person. Jana's father would notice the change and might feel as if a stranger were living in his house. Sperancia recommended that she find a new place to live, but that would leave Papà alone.

Jana tried to bring up rope making, but Papà dismissed the topic. "Just get Sperancia to move the rock."

"But she has so much else to do."

"Then gather a group of men to do the job."

Jana bristled at this. A group of women could do the job just as well. Even if they weren't as strong, on average, they wouldn't waste time uselessly grunting and straining against the boulder. But even more so, Papà didn't understand how people responded to her. Papà could go to the town square and rally workers as easily as he could pluck mirto berries. So could Filumena, for that matter; in two seconds she'd have a dozen amorous volunteers begging to do her bidding. But people didn't respond to Jana that way. Maybe they were a little scared of her because she would presumably be the next maghiarja, but they didn't love her the way they loved Papà and Filumena.

She was different. She wasn't one of them.

But Papà loved her, so she let it go and returned her attention to making dinner: a tomato stew, potatoes fried in olive oil, hunks of soft sheep cheese seasoned with oil, vinegar, sea salt, and fresh basil.

After they ate, she started to clean, but Papà took over. "Let me do it.

You must be tired from plowing the field all day. And from what you said, Cristo and Antonio weren't much help. I'll talk to Iginu."

"Please don't, Papà. It won't help."

He grunted noncommittally, making no promises, but Jana hoped he would stay out of it. She could handle those boys on her own, and she didn't want relations between Cristo and Iginu to sour any further.

She told Papà she was going to visit Sperancia and would be back soon. Her muscles *were* tired from the labor, and her back was sore, but her mind was wide awake. She imagined greeting the visitors in the morning, and what questions she would ask them. And she was curious as to what Sperancia wanted to show her.

Sperancia lived in an ancient stone house at the top of the hill, practically in the shadow of the castle ruins. She owned several goats, a dozen chickens, and tended a large garden. But the maghiarja received even more food from townsfolk paying her for services: healer, teacher, advisor, strongwoman. Sperancia opened the door seconds after Jana knocked and wordlessly led her to the roof.

Jana had been to Sperancia's rooftop only a few times. In the moonlight she saw a few familiar things: an herb garden, a small wooden table and chair, a cistern. But there was something new as well: a long, tapering tube mounted on a sturdy stand.

"It's called a telescope," Sperancia explained. "I've been grinding the lenses by hand, for weeks, from glass. Pietro's father built the casing for me."

"Like a giant spyglass?"

"Precisely. Have a look." Sperancia pointed to the eyepiece on the narrow end of the tube. "Be careful not to touch it or move it."

Jana looked through the eyepiece, expecting to see a blurry smudge of light, a star or planet or ring, or maybe the crescent moon. But instead she saw a clearly defined oval ring of light. She gasped when she realized what it was: a giant structure, slowing turning on a central hub, high in the sky.

"The rings are machines!" she said. She'd seen the rings in the sky, several of them, her entire life. Each was a slightly different shape and color, and occupied the same place in the sky, staying still even as the rotation of the planet made the constellations appear to move. The rings were dimmer than the stars and planets, but were visible on clear nights, even without a spyglass. "You always suspected they were machines, but this proves it."

"I always *knew* they were."

"What do you mean? If you knew, why didn't you tell us before?"

Sperancia furrowed her brow. "I couldn't prove it. And I didn't know if it would help anyone, or do any good. But maybe I should have."

"The visitors – are they from the rings? Have they come down from the sky?"

"Maybe. It seems likely."

"Tell me everything you know about the rings."

Sperancia explained that in the century of economic and political collapse triggered by climate disruption, reduced birth rates, and political corruption, some enterprising nations, corporations, and wealthy individuals had collaborated to design and assemble vast ringships. These orbiting habitats contained everything needed to support life for thousands of people. When the great Campi Flegrei eruption dealt the final, eventually fatal blow to global civilization, those in the ringships were fully protected.

"The knowledge that I have preserved in my many selves – it is only a fraction of what they must possess. Medicine, biology, physics, mathematics. And not just the sciences, but the arts. They still have *everything*."

Sperancia sounded envious, which Jana didn't understand. Their lives in Bosa were rich and good. Most people were happy and everyone had plenty to eat. From what Sperancia had taught her of history – wars that lasted centuries, horrible plagues, the destruction of nature, terrible crowding, human cruelty beyond imagining – life on the island was blessed and relatively free of strife. So why would Sperancia lust for lost knowledge? What good had it done their ancestors?

She said as much. She wasn't afraid to express herself freely around Sperancia.

"Yes, our lives are good. But everything depends on knowledge, and how it is passed along. Imagine if we didn't know how to fish, or grow food in our gardens, or treat the sick."

"We'd be hungry and miserable."

"And far fewer in number."

Sperancia didn't need to spell it out. When she referred to knowledge, she referred to *her own* knowledge, though she shared most of what she knew freely. Whenever people had a question, they came to the maghiarja. How to cure a sty? Ask Sperancia. How to grow beans? Ask Sperancia. Even the mirto liqueur that Micheli distilled from berry mash – Sperancia had taught him how to do that. Micheli had remembered his great-grandmother making the stuff but had no idea how. Sperancia had remembered the exact recipe and methods.

Without Sperancia, they would be a poor, wretched, hungry lot, like the Corsican savages. As a child she'd once seen Corsicans fishing on a crude raft. Even from far away the north islanders looked dirty, ungroomed, dangerously thin. They'd stared at her and Papà, in her father's newly painted red fishing boat, with resentment and hatred. She'd started to wave but Papà had scolded her. "They're not like us," he'd explained. "They're not friendly. If they could, they'd run you through with a spear, roast you over a fire, and eat you with pepper sauce."

To this day she wasn't sure if the Corsicans were truly cannibals or if Papà had just been scaring her for her own good. And what was *pepper sauce*, anyway?

Sperancia had been adjusting the telescope. "There it is," she said. "Have a look."

Jana lowered her eye to the eyepiece again. This time, instead of a slowly spinning, dim, yellow-orange ring, she saw a bluish, rotating cylinder. "What is it?"

"Another space habitat. I can't be sure, but I think it appeared for the first time only three days ago."

Jana stood straight and tried to find the object without the aid of the telescope. Sperancia pointed to a still blue dot, with no starlike flicker. Jana didn't have the same knowledge and perfect memory of the sky as Sperancia, but it did look out of place. "I think I would have noticed that before."

"So do I," said Sperancia.

"Do you think its appearance has something to do with the visitors?"

"Maybe we should expect more than one group of visitors."

Sperancia offered Jana herb tea with wildflower honey, which she politely declined. There were many more things she wanted to ask the old woman, but she needed some time alone to think.

"Sperancia – I have a favor to ask, though it's nothing urgent. If you're too busy I can probably find another way."

"What?"

"There's a large boulder in the field I'm plowing...."

"I'll move it tomorrow, after we talk to the visitors. Whatever you need, child. You should never hesitate to ask."

Jana thanked her, though she didn't understand Sperancia's constant willingness to help her, no matter the inconvenience. Certainly that wasn't true for everyone in town; most had to pay fairly, if not dearly, for Sperancia's assistance.

Though it made sense in a certain light. They were separate people now, but after the Crucible ceremony, they would become one. By helping her, Sperancia was helping her future self.

CHAPTER TWO

Jana and her father arrived at the docks early, but so had everyone else. Half the town was there, at least, talking excitedly in anticipation of the visitors. She was as curious as everyone else, but this was too much – too many people in too small an area.

As she turned to leave, Sperancia roughly grabbed her arm from behind. "You need to be here. Suppress your feelings, for now."

"You're hurting me."

Sperancia instantly released her. "I'm sorry. Can you control yourself?"

"Of course."

"Stand over there, away from the crowd." Sperancia pointed to an empty fishmonger's stall. "When the visitors come, force your way to the front, and find me."

Jana nodded and did as Sperancia asked. The stall had a pungent smell and the wooden counter was slick and glistening with fish scales, but no one bothered her there.

She watched the crowd. Some of the young men had brought weapons: Cristo was carrying a crossbow; Antonio was hefting a long pike that looked far too heavy for him. Jana thought that was ridiculous. If the visitors had a boat that could fly, then surely they had weapons that outclassed bows and spears. Guns or missiles, maybe, as their ancestors had used in wars that spanned the planet. Those who wanted safety should have stayed at home.

Though maybe there was sense in not appearing defenseless. Bows were enough to ensure the Corsicans kept their distance.

Whatever the visitors had meant by 'morning', they had not meant dawn or any time close. Two hours passed without any sign of them. What if the whole thing had been a distraction, and the visitors were attacking the old town even now? She shared this thought with Filumena when her friend stopped by to say hello.

"You sound like Iginu with your suspicions."

"But admit it, we're acting like sheep. All gathering here at the docks, exactly as they asked."

"They didn't ask us all to gather here. Besides, the men are well-armed."

"The visitors could have better weapons. They probably do."

"You worry too much. And you look like a fishmonger with no fish." Filumena laughed, which made her even more beautiful.

Jana laughed with her because there was no meanness in her friend, only playfulness. But maybe Filumena was right about her worrying too much. "I worry that you're too trusting," Jana said.

"You're not trusting enough."

"I trust you."

Filumena gave her a serious look that she had trouble interpreting. Was it sadness, or regret? But both women were distracted by the noise of the crowd. The visitors had arrived.

Jana and Filumena ran down to the dock. Jana waded through the crowd toward the front, which was not as difficult as she'd expected. She was tall, with sharp elbows, and people made way with only a few resentful grumbles. And Jana carried some of Sperancia's authority by proxy.

As Jisepu had described, the visitors were on a floating vehicle. They slowly glided over the water, about twenty meters away. Directly beneath their *hovercraft* – as Sperancia had called it – the water was turbulent; a down-blowing wind was keeping them in the air.

Jisepu had described three people, but there were four today: two women about Papà's age, one with orange hair and one with brown hair streaked with gray; a handsome man with light-brown skin and long, dark hair, older than Cristo and Antonio but still young; and a pale woman with long, black hair, a broad face, and attractive but unusual features.

"Hello!" shouted the woman with orange hair, in Italian. "My name is Ingrid. These are my companions, Lydia, Tem, and Maggie." She gestured to the older woman and the young man and woman in turn. "We need to give you some blood tests before we get any closer. Can I get a few volunteers?"

Sperancia stepped forward. "Why do you need blood tests? We don't consent to genetic testing." Jana recognized the word – *genetic* – from Sperancia's description of Pietro's disease, but she didn't understand its exact meaning.

"We need to test for various antibodies, to get a picture of your general immune profile. We'll look for indicators of your virome and phage ecology. We might be carrying pathogens that are harmless in our own bodies, but that could make you sick. We only need a drop of blood from three or four people."

Sperancia appeared to understand this explanation. "How will you collect the samples?"

In response, the young black-haired woman produced a canister and sprayed a liquid over a number of small objects. She then picked up the pebble-like objects and tossed them in the air. Jana expected them to fall to the water, but the pebbles took flight. Moments later a tiny swarm of metallic black beetles were buzzing around them. Jana stepped back instinctively.

"Extend your arm, if you're willing," Ingrid shouted. "The drones will take blood samples and return them to us."

Jana looked to Sperancia, who nodded. Jana extended both arms, palms up. One of the beetles landed on her left forearm; a moment later she felt a quick, almost painless prick. Up close the beetle was iridescent, and glimmered as if wet. It lifted a double set of wings, perhaps to say thank you, and flittered off. Jana examined her arm but there was no blood nor redness. And no lingering pain.

Cristo handed his crossbow to Antonio, who had some trouble taking it while maintaining control of his long pike. Cristo stepped forward, slightly jostling Jana, rolled up his sleeves, and extended his arms. Jana noticed his hands were trembling slightly, but she took no pleasure in this observation. It made him braver than her, that he was actually scared. She'd felt no fear at all, not even a trace. Her body – it was just a thing, a vehicle for her mind. She realized most people didn't feel the same, that her sense of complete duality was unusual. To them, body and self were one. When Filumena saw her reflection in a mirror, she saw *herself*. But when Jana passed a highly polished surface, she felt no connection to the image she saw. And that disassociation extended to all of her bodily senses, including pain. It was nothing, pain, just signals traveling within her nerves, like the vibrations of a horn transferring to the air and making sound.

After Cristo's show of bravado, two other young men stepped forward and let the beetles sample their blood.

"Can we get one more person, please?" Ingrid called from the hovercraft. "A woman, someone older?"

Several people looked to Sperancia, but Jana knew better. It wasn't that the old woman was scared, but she wouldn't let the visitors read her blood. Her body was different, on account of the fine threads that were visible beneath her skin. Those threads had penetrated every millimeter of her flesh, including her brain. Sperancia had explained it all to Jana, how the Crucible worked.

"I'll do it." Vissenta, Cristo's mother, stepped forward, but not before shooting a look at Sperancia, which garnered no reaction. Vissenta cried out and stumbled as the beetle raised its wings and flew off. Cristo rushed to support his mother, cursing loudly.

"I hope you have what you need!" he shouted at the visitors.

"We do, thank you," Ingrid replied, either not registering or ignoring Cristo's hostility. "We'll need a few minutes – please be patient."

Jana watched them closely. The older brown-haired woman – Lydia – was busying herself with the beetles, doing some kind of fine work with small tools. Perhaps she was a doctor or healer, like Sperancia. Ingrid sat on the edge of the craft and smiled at the townsfolk of Bosa, waving back at several small children in the crowd who waved and cheerfully shouted at her. Ingrid was the face of the visitors, and their tongue. The two younger visitors spoke quietly with each other. Jana wondered what their roles were.

"Good news!" Ingrid called out. "It's safe for us to get closer. May we approach?"

Gregoriu, the mayor, finally stepped forward. He was a short, slight man, older and balding, with tiny tufts of black hair sprouting from his nostrils and ears. He was timid, but thoughtful and unwaveringly fair, which had led to his election five times. Not five times in succession; Micheli had been elected for a single interim term. But that had gone poorly, and the townsfolk of Bosa had reinstated Gregoriu as soon as was possible.

"Yes, you may approach," shouted Gregoriu in a wavering voice. "I am Gregoriu Serra, mayor of Bosa. Welcome to our town, and welcome to Sardinia!"

The crowd shuffled back as the hovercraft glided in, spraying the front line with sea mist. Tem, the young man with long hair, nimbly jumped to the dock and tied the craft to a post with a length of black line. Jana eyed the rope enviously. It was thin but she guessed it was strong, much stronger than the scratchy oak-bark rope that had snapped at Pinna's first heave.

"Thank you for the kind welcome," said Ingrid. "We are from a town called Ilium, in the Po Valley, approximately seven hundred kilometers to the north."

"Ilium," Sperancia repeated.

"Have you heard of it?" Ingrid asked. Too casually, Jana thought. Maybe Ingrid was not as simple and naïve as she appeared.

"No," Sperancia replied, with a stubbornness that made Jana sure that she had.

"It is not as beautiful as Bosa," Ingrid continued, "with your castle and colorful houses and wonderful stonework. We are a very young town, only thirty years old, about as old as Tem here." She gestured to the long-haired man, who was watching Sperancia closely. Had he noticed something different about her?

"Why are you here?" asked Iginu. It was a blunt question, but a fair one. Everyone wanted to know.

Ingrid nodded. "The short answer: we are here to trade. We'd like to exchange both knowledge and goods. We can help each other. We have medicine that can heal your sick—"

"We already have a healer," Iginu interrupted. He pointed with his chin at Sperancia, who looked displeased.

"Let her speak!" The angry voice was from Enzo, Pietro's father. Pietro himself, unable to walk, was not there, though Jana was sure he would want to be; the boy was curious and adventurous.

"We have medicine, we have supplies, and most of all we have knowledge of the world we would like to share with you."

"And what do you want from us?" Gregoriu asked.

"We want to know what you know," Ingrid answered without hesitation. "Your history, your way of life, exactly how you have survived through the ages."

"I think you already know," said Iginu accusingly. "You've been spying on us, haven't you?"

To Jana's surprise, Ingrid nodded. "Yes. For many years we watched you from a distance. Never too close, but there were people on the island observing you, taking notes. Anthropologists. But they meant no harm – they were only there to learn."

"I knew it!" Iginu shook his fist.

"But that was many years ago. We stopped that practice long ago. We decided among ourselves that it was unfair, unethical." Tem leaned in and said something to Ingrid in a language Jana didn't recognize. Could Tem understand Ingrid's Italian, but not speak it himself? "And yes, as Tem points out, it was a decision made after one group in particular expressed their displeasure."

"How many groups are there?" Sperancia asked.

Ingrid smiled. "We don't know. Far more than we initially thought. So far we are in contact with six communities, including yourselves. We guess there are far more, possibly hundreds."

"That's all you want?" Gregoriu asked. "Knowledge of how we live?" The mayor sounded relieved.

"Mostly. We'd like to trade foodstuffs as well. We get tired of eating the same foods all the time."

"We don't," Vissenta bragged. "We eat well."

"You especially," quipped Iginu. Vissenta flicked his ear, eliciting a howl of pain from her husband. But the tiff provided a moment of entertainment and levity at the old couple's expense. The crowd's mood lightened.

"Would you be willing to give us a tour of Bosa?" Ingrid asked. "And after that, maybe we can sit somewhere and talk, the four of us with four of you? Yourself, Gregoriu, and others who make decisions?" She looked pointedly at Sperancia even though the maghiarja had said little.

"Yes, of course. Please, make some room for our guests. Let them through!"

The visitors left their hovercraft tied off and unattended, though a clear glasslike shell slid over the passenger compartment as they walked away. The machine probably had its own defenses, and she hoped Cristo and the others would not be foolish enough to attempt boarding it. The young men loitered on the dock, stupidly holding their weapons, as the town elders led the visitors toward the old town.

"Antonio, lend me your knife," she said when the visitors were out of sight.

"Why?"

"Just give it to me."

Antonio frowned but reluctantly handed Jana his knife, a dark steel blade with a polished handle that his father had fashioned from a sheep's horn.

"What are you going to do?" Cristo asked.

"What are *we* going to do. We're going to move that rock."

There was a long coil of the black rope on the dock next to the post where Tem had tied off the hovercraft. Despite the sharpness of Antonio's blade, it took her over a minute to cut through its tough fibers.

"What are you doing?" Cristo shouted. "You'll start a war!"

"You'll ruin my knife!" Antonio protested.

"Don't worry, boys. They don't seem very warlike, do they? And I'm sure they have plenty of rope." She examined the edge of Antonio's knife; it looked duller but undamaged. "Just needs a good sharpening."

"If they have plenty of rope, they'll be happy to trade for it," said Antonio. "You shouldn't steal."

"Didn't you listen to what the woman said?" Jana protested. "They've been spying on us for years. They owe us."

Cristo and Antonio agreed to meet her at the field after they put away their weapons, and somewhat to her surprise they arrived soon, with Pinna the red ox in tow, ready to work. All three of them were happy to have something to do while the elders met with the visitors.

"Who did Gregoriu pick to represent us?" Jana asked.

"Council members," Antonio answered. "Sperancia, Micheli, and my father."

Those were good choices, if predictable. Micheli was popular, Antonio's father, Austino, was rich and an active trader, and Sperancia was the oldest, wisest, and most knowledgeable person in Bosa.

"I don't trust them," Cristo said.

"You sound like your father," said Antonio.

Cristo shrugged. "Maybe he's right this time. They admitted to spying on us, didn't they? It's a good time to be cautious."

"But they admitted it," Antonio protested. "They said they knew it was wrong, to watch us without our knowledge. Don't you think that means they want to have honest relations with us now?"

"Maybe. But it might be more lies. Jana, what do you think?"

"I don't think they're lying to us. But I do think they're hiding something. If they've known about us for a long time, why wait until now to contact us?" She was thinking of the blue cylinder she'd seen with Sperancia's telescope, a new object in the sky.

With strong rope, the work was easy. Pinna hauled the boulder aside, and taking turns at the plow they readied the field for planting well before sundown.

"You lead Pinna back," Jana instructed Antonio. "I'll return the rope."

She hadn't been worried at the time, but doubt had crept in as they'd worked. It was probably unwise to anger the visitors, even if they had plenty of extra rope.

"You'd better not blame it on us," Cristo said.

"Do you really think I would?"

Cristo would not admit it, but she knew that he trusted her, even if he didn't like her.

The dock was deserted when she returned. She brushed as much dirt as she could from the rope and left it in a neat coil next to the post. She didn't see anyone around, but several young men had seen her cut the rope. Antonio and Cristo might not rat her out, but someone would likely gossip.

That was fine. She would defend what she'd done – the visitors did owe them. And now they had two lengths of rope when before they'd had one.

That night, after dinner and cleanup, she told Papà that she was going to visit Sperancia. He did not discourage her. Though he did not say so, she guessed he was also curious as to what had been said in the meeting with the visitors. What terms, if any, had been agreed to? She knew only that the meeting had lasted nearly four hours, and that the visitors had returned to their hovercraft and left unceremoniously, looking neither jubilant nor dejected. They'd left a length of rope, as a gift, someone had said, which Vissenta had helped herself to.

News spread like wildfire through Bosa, but apparently none of those present at the meeting had revealed anything. Maybe they'd been too tired after the lengthy discussion. But she knew Sperancia would still be up; the old woman slept little.

"Ah, I'd hoped you'd visit," Sperancia said as soon as she opened the door. "Come in, have some tea."

Sperancia's kitchen was lit by several tallow lamps. A large, ancient book was open on a round oaken table. A book of maps. "Here." Sperancia pointed to a spot on the map that Jana recognized as the east coast of the Mediterranean Sea. "That is where Ilium was. An ancient city that they've named their new town after. It's mentioned in Greek myths."

Sperancia had told her some of the Greek myths. The stories were memorable: Pandora's box, the Minotaur's labyrinth, the flight of Icarus. So were ancient myths from other cultures: Sumerian, Egyptian, Norse, Celtic. "Does that mean their ancestors were Greek?"

"Maybe some of them, but the visitors have ancestors from every continent on Earth. Before they settled in Ilium they lived on a ringship called the *Stanford*."

"The spinning yellow-orange disc?"

"Yes, that one. Though they consider themselves independent now."

"How many ringships are there?"

"They mentioned five. The *Stanford*, the *Liu Hui*, the *Al Hazen*, the *Hedonark*, and the *Michelangelo*."

"The blue cylinder we saw…."

"That's the *Michelangelo*. They're worried about that one." Sperancia placed a steaming mug of tea in front of her. Sage, from the smell of it, and maybe dandelion.

"Why?"

"From what we remember of the *Michelangelo*, it was a museum ship – a project meant to house and protect humanity's great works of art."

Jana was used to Sperancia's use of *we*, which she tended to use when discussing the distant past. "Why are the visitors concerned? A museum ship doesn't sound very threatening."

"The *Michelangelo* has been in the outer solar system for a long time, isolated from the other ringships. Unlike the *Stanford*, the *Michelangelo* doesn't use sunlight for heat and energy, so it's not confined to a close geosynchronous orbit."

"I don't know what that means."

"I'll explain it to you sometime, but the point is that they've been away, and now they've come back, and that has the other ringships worried. The *Michelangelo* won't communicate – they've been dead silent. But they're sending down shuttles to explore the planet."

"So the visitors were lying about wanting to trade with us?"

Sperancia looked at her sharply. "You don't trust them?"

"They seem friendly, but no, I don't. But only because I don't understand them. I trust Iginu because I know he wants to be safe. I trust Vissenta because I know she wants a full pantry. I trust Cristo because he wants to fuck anything pretty."

Sperancia laughed. "You have that family figured out."

"And I trust you, because I know you want to learn everything you can, and you want what's best for Bosa. But I don't know what the people from Ilium want, not really."

Sperancia nodded. "Nor do I. But I sense they are good, virtuous people. In any case, we have a decision to make. They want to offer us medical care."

"Will you allow it?"

"I'm tempted to. Zicanna has blood cancer, and while I might be able to keep her alive for many more years, I can't cure it. And I've done what I can for Pietro, but his muscles keep wasting. In a few years he'll be too weak to breathe."

Zicanna was Filumena's mother. She'd been sick for years, mostly confined to her house and very weak, which meant more work for Filumena. More work and more tears.

"They say they can cure them, completely? Both Zicanna and Pietro? Pietro would walk again?"

"For the most serious cases, our ill would need to travel to Ilium to receive treatment. But yes, I know for a fact that the disease Pietro has, they could cure it. Completely. The cure – a small genetic edit – has existed for centuries. And they've kept that knowledge alive." Again, Jana heard a tinge of envy in Sperancia's voice.

"Pietro's father would never allow it."

"They would go together. Maybe his mother as well."

"Pietro would love that. He has an adventurous soul. But Zicanna – I don't think she'd be brave enough to leave Bosa. Can't they help her here?"

"Maybe. But I believed them when they said they could cure her in Ilium."

Jana sipped her tea. Sperancia had a difficult decision to make. But for young Pietro, some chance at a long, rich life seemed better than certain death in a few years. "What else did you discuss?"

"Trade. They seem serious about that – they're interested in the food we make. Gregoriu brought them some of his pecorino, which they loved. And Tem had many questions for Austino – where he obtained his goods, how Bosa's blacksmiths made their steel, and so on."

"And what about the *Michelangelo*? Should we expect more visitors?"

"Perhaps. They don't know. A shuttle landed to the south, in the ruins of Tunis."

"Isn't that very far away?"

"It's closer than Ilium. Only five hundred kilometers south of where we stand. If there were another island the size of Sardinia directly to the south of us, you could walk to Tunis." Sperancia showed her on the map. To Jana, their island seemed very large. In all her life she'd only seen a small part of it. And yet within the Mediterranean Sea, Sardinia looked tiny. The Earth was truly vast in size.

"This tea is making me sleepy." Maybe it was the tea, maybe it was the work in the field, maybe it was the events of the day. She felt as if everything in her world had shifted and was now balancing on a precipice.

"Then sleep, child. It will be a week at least before the visitors return, so we have time to talk. Time to decide."

"Should I keep what you told me a secret?"

"No. If I know Micheli, everyone will know everything by midday tomorrow. At least they'll know Micheli's version of it."

"One more question – did you tell them about yourself? I mean, did you tell them about the Crucible?"

"No. But Tem – the young man – he was looking at me intently." Sperancia touched her temple where the black threads were most visible beneath her skin.

"Curious, maybe?" That seemed a natural reaction to Jana.

"Maybe," said Sperancia, getting up to clear the table. "Maybe that's all it was."

CHAPTER THREE

Tem Ganzorig-Espersson was nervous. It had been three years since he'd last set foot in Happdal, in the Harz mountains of what had once been Germany. The village where his father had been born, and where his parents had met and fallen in love. The village where he'd lived the first nine years of his life.

But he was also excited to see his uncle and aunt, Farbror Trond and Tante Katja. And his grumpy, fierce grandmother, Farmor Elke, who somehow defied age and weakness. What did they all think of him, of his decision to live on the *Stanford*? Did they feel forsaken and resentful? He knew that Farmor resented his mother, Car-En, for stealing her favorite son away, but over the years his mother and grandmother had reached an uneasy truce. Farbror Trond – now *Jarl* Trond – always seemed happy to see him, and was too busy with his own large family, the smithy, and his duties as jarl to spend time nursing old hurts. As for Tante Katja, she mostly kept her emotions hidden. She hadn't always been that way; he remembered her as playful and expressive when he'd been a child. But her experience with Raekae – the slaver who had taken possession of her body with a centuries-old technology – had scarred and changed her.

He had something important to discuss with his aunt. Something he'd seen, and was worried about. She, of all people, might know what to do.

He navigated the hovershuttle carefully over the dense green canopy. The craft had layers of redundant safety mechanisms, but he was alone. Reckless maneuvers could get him in serious trouble.

Maggie, curious about Happdal, had offered to come with him. He'd tried to scare her off with tales of his fearsome grandmother, of meals of rare venison and sour berries, of the complete lack of plumbing and hot water. His scare tactics hadn't worked, but Maggie had sensed the truth – that their relationship was too new for her to meet his extended family. It would be stressful for him to be with her and his Happdal kin at the same time. She'd let him off easy, gracefully, without forcing the issue. And he knew that she wouldn't hold it against him. He loved her for that, for her emotional generosity.

He landed the hovershuttle in the clearing a few kilometers north of Happdal near the natural Three Stones formation. The walk would do him good, give him time to stretch his legs and acclimate his mind. As he followed the old path, he recognized landmarks: familiar boulders and gnarled trees that were far older than himself. His emotions came in waves, and he did nothing to control them. There was nobody around, no reason not to shed a tear or laugh aloud as the urge struck him. He felt a poignant nostalgia as he heard the cry of a lynx, and an echo of fear as he neared the spot where he and his mother had been captured by Svein, jarl of Kaldbrek. For weeks he'd been pressed into servitude by the cruel smith Völund, not knowing the fate of his mother. His father had rescued them both, killing Völund in the process. And that had been only one of his life-changing adventures that year. It was a miracle he'd survived his childhood.

He was dressed in simple, drab clothes – nothing bright or colorful so he would not stand out in Happdal. But the synthetic, intelligent fabrics were anything but simple; they regulated his temperature, monitored his biosigns, and were near impossible to tear or pierce. He had his godsteel knife, Squid Cutter, that Farbror Trond had given him as a child. It was his only possession from that time. What had happened to his clothes, when he'd come aboard the *Stanford*? He couldn't remember. They'd probably burned the filthy garments.

His parents were still on the ringship. They visited Happdal as well, every few years. At first they'd all come every year, but the visits had become less frequent since he'd grown up. This was his first trip on his own – another reason he felt nervous. Everyone was always delighted to see Esper Ariksson, his handsome, charismatic father. And his mother had lived in Happdal long enough to make her own friends. And so had he, but for some reason he felt insecure.

As he neared the village his thoughts returned to Bosa and the strange old woman Sperancia. When he'd first seen her, the black lace visible beneath her skin had reminded him of Tante Katja, before her body had reabsorbed the synthetic material. But nothing else about Sperancia had matched Katja's recounting of being possessed by Raekae.

Tem had joined the Sardinia delegation as a representative of the *Stanford*'s Repopulation Council. Gradually, over the past twenty years,

Repop's Non-Interventionism policy (which his mother had so famously violated) had shifted to the 'Three R's': Responsible Repopulation and Reclamation. Tem had his doubts about the new approach, even though he thought Director Balasubramanian, its progenitor, was well-intentioned.

Responsible made sense; responsibility was a core value of the ringstation citizens, and everyone on Repop took their job seriously. The planet was giving human beings a second chance, and it was of paramount importance to not screw up this time.

Repopulation was obvious; that was the point of the council. But when Repop had been founded, no one had known there were many existing communities on Earth – possibly hundreds – each with its distinct culture, with varying degrees of technological sophistication. For centuries the Ringstation Coalition had discussed repopulating Earth as if the planet were a blank slate, home to abundant flora and fauna but scant human life. But that was no longer the case. Repopulation would include contact, integration, and politics.

Reclamation was the R that made Tem the most uneasy. There was the environmental sense of the word, in terms of restoring ecologically damaged areas. He had no problem with that; there were still dozens of nuclear waste and power sites that needed containment, city ruins and ancient industrial sites that had to be decontaminated, and so forth. To a great extent the planet had cleaned itself over the centuries – especially the oceans – and much of civilization's remnants were buried under ice fields or covered in dense forests or jungles, completely inaccessible. But there was still work to be done.

But there was another sense of the word, definitely intentional. Human beings were in the process of reclaiming the planet as the still-dominant species. Earth had had a break from humanity's hordes, from global consumer culture, from cargo ships and planes that belched pollution into the atmosphere, from billions of hungry mouths that stripped the ocean of life and the soil of minerals, from sprawl and blight that crowded out other animals and even insects. That break, dated from the massive Campi Flegrei eruption that had triggered the planet's cooling phase and the ultimate unraveling of global civilization, had lasted nearly four centuries. Now their ancestral home was teeming with life, mostly pristine, with most of humanity's sins and transgressions either faded by time or buried by ice or trees.

But would they make the same mistakes all over again?

Not only was there the question of repeating past environmental mistakes. There was also the question of *who*, exactly, would be doing the repopulating, under what terms, and how Earth's current inhabitants would fare during that process. There was no central plan, no constitution, no guiding set of values beyond the Ringstation Coalition's grandly worded but unenforceable charters. It was up to each community to govern themselves as they saw fit. There was nothing to prevent the rise of despots and tyrants, nothing to prevent a repeat of Earth's bitter history.

Adding to this uncertainty was the return of the *Michelangelo*. Tem had heard stories, growing up, of a ringship inhabited by artists gone mad, isolated in the outer solar system, paranoid and armed to the teeth. Now the *Michelangelo* was back in geosynchronous equatorial orbit, only a few thousand kilometers away from the *Stanford*, right over Lake Victoria in eastern Africa. But ignoring all hails.

He'd descended into Happdal's flat basin. Passing fields of wheat and rye, he waved to a farmer. The man gave him a long look but finally waved back. There was no watch or guards, which Tem took as a good sign; relations with Kaldbrek, the neighboring village, were still peaceful. There'd been no trouble since Saga had replaced Svein as jarl, many years ago. Though Svein was still alive, which meant that trouble could easily return.

He was nearing Farfar Jense's smithy, but saw no smoke, nor heard any hammer clanging. The last time he'd seen Jense, his uncle's father had been griping about his aches and pains. A pit of worry formed in Tem's stomach as he considered that Jense might have died, just as Farfar Arik – his biological paternal grandfather – had passed away. Fortunately, Esper had been with Arik at the time. Those that knew Jarl Arik insisted that the old man had clung to life by a thread, for months, until all his children could be at his bedside. Tem wouldn't be able to forgive himself if Jense died before he could say goodbye. He owed the old smith so much, in terms of the man he'd become….

So it was a relief when he saw Jense arguing with Lars in the middle of the road. He couldn't yet hear what they were saying, but Lars, who had one wooden leg, was swaying precariously, shaking a finger in Jense's face. The old smith kept batting Jense's finger away, but Lars's finger kept returning, getting close to Jense's thick mustache each time.

"Fuck you, you old pumpkin fucker," Lars was yelling in Norse. "I paid you for those hinges months ago."

"You paid me for the nails, and you shorted me," Jense said, his voice short on patience. "How could you have paid me for the hinges when they weren't yet done?"

Lars looked confused. "I paid you in advance."

"You did no such thing, though the next time you need my services you *will* pay me in advance. You're not getting those hinges until you bring me the boar hides, as agreed. Or you can pay me in silver like everyone else."

Lars hawked and spat on the ground, probably intending the spittle to land near Jense's feet. But a thick glob of mucus landed squarely on Jense's boot. Lars looked up just in time to see Jense's fist closing in on his face.

Tem sprinted to close the distance, but by the time he reached them the old men were scuffling in the dirt. Tem grabbed Jense by his leather smock and heaved, but failed to pull the huge man off of poor Lars, who was getting the worse of the exchange. Lars was laughing uproariously through a mouthful of blood.

"Farfar, get off of him! You know you can't hurt him."

Lars had a genetic mutation that prevented him from feeling any pain. It made him an eager fighter and an adventurous hunter, but both activities had resulted in numerous injuries over the years.

Jense looked at him, first in anger, then with the shock of recognition. He released Lars and stood to embrace Tem. His farfar smelled of smoke, iron, and sweat – comforting smells.

"Look who's here! This reminds me of when I pulled you off Hennik, years ago, when you were beating him to a pulp in this very spot."

"I remember," Tem said. Though it had been Hennik beating him, not the other way around. He wondered what else had been lost in Jense's memory.

"Look at you," said Jense, cupping Tem's face with both hands. "What a beautiful man you are. The best of your father and mother's features. But you look like a woman, with your long hair and bare face. Aren't you old enough to grow a beard? Or is there something in your mother's blood that prevents that?"

Tem laughed. He was quite sure that he didn't look like a woman, and he knew there was no use in trying to explain to the old smith that there was nothing wrong with a man looking like a woman in the first place, if he happened to or wanted to. "I don't look good with a beard, Farfar. I tried it once, but my all friends said my face looked dirty."

"Hello, Tem!" said Lars from the ground. Tem reached down to help him up, and Jense helped as well, anger forgotten. "I'll let the two of you catch up." Lars left them, swaying unevenly and perhaps drunkenly, but making good ground toward the center of town, where he would surely spread news of Tem's arrival.

"You're too old to be fighting, Farfar. But you look well. I'm glad to see you."

"I'm not well. Every joint aches. I have a year left at best. It's time for me to join Arik and Bjorn in Valhalla."

"Not for a long time, I think. Why don't you come to the *Stanford* for a rejuv?"

"How much would that cost me? My weight in silver?"

"It would cost nothing but the lice in your hair."

"I don't have lice, you little squirrel – I wash and comb my hair every month!" Jense punched Tem playfully in the chest, causing him to stagger back and nearly fall. The man was a solid brick of muscle. Like Farbror Trond, Jense's body produced almost no myostatin. Many of Happdal's residents harbored wildstrains, remnants of genetic engineering mods from the Corporate Age.

Jense wrapped a brawny arm around Tem's shoulder and ushered him into Happdal. It was hard not to feel like a ten-year-old bellows boy again, being held by his bearlike farfar. His uncle and father had different fathers – Jense and the late Arik respectively – and thus Jense was not his real grandfather. But he had grown up in Trond and Jense's smithy, back when the two smiths had worked under a single roof, and he loved both men as fiercely as he loved his own parents.

Elke's house was their first stop. His grandmother looked at him without smiling, and he felt a stab of fear, as most did in her presence. But she hugged him long and tight, without saying a word, and he was reassured that her love for him was stronger than any resentment.

"You haven't aged, Farmor."

"Of course I have. Come, sit and have something to eat, and some *öl*." Elke's hair had gone completely gray, and the lines in her hard face were deeper, but otherwise she looked the same as she had twenty years ago, beautiful and formidable.

Elke brought out pickled vegetables, smoked trout, hazelnut cakes, and *öl* for everyone. Lars had delivered news of Tem's arrival quickly and enthusiastically, and within minutes Elke's house was packed with visitors, all wanting to touch and talk to Tem. He surrendered to the process, already feeling a buzz from the *öl*, and tried to shake the rust off of his Norse. Soon his mouth hurt from smiling and forming words that he had not uttered for years, round vowels and lingering consonants. He felt happy and drunk and loved.

But where was Trond? Was his uncle not eager to see him? And where was Tante Katja? He needed to tell her about Sperancia, about his suspicions....

"Where are my aunt and uncle, Farmor? Are they too angry with you to set foot in their childhood home?"

Elke took a puff on her pipe. "You know Katja doesn't like crowds. You can find her with her nose in an old book, as usual. And Trond is meeting with Saga, at his home, discussing Summer Trade."

"He's a good jarl, your uncle," said Lars. "The best in the Five Valleys. We've had peace with Kaldbrek for years."

"That's thanks to Saga as well," Elke pointed out.

"Two smiths as jarls," Jense added. "Smiths are sensible people."

"How is Saga?" Tem asked. He had a complicated history with Kaldbrek's jarl.

"Can she make a decent sword yet?" Lars asked. There was still dried blood in his beard from his fight with Jense, now mixed with pickle juice.

"She's getting better," Jense said. "What about you, Tem? Are you forging steel on the ringship? Esper told me they have furnaces as hot as the sun."

"I haven't for a long time." As a child he'd dreamed of being a smith. More than that, he'd *known*, deep in his bones, that he would spend his life in the smithy, exhausting and strengthening his arms with thousands of hammer blows each day. And yet here he was, a diplomat. He had studied and experimented with metallurgy on the *Stanford*, and Jense was right – he had access to materials and resources that would seem miraculous or magical to the village folk. But he'd yet to forge a decent sword.

The floor shook. A huge man had burst through the door. The giant towered over everyone and looked directly at Tem. What Tem saw was an impossibility: his uncle Trond, but as a young man again, without a single gray hair in his thick red beard.

But of course it wasn't Trond. It was Sigurd, Trond's firstborn son, now a full-grown man. Last time he'd visited Happdal, Sigurd had had his full height, but not his breadth nor his thick beard.

"Cousin!" Sigurd shouted, quite unnecessarily, as everyone had gone quiet. "Tell me everything that has happened on your ship since I last saw you, and start from the beginning."

It was late by the time Elke, unwilling to tap an additional barrel of *öl*, had kicked everyone out of her house. Jense had disappeared, and Tem vaguely wondered if he was asleep in Elke's bed, and what everyone else might think of that. But if Jense and Elke had rekindled their old love, what business was that of anyone else? Arik was long dead.

Tem followed Sigurd in the dark toward Trond's house, stumbling frequently. The night was clear but the moon was new, and only dim starlight and ringlight illuminated the path. And he was drunk, far drunker than it was even possible to get on the *Stanford*.

"What's that sound?" he asked Sigurd in slurred Norse. "A smith's hammer? Is someone working at this hour?"

"Sometimes Father works when he cannot sleep. His mind does not rest as easily as it did when he was young. Every worry of every person in Happdal, he carries with him. Your father is lucky not to be jarl."

"It's what Elke wanted for him."

"I know," Sigurd said, without a trace of anger. Everyone knew that Esper was Elke's favorite – it was just a simple fact.

"Can I go visit him?"

Sigurd laughed. "You don't need my permission. This is still your village, cousin. Do as you like. If you get lost coming home, just knock on any door – they'll take in Esper's son and feed you in the morning."

Tem bid Sigurd good night and made his way in the dark, stepping carefully, vaguely cognizant that falling and splitting his head open would be deeply unwise this far from the medical facilities on the *Stanford*. He followed the sound of metal clanging on metal toward the 'new' smithy, as he still thought of it, and from the rhythm and timbre of it he decided his uncle was making a sword.

He opened the smithy door to see a blade, glowing white, but it was not his uncle holding it. It was a woman, her long, dark hair pulled back, pale skin and flushed cheeks, hammer raised. She glared at Tem with naked rage, livid at being interrupted, but when she recognized him her anger melted into a sly grin.

"Hello, Tem."

"Saga. I'm sorry…I heard the hammer. I thought it was my uncle working."

"Jarl Trond told me I could use the smithy tonight. And I would guess right now he's snoring loudly after making love to his plump wife."

Tem was taken aback by this blunt assessment, but he had to admit it was likely true. "I'll let you get back to work."

"No. Stay a minute. Look at this, let me know what you think. You were a bellows boy once. And I remember you holding Völund's hammer."

Did she also remember Völund keeping him locked in a hole? Did she also remember his father cutting Völund's throat? But it was true – the Kaldbrek smith had let Tem take a turn at the anvil long before his uncle or Jense had let him hold a hammer.

"Come closer. I won't bite. You're drunk, aren't you?"

"A little. Elke's öl is strong."

She laughed. "Not really. Ringship life has weakened your liver. But really, tell me what you think. Your uncle has been teaching me. He's less stingy with his knowledge than Jense."

"Jense regrets not teaching Trond to forge godsteel sooner." He took the glove Saga offered him, and held the sword, still faintly glowing orange, by the tang. It was a one-handed blade, more-or-less a Viking-style sword, light and well-balanced.

"This is good." He was envious, he realized, but also impressed. Saga had put in the time and effort, and it showed.

She smiled. "I know." And then her hand was on his crotch, squeezing gently. "It's good to see you. I've missed you."

He pushed her hand away, but he'd waited a moment, and she'd sensed it. Against his will he stiffened, and she noticed that too. His first time had been with Saga, and several times after that, long before Maggie.

"I'm…with someone."

"Right now you're with me."

He couldn't argue with that, he thought, as she cupped the back of his neck, pulled him close, and kissed him. Well he *could*, but he didn't want to. It was exhilarating to touch Saga, as exciting as the first time. She smelled of charcoal smoke and sweat and metal, good smells. And he was here, in the Five Valleys – why shouldn't he be with Saga?

Things were different here. Life was more brutal, and potentially much shorter. There were none of the layers of redundant safety mechanisms that made ringship life possible, triple airlocks and boarding decontamination procedures and endless safety checklists. Everything safe. Everyone responsible. Everything planned and analyzed, measured and managed.

It was a burden sometimes.

"Stop thinking. Be with me."

He did as she told him. Then, and for several hours after, in the hay-lined nap nook, until they collapsed unconscious, filthy and exhausted.

CHAPTER FOUR

When Tem woke, Saga was gone. There was no fire in the furnace, though the coals still glowed warm. Every tool was in its place, the floor swept.

He dressed and poked his head out the door of the smithy. It was early still, though he had no idea of the exact time. Any means of communicating with the ringship were back at the hovershuttle.

He crept down to his old fishing spot on the bank of the Upper Begna, removed his clothes, and took a quick dip in the frigid water. It wasn't the same as a hot shower followed by a cup of coffee, but he was just as awake. He dressed, still wet, but the intelligent material of his clothing wicked the moisture from his skin and dried itself.

He knew he would probably regret his tryst with Saga, but he didn't yet. The memory of her was too fresh in his mind. He wondered how much she had changed. Now that she was jarl, was she less impulsive, less prone to outbursts of rage? Maybe she had mellowed a little, become more sensible.

Or maybe not. It still *felt* dangerous to be near her. That was part of why it was so exciting. And yet he felt a pit in his stomach when he thought of Maggie.

He trudged up the trail, feeling a chill from his wet hair, despite the warmth generated by his clothes. Tante Katja's cabin was not far from Trond's large house. He was worried she might still be asleep, but his aunt answered the door moments after he knocked. She looked at him with bemused skepticism.

"Gone for a swim this early?"

"Let me in – it's freezing out here!"

Katja had looked alarmingly lean the last time he'd seen her, but she'd filled out since then, and her skin had some color. She looked healthy. The black threads had completely faded away over the years.

"What a racket last night. First Elke's house, and then a great deal of noise from Trond's smithy."

"Saga was working late."

"Someone was. It's quite close to here, and sound travels."

He looked away. He'd thought they'd been relatively quiet. "Why didn't you come to Elke's last night?"

Katja sighed and rubbed his shoulder. "It's difficult between me and Mother. You're lucky to get along so well with Car-En."

"Not all of the time." He'd had his conflicts with his own mother over the years, but ultimately he'd been glad of her decision to uproot their lives and move to the ringstation. Though even now he had mixed feelings. He would always be of two worlds because of that choice she had made for him, to bring him to the *Stanford*.

Tante Katja made them breakfast: oat porridge, strips of salted venison, and dried apples. It had been a week now without coffee and he was beginning to adjust – he felt alert, with no headache. Other ringstation citizens might not suffer from caffeine withdrawal; most had implants that closely monitored and managed their physiological responses. But his mother had forbidden such technologies for him, and as an adult he'd just never gotten around to the necessary medical procedures. Maybe he was holding on, in some way, to his 'natural state' as an Earth-born child. He didn't even wear a m'eye lens.

Over breakfast they talked about family. He told her about Esper, how his father was teaching archery to ringstation children. In turn she told him about Trond's many children, his cousins, and who they took after. Her cabin was as he remembered it. Biter – a godsteel longsword forged by Stian, the first smith of Happal – hung on the wall. A shelf of ancient books she'd retrieved from nearby ruins sagged with weight. Another shelf housed a spyglass that Happdal lookouts had once used to watch for Kaldbrek raiders, in darker times.

"I need your advice," he said after they'd eaten and cleaned up. "I was part of a contact delegation to Sardinia—"

"How did that go? What are they like?" Katja asked, switching to Orbital English. She'd learned the language from Esper, Car-En, and Tem, and tended to use it when discussing anything outside of Happdal. His aunt showed more interest in the greater world than most villagers. She'd never expressed any desire to visit the *Stanford* or any other ringstation, but the lives of ancient peoples fascinated her. The few known surviving communities on Earth were windows into that past.

"They're surprisingly resourceful. We knew they were gardeners and herders from Svilsson's and Han's early observations, but somehow they've developed a full-blown agricultural tradition in the last fifteen years. They're much richer and more technologically advanced than we thought."

"Do they have flying machines?"

"No. Not that advanced. But there was an old woman there – Sperancia – who I think has a greater understanding of science than the others. I suspect she's introducing new technologies to their community."

"Is she from one of the ringstations? The *Liu Hui*?" Katja was familiar with all the members of the Ringstation Coalition.

"No, I don't think so. I think she's lived in Bosa – their town – for a long time. She's been there since Han's field research, at the very least."

"Then how does she know so much? Books?"

"Maybe. But I noticed something about her appearance." Tem described the faint black threads he'd noticed beneath Sperancia's skin. The same as he'd seen beneath Katja's skin before her body had reabsorbed the remnants of the artificial parasite.

Katja paled. "You think she's a gast." That was what the villagers had called Raekae, and the long line of bodies he had possessed.

"I can't be sure. There are so many things we still don't understand about technologies from that age. Rogue experiments, real mad scientists – it was a wild time in history. But there were enough clues…."

"You must have been terrified."

Her reaction gave him pause. It wasn't what he'd expected, but of course it made sense. Given what had happened to him as a child – his experience with Umana – it would be understandable if he'd felt uneasy at seeing evidence of another Crucible host. Umana – the 'Squid Woman' – a psychopathic tyrant with cybernetic tentacles, had used the Crucible technology to enslave previous hosts within her mind. Among her many heinous deeds, Umana had kidnapped Tem in an attempt to get at his mother. And come to think of it, maybe he had experienced a brief flash of panic when he'd first seen Sperancia up close.

"No – I wasn't terrified. She was nothing like Umana. She seemed like a kind and sensible person, and the other Sardinians looked up to her."

"But still – you know what's possible."

"Of course."

"And you want my advice?"

"You're one of the few people in the world who understands what the Crucible is. Who *really* understands it." Katja had lived through the Crucible taking over her body, hijacking her senses, and attempting to map and virtualize every neuron in her brain. But she had found an ally, Zoë, a previous host who had been trapped, existing as a copy of herself within the Crucible's quantum core. Zoë had created a world within a world, escaping control of the slaver Raekae, and had orchestrated an escape for Katja. That escape had cost Zoë's life, and the lives of every other previous host enslaved by Raekae, as well as Raekae himself. Katja had not survived unscathed. But she had lived to tell the tale.

"You need to kill her," Katja said flatly.

"*Kill* her? No. That's impossible. We just made contact with the Sardinians. And Sperancia hasn't given us any reason to believe she's anything like Raekae or Umana. If she is a Crucible host, it's somehow different. Maybe with Sperancia, the Crucible is operating as planned: a community of minds inhabiting a single body, with shared control."

"But even if that's true, what happens with the next host? All it takes is one person, hungry for power, and then you have a monster. Umana slaughtered a whole town. She would have killed all of us if we hadn't stopped her. Everyone in the Five Valleys, everyone in Ilium. She wanted Earth as a park, with no people at all. And the Crucible let her rise to power. Without it, she'd probably have lived out her natural life without causing too much harm. It turned her into something else."

"There's no indication Sperancia is looking for a new host."

"You said she was old, didn't you? That's reason enough. As the host ages, the Crucible master looks for young bodies to steal."

Katja herself had been young when Raekae had taken over her body. The mad inventor, in his quest for immortality and power, had stolen her youth. The young woman Tem remembered as a child, laughing and carefree, had never returned.

"We're meeting with them again soon – this time to trade. Maggie is in Ilium gathering supplies now. I promise I'll keep an eye on Sperancia. When the time is right I'll ask her directly about the Crucible, see what she knows. Or at least what she's willing to admit."

Katja adjusted a vent that fed the cooking fire, stretched, and then gestured to a pair of wooden swords leaning against the wall. "Fancy a quick spar?"

"Sure. But I'm a little rusty, so go easy on me." He always enjoyed sword fighting with his aunt, and he was relieved for a change of subject. Maybe it hadn't been a good idea to tell Katja about Sperancia, given her immediate visceral reaction. Too much trauma there – his aunt wasn't thinking rationally.

The wooden longswords were made of hard oak. Katja let Tem take his pick, though the weapons were of approximately the same length and weight. Tem took the one that felt more balanced.

"Good choice," Katja said. "Sigurd made both of them – practice before Trond let him work with metal. But that one is the second he made, and the better one."

Outside, on the hard-packed earth in front of her cabin, Katja took a defensive stance. She let him attack, easily defending against his blows with short, efficient parries, always keeping the point of her oaken sword in line with his body. But his aunt seemed more chatty than combative.

"So you came alone? How did you get here?"

"In one of the Ilium hovershuttles."

"It's nearby?"

"It's near the Three Stones. I didn't want the village children messing with it." That had been a problem in the past. The hovershuttle didn't respond to Norse, but some of the villagers had learned enough English to issue it commands, and one joyride had come close to ending in a collision with a tree. In Bosa, someone had severed the rope he'd used to lash the hovershuttle to a dock post, though fortunately they hadn't managed to activate the craft.

"Does it remember where it's been, like a bird?" she asked.

"Of course. It records every route and shares that data with computers in Ilium."

"So everyone knows you are here? There's no way to travel in secret?"

"I could, if I wanted to, though I have nothing to hide." Even as he said the words he felt a stab of guilt in his gut. "Why are you so curious about the hovershuttle?"

"You know I have a love for such things, and how they work. Did Trond tell you I designed a system of vents for his furnace? There's no more need for a bellows boy to wear out his little arms for all hours of the day."

"I haven't seen Trond yet – he didn't come to Elke's last night. I'll visit him next, and I'm sure he'll give me a tour of the smithy."

Katja grinned, knowing full well he'd already seen the smithy, and lunged at him. He leaned back but her wooden blade still clipped his shoulder. "Slow as ever, nephew." He wasn't slow at all – his reflexes were quick enough to have won him several fencing tournaments on the *Stanford*. But Katja had always been preternaturally fast.

The pain stirred his blood, and he struck back against his aunt, countering her quick strikes with powerful swings. She was faster, but he was younger and stronger. Not as strong as his father or Trond, but still strong, and the two-handed techniques were coming back to him.

"Not bad, little son-of-my-brother!"

Farbror Trond had more gray in his beard, and dark circles under his eyes. But he looked as massively powerful as ever, and happy. He embraced Tem in a bear hug, wooden sword and all, and kissed his forehead. "Sorry I could not join the festivities last night to welcome you. Jarl's work."

"I'm happy to hear Summer Trade is still happening."

"Happening? It's thriving! Saga is a fine jarl, and Kaldbrek and Happdal are both richer for it. Our cheese for their wool, our steel for their silver, and so on."

"I hear you are teaching her."

His uncle furrowed his brow. "Are you jealous, nephew? You know you are always welcome in my smithy, even to this day."

"I know, Farbror." He felt his face redden. Why did the village make him feel like a child again?

Trond insisted he visit the big house and see everyone in his family, including Trond's youngest daughter, Gunborg, who was already two and walking, though Tem had yet to meet her. Katja embraced Tem and kissed his cheeks and thanked him for the sparring session, but did not accept Trond's invitation to join them. There were always too many goings-on at his house and the ceaseless noise hurt her head.

★ ★ ★

Lissa, Trond's wife, embraced him. She smelled like milk, goat's milk and probably her own, and insisted Tem eat breakfast with the family. He'd eaten a full meal only an hour ago, but somehow he was hungry again. Trond and Lissa's brood were overjoyed to see him. The children were Sigurd, Baldr, Mette, Erica, and little Gunborg: two boys, both with their full height, and three girls who seemed incapable of normal speech. The girls only shouted, even within a pace or two of each other, though neither Trond nor Lissa nor their brothers seemed to notice. Tem filled his plate with oatcakes, honey, sausage, and bitter greens. Lissa brought him a ram's horn filled with warm goat's milk, spiced and honeyed, and though it was delicious the grassy smell and sweetness were overwhelming.

"I think I need some fresh air."

"Come work with me," Trond said. "Maybe you can swing a hammer for a few hours, since you seem to remember how to swing a sword."

His uncle took him back to the smithy, where he'd woken in a pile of hay only hours before, and Tem was thankful that Saga had tidied up. If Trond had heard anything besides Saga working steel the night before, he gave no indication of it. And though Trond had many gifts, guile was not one of them; you could see his thoughts written on his face as plain as day.

Trond showed him the new vent system for stoking the furnace, and a foot bellows, and an upgraded hammer rack, and many things that he'd seen before. Tem enjoyed his farbror's long-winded, loudly spoken explanations; it was comforting to hear Trond's voice and to know that his enthusiasm for heating and shaping metal was undiminished. If Trond's duties as jarl weighed heavily, he gave little indication of it.

"Where is Nine-Finger Pieter?" Tem asked. "Do you no longer share a smithy?" Pieter had once been Trond's apprentice, a role Tem had long coveted.

"He fell in love with a Skrova girl. And after old Orvar died, Skrova needed a smith. I was sad to see him go. But with Jense refusing to put down the hammer, Happdal did not need three smiths."

"And what about Saga? Did she return to Kaldbrek?"

Trond nodded. "Her plan was to leave early this morning. Though maybe she is with Hennik."

"Hennik?"

"I'm glad she's taken a lover in Happdal. It can only help forge a stronger bond between our villages. Summer Trade is a start, but there is still much bitterness because of Svein. And many of the Kaldbrek elders still remember Völund fondly, though most consider Esper's actions justified."

"Saga is with…Hennik?"

"I doubt it will last. He is too stupid for her, or she too cunning for him. Though maybe she will give him a child, and then we'll see. It is not too late for her to start a family."

Tem had a lump in his throat. All at once he felt jealousy, guilt, and fear. *Give him a child.* Saga had wrapped her arms and legs around him when he was close to finishing, pulling him in with limbs like iron bars. He hadn't thought to resist. His first time with Saga, he'd done what she'd told him to do, including pulling out. But with every other woman he'd been with (which was only a few), they'd had complete control of their own reproductive process via implants. On the *Stanford*, it took a willful act to create a child. But here, nature could take its course....

"What is it, nephew? Ah – I had forgotten – you once had eyes for Saga. And maybe she for you. But forget that. You are Messenger to the Jarls, are you not? Don't make your life more complicated."

The *Stanford*'s Repop Council had given him the title as a child, more of a pacifying honorific than anything else, but he had done his best to keep relations between the Five Valleys villages and the Ringstation Coalition honest and fruitful. And now he was a full-fledged council member. His uncle was right; he had responsibilities. And because he was in Happdal, he should take those responsibilities more seriously, not less. The thrill of the previous night was wearing off, replaced by the weight of his duties and a dark veil of shame.

"Do you want to shape metal with me, nephew? Nothing exciting today, just mudsteel jobs. But you could roughen up your hands."

"Yes, I'd like that."

Trond stoked the warm coals and added fuel. He listed the day's work: hooks, nails, a shovel head, a set of chisels. Tem took his turn at the anvil, turning out clumsy work at first. But his uncle only encouraged him, and a few hour later Tem had shaped a hay hook that filled him with an unreasonable amount of pride. It was good to feel something besides shame, and Tem relished the soreness in his muscles and the satisfaction of working next to his uncle. Mette and Erica brought them cool spring water to drink, with little Gunborg tagging along, shouting at each other about how Tante Katja had bid them goodbye – she had left on a long journey and wouldn't be back for weeks.

"She was carrying Biter," Mette loudly proclaimed, "a soulsword containing the spirit of a wolf, forged by Stian, first smith of Happdal. Do you know all the smiths of Happdal? I do. First was Stian, from the northlands. Then Jakob the Bold, then Kai, then Baldr – my brother Baldr is named for the smith Baldr – then Farfar Jense, then Father—"

"Weeks? Where has she gone?" Tem asked.

"To an island!" Erica practically shouted. "To kill a monster, she said. And not to tell you until the sun was high."

He ran to the Three Stones, cursing himself the entire way. As he had feared, the hovershuttle was gone. There was no trace of it, nor of his aunt.

How could he have been so stupid?

He trudged back toward Happdal, still absorbing the scale of his idiocy. Katja had not changed the subject because she'd tired of it – she'd simply realized she would not change his mind. She'd made a decision, in that moment, to take matters into her own hands. If there was another living gast – a body snatcher – then she intended to kill it before it could do more harm.

And yet Sperancia was no monster. He was sure of it. She was a true wise woman, a font of knowledge for the community of Bosa. She was their treasure.

And now he'd inadvertently sent his aunt to go cut off her head. A fine diplomat he was.

"Tem."

A broad-shouldered man blocked his path. Tem recognized the brutish features, the thick mop of blond hair, the pale, freckled skin.

"Hennik. It's been a long time."

Hennik stepped toward him, with a dark look in his eyes. Tem reached for the knife at his belt.

CHAPTER FIVE

Jana had finished planting the barley with her father that morning, and was now helping Sperancia prepare a garlic extract for Pietro. The medicine would not cure him, but it slowed his wasting and made him stronger. And the boy would need his strength for his journey to Ilium; his parents had decided to accept the visitors' offer.

On the way down the hill from Sperancia's house, still in the shadow of the castle, Jana noticed a golden glint in the sky. Traversing the narrow cobblestone streets of the old town, she lost sight of whatever was producing the reflection. But after delivering the garlic extract and a basket of eggs from Sperancia's chickens to Pietro's family, she made her way to the town square and caught sight of the flickering light again. This time it was bigger and brighter: a golden orb slowly descending toward Bosa, from the south.

Whoever or whatever was approaching them had not taken a subtle approach, and Jana soon found herself in the midst of a small crowd, also tracking the golden object toward its anticipated landing place. Which, to her dismay, turned out to be right in the middle of her freshly planted field of barley.

"What could it be?" Filumena asked her. "The visitors returning, by sky this time?"

"Maybe," said Jana. "But perhaps someone else entirely."

The orb was vast, a glittering golden balloon. Jana could make out three figures in the basket, two men and a woman, naked from the waist up, with olive-gold skin. The men and women looked down imperiously, unsmiling, at the townsfolk gathered below, who were standing without a thought on her freshly planted barley seeds. But Jana was dumbstruck too, and could not even open her mouth to complain.

They were the most beautiful people she had ever seen, tall and muscular, with large eyes, strong noses, and high cheekbones. All of them had thick black hair, oiled slick, precisely cut and styled. And the balloon itself was a work of art, covered in shimmering layers of thin gold leaves.

Actual gold, from the look of it, hammered thinner than paper, interspersed with other metallic leaves: gleaming silver and bright copper. But mostly gold. More gold than existed in all of Bosa, a thousand times over.

The basket, a delicate structure woven in intricate patterns of wicker and brass wire, touched down, and a moment later mechanically unfolded. The golden people strode toward them, unarmed and half-naked but completely unafraid, saying nothing. None of the Bosa people had weapons either, not even a staff.

The tallest of the sky visitors stopped a few paces away, and scrutinized the townsfolk, one by one, appraisingly. His eyes lingered on Filumena, which was only natural given her beauty. But another thought crept into Jana's mind, an observation she might have considered an impossibility only minutes ago. Filumena, even with her pleasing features and glowing skin, looked almost plain compared to the angelic, otherworldly beauty of the three.

"I am Maro Decimus," said the tallest of them in Italian, his voice deep and resonant. To Jana's surprise, she realized he was addressing her directly. While the others had stepped back, she had stepped forward, blocking his view of Filumena.

"What do you want?"

He regarded her coldly, and his right hand twitched. She stared back at him, defiant, unafraid of being struck. He looked strong, but not strong enough to kill her with a single punch. And what was a little pain, a bloody lip, or even a lost tooth? Those were just parts of her body, not *her*. On some level she knew that when the vessel perished, so would her mind, her self, her soul. But she could not make that logic match the way she felt, that her body was just a thing, sometimes useful but not at all precious. So she felt no physical fear, and showed none.

A snakelike smile crept over Maro's face, and out of nowhere she remembered the time she had seen Sperancia kill a sick bull with a single short blow to its skull, and the cracking sound that had resulted, stone on stone. Soon she would have Sperancia's strength, and maybe then this handsome, arrogant man, whoever he was, would come to fear her.

"What do *you* want?" he mimicked. "We come not to take, but to give."

"We want to know why you're here. I want to know why you landed on my barley field."

Maro knelt, took a handful of black soil, crumbled it between his fingers, and inhaled the scent from his palm. "Still rich in silicates, from the ancient eruptions." He stood and brushed his hands together. "You will be compensated for any damage. As a start, we have brought these gifts."

Maro nodded to the other man, who returned to the balloon basket and retrieved a wide, flat tray. He removed the lid, revealing an assortment of what appeared to be pastries. "Please, help yourselves," he said in a velvety voice. "Try some of our chocolates. And if you like, offer us some of your own delicacies in return."

The other visitors had taken precautions against spreading disease, but these three seemed unconcerned, and before Jana could protest the man was moving through the crowd.

"Wait!" Jana managed to say, but Filumena already had a pastry in her mouth. Jana wished Sperancia were present. She had no idea how to handle these people, no idea if they could be trusted.

"Holy Mother of God!" Filumena's eyes widened, tasting the dessert. "Jana, you have to try this. It's amazing." Others made similar proclamations as they tried the confections.

"Enough!" Jana shouted. "Don't eat any more of that. We don't know what's in it. We don't know these people."

Embarrassed, the Bosa townsfolk fell silent, and several covered their mouths. But nobody threw away any bit of pastry they had already taken.

"You are right to be cautious," Maro said. "But I promise you we mean no harm. Will you invite us to your town, and let us see how you live?"

"Absolutely not. You may wait here until the elders come – the children have already run off to fetch them. When they arrive, you may speak to our mayor and plead your case. But first, tell us who you are."

Maro bowed. "Of course. Things in the right order. I was presumptuous."

Maro introduced his companions, Livia and Felix, and explained that they were from the *Michelangelo*, a vast worldship housing its own small sun. Their ship had resided in the outer solar system, beyond Jupiter, for nearly a hundred years, and though the *Michelango* was a miraculous moving world that provided everything required for life and happiness, Maro and many others believed that they had become too isolated. It was time to reach out, to form new friendships and forge new alliances.

"So we are here to invite you to visit the *Michelangelo*, to teach us your way of life. And also, if you wish, to learn from us."

"Are you the leader of this *worldship*?" Jana asked.

Maro bristled. "We have many leaders. But I am *a* leader, a senator."

"You said *many others*. So not everyone on the *Michelangelo* agrees you should be here?"

"My faction commands the majority. It is the right thing, for us to be here. Right for us, and right for you."

"Why us? There are people living on the island to the north of us. There are people in Ilium." She watched Maro's face for any reaction, but he ignored her mention of the ringship settlers.

"There is an answer to your question, but perhaps I should share it with your elders, when they arrive. Everything in its proper order."

"Well, until then, can you cover yourselves?" Jana requested. "It is our tradition to fully cover our bodies with clothing." It was hard not to stare at their strong, lean bodies, their hairless, gold-toned skin, shining from sweat or oil. She felt slightly embarrassed, but also irritated that Filumena was openly gazing at Maro's muscular torso.

"That's not necessary, is it?" Filumena said. "They have their own ways. They needn't do exactly as we do. I'm not offended, in any case." Filumena smiled at Maro, who raised an eyebrow.

"We wish to make a good impression on your elders," said Livia, speaking for the first time. Her voice was nearly as low as Maro's, and just as pleasing. "Felix – bring us some robes from the gondola." Felix, evidently the lowest ranked of the three, obliged, producing three robes of shimmering translucent material that concealed little. The effect was erotic, not modest, and Jana felt an annoying stirring in her loins. She averted her eyes, especially from Livia.

Micheli arrived, with Cristo and Antonio, all three of them with wine-reddened eyes though it was still early in the afternoon. Gregoriu and Papà came soon after, and then Sperancia, who appeared calm but alert, and listened patiently to Jana's recounting of the situation. The three *Michelangelo* visitors retreated to their gondola, where they stood quietly, watching the townsfolk, occasionally exchanging a quiet word.

"They appear to have peaceful intentions," Gregoriu said. "Though it seems unusual to encounter two new groups in such quick succession."

"I guessed there were other people in the world," said Micheli, "but we've only ever seen the Corsicans. And now we have the people in the flying boat, and these others who arrive in a balloon, and claim to live among the planets."

"They may be telling the truth," Sperancia said. "There is a new ringship visible in the sky – it could be the *Michelangelo*. I saw it with the telescope Enzo helped me build."

"Is it safe to invite them to our council, to hear them out?" Gregoriu asked Sperancia. Micheli looked to the maghiarja as well. On other town matters, both men were happy to argue with Sperancia until they were blue in the face. But both were wise enough to defer to the much older woman when confronted with the unfamiliar and strange.

"It may be the only safe thing to do," Sperancia said quietly. "I don't know their true intentions, but we are at a disadvantage. I am sure they have machines that could destroy us – destroy this entire town – if they wished."

Jana had been edging closer to the elders, to eavesdrop. "I should be there," she blurted. "At the council, to hear what the visitors have to say."

Gregoriu looked at her, surprised and frowning, but Micheli shrugged. "She will be the next maghiarja, so why not?" said the ex-mayor.

Sperancia gave a quick nod, and it was decided.

Gregoriu officially invited the *Michelangelo* visitors to tour Bosa, and to present their proposal before the town council. What followed next was a sort of parade, with Maro, Livia, and Felix at the center of it, in their shimmering gauzy robes that did little to hide their lean, muscular bodies. As the visitors strolled down the hill, surrounded by townsfolk, they answered questions and handed out small gifts to children: balls, tops, and small dolls. The toys appeared to be handmade, out of materials that the townsfolk themselves could have produced: wood, leather, string, wire, and cloth.

"How old are you?" a little girl asked.

"Older than I look," Maro answered. "Much older."

"Are you married?" a boy of about ten asked Livia.

"Why? Are you interested? What will you do to impress me?"

"Do you have more pastries?" Filumena asked Felix. "What did you call them? *Chocolates*?"

"On the *Michelangelo*, we have thousands of delicacies, from every cooking tradition that has ever existed on Earth. Coconut ice cream, lemon tarts, and of course *tiramisu*. Do you still have tiramisu, here in Bosa?"

"I've never heard of it," Filumena said.

"I have," said Sperancia, in a voice that sounded deeper than usual. "Though I haven't even thought of it for many years."

"Maybe you will both visit us and try everything for yourselves," said Felix, but Jana noticed Maro give Sperancia an appraising look. He said something in a language Jana didn't understand, though it sounded similar to Sardo, the old language. Sperancia kept walking, eyes straight ahead, as if she hadn't heard.

The visitors, but Maro especially, seemed to take in every little detail of Bosa as they walked, devouring the town visually. They said little, except to answer questions, but gave each other meaningful looks.

Jana decided she didn't trust them. Not one bit.

The town hall was a new building, only thirty years old, built from salvaged stone and oak beams atop the cleared ruins of what had once been a church. Though some still prayed to the Virgin Maria and various saints, the formal practice of religion had been lost over the years. Still, the new town hall was a handsome building, both solid and pleasing in its proportions and design, and Jana imagined that it might feel something like what the ancient church must have felt like, especially when the light streamed through the blue and green tinted glass of the high windows.

The visitors sat on one side of a long table. Seated on the other side were Bosa's mayor and council: Gregoriu, Micheli, Sperancia, and Austino. Jana herself sat at one end, feeling out of place and awkward. But she often felt that way, and was used to it.

"On the *Michelangelo*," Maro began, "we take history and the preservation of both knowledge and art very seriously. We preserve all manner of recordings, photographs, and artifacts, including many great works of art rescued from Earth museums before they could be stolen by looters or destroyed by vandals. Or lost to time and neglect.

"But we are not simply interested in preserving old things. We want to *live* the old ways, to fully comprehend the minds and attitudes of our ancestors, so that we may fully understand the arc of our own history. We learn and converse in ancient languages: Latin, Greek, Canaanite, Aramaic, and many others. We grow and prepare food using traditional historical techniques. We maintain a vast library of seeds, not only for emergencies and protection from agricultural diseases, but to experience the entire range of what nature has provided over the centuries. We eat dates from trees that once thrived in the Judean desert five thousand years ago."

"You eat five-thousand-year-old fruit?" Micheli asked, uncomprehending.

"I am simply trying to give you an idea of what we value. We are not so different than yourselves, in this way. We can see that you preserve the old ways of doing things. The way you build, for example, is not so different than the ruins of the castle on that hill." He gestured toward the Malaspina castle that overlooked Sperancia's house.

"We value new things as well," Sperancia said. "There are many things we could learn from you. Our ancestors grew grapes and made wine, but they also powered lights with electricity. We have forgotten how to do that. Could you help us regain the knowledge we have lost?"

"Of course," Felix answered, "but gradually. Slowly, so that it does not disrupt your way of life."

Maro glared at Felix. "That is not our decision, what they do with the knowledge we share." And then, to Sperancia: "We are proposing an equal exchange. Both sides, teaching and learning. A cultural trade, spanning the artistic, the scientific, the mathematical…nothing off-limits."

"Nothing off-limits?" Jana repeated.

Maro turned to her and smiled, but she caught a flash of irritation in his eyes. "Who is this?" he asked. "The youngest member of your council?"

"Jana is my protégée," Sperancia replied.

"Yes, Jana, we would open our libraries to you, without limitation. And we would provide instruction and other resources you might require to put that knowledge to use. As you may now be realizing, we are offering your community an enormous amount of power."

"How did you find out about us?" Austino asked. "Have you been spying?" It was the same question that Iginu had asked, but it no longer seemed paranoid. The Ilium visitors *had* been spying on Bosa, for years, though they'd claimed they had stopped.

"We have been observing you from the *Michelangelo* with powerful telescopes. But most of what we know of your culture is from history. It is fascinating to us that you survived, largely unchanged, when so many others perished. And Mediterranean cultures are of special interest to us."

"Why?" Sperancia asked.

"The greater Mediterranean area is the birthplace of civilization. The Mesopotamians, the Sumerians, the Egyptians, the Greeks, and later the Romans—"

"What about the Indus Valley and the Chinese?" Sperancia interjected. "And the ancient civilizations of the Americas – the Maya and the Aztecs? We have some understanding of history ourselves, you know. Human civilization arose in many places simultaneously, taking different paths."

"Yes, of course," said Maro. "But those civilizations are long dead, as is everyone descended from them. You are still thriving, a living link to the ancients." There was something hungry in his voice.

"Look," Maro continued, "what we are proposing is simple: an exchange program. Some of you come live with us for a time, while some of us live with you. Only volunteers, of course, though after meeting some of you, I don't think volunteers will be in short supply – you are a brave and curious people. And just for a short time, at first. A few months."

Gregoriu turned to Micheli. "It would be safer that way."

"Would we have any way to talk with our people?" Sperancia asked.

"How could they?" said Micheli. "Their world is high in the sky."

"We have machines that would allow that – yes. You could communicate with your people easily, every day if you wished. Our guests in Bosa could facilitate that."

A lump of tension was rising in Jana's throat. How were they discussing this so calmly, already working out the details, as if everything was agreed? She desperately wanted to speak with Sperancia alone, to share her feelings of distrust. To her it was as plain as day that Maro and the others were hiding something. But the council members seemed not to see it, or to care. And it was not her place to interrupt her elders.

The initial discussion concluded with an agreement to meet again the next day, with the second meeting to include more townsfolk. But Jana sensed that both sides had already decided the arrangement would be mutually beneficial. Sperancia was the hardest to read, but Gregoriu, Micheli, and Austino had all taken an obvious liking to the visitors. The men were all charmed by Livia's symmetrical face and sultry voice, but also seemed ready to fall in line with anything Maro suggested. Even Jana found that part of her wanted to surrender to the *Michelangelo* senator's commanding presence, to accept his reassurances at face value.

But she knew better. Why didn't the others?

Many of Bosa's residents were gathered outside of the town hall as they emerged, and Jana wanted no part of the parade back to the golden balloon. Too many people, too close together, and she would have to replant a good section of the field when it was all done.

"Sperancia," she hissed, grabbing the old woman's arm. "Can we talk? In private?"

Sperancia shrugged her off. "Later, child. Meet me at my house."

As the parade disappeared from sight, she was surprised to see Cristo hanging back. He looked how she felt: worried and irritated. "You don't trust them either," she said.

"They remind me of wild horses," Cristo said. "Sleek and strong and pleasing to the eye, but they also bite and kick."

"They didn't threaten us, or make demands," Jana said.

"And yet you sensed it, didn't you? That they're dangerous?"

Jana nodded.

"Filumena is too trusting," Cristo said.

Jana noticed something in Cristo's voice, a tenderness. "You care about her, don't you? I mean, I know you think she's beautiful. So do I. She *is* beautiful. But...you don't want her to get hurt."

Cristo grunted. "Of course not. She's a good person."

"Is it more than that?"

Cristo wouldn't meet her gaze.

"You're still engaged to Sabina, aren't you?" Jana regretted the words as soon as she'd said them. It wasn't a real question – she knew Cristo and Sabina were still engaged. Everyone would know within hours if they were not; gossip travelled faster than fire in Bosa. She was just being cruel, goading him.

Cristo narrowed his eyes and spat in the dirt, but didn't deny his feelings for Filumena. "Sabina will make a good wife, and I'll be faithful to her. And you should consider your own feelings before you stick your nose in mine."

Cristo strode off with his usual arrogant swagger, head held high, in the direction of the docks. Jana stared at the cobblestones, feeling ashamed. Of course he was right. She loved Filumena, and it was probably obvious to everyone. Once, on a beach beneath some cliffs, they had kissed and pressed their bodies together. But to Filumena it had been pure playfulness, a game, while to Jana it had meant everything. Filumena had been serious the next day, realizing her mistake, and had reassured Jana that their friendship was the most important thing in Filumena's life, and that she hadn't meant to toy with Jana's feelings. But she didn't feel the same way. Filumena had only ever felt romantic love toward men, and never expected to feel differently. If only Jana were a man....

It had taken some time for their friendship to recover, but it had. Jana had tried to bury that afternoon on the beach in the deepest recesses of her mind. But here it was again, popping up, the smell of Filumena's hair, the softness of her skin, the smell of mirto on her breath – they'd both been a little drunk.

Jana forced herself to start walking, to get out of her head, and the exertion of climbing the steep streets toward Sperancia's house helped. She pushed her pace until her thighs and calves burned. The pain was preferable to rumination and worry.

Jana let herself into Sperancia's yard. It would be some time before the maghiarja returned, and there was always work to be done. Jana fed the chickens and brushed the goats clean with a stiff hedgehog-spine brush. While she worked, she thought about the Crucible ceremony. Only Sperancia herself knew exactly what to expect; the last Crucible ceremony had occurred over one hundred years ago. But the way Sperancia described it was not at all reassuring. The Crucible, a kind of ancient machine that resided inside of Sperancia's body – a machine that she had become dependent upon to sustain her life – would be forcibly ejected. Jana would then be expected to ingest the Crucible even as Sperancia died in front of her. Except that Sperancia didn't describe it as dying. She used the phrase 'physically expire'. Sperancia insisted that she would live on, complete and whole, within the Crucible machine. Within Jana.

But it would take time. Over weeks or months, the Crucible would adapt to Jana's body, and eventually transform it, bestowing her with great strength and perceptive powers. It would weave its way into her mind as well, and gradually Jana would become aware of the previous Crucible hosts – Sperancia and three others – and be able to communicate with them.

She would become part of a community.

Or so Sperancia said. It was all so difficult to imagine. Jana wasn't even sure if she believed her mentor. Maybe the old woman had gone crazy, beset with dementia. She was extremely old; that was indisputable. Every nonna and nonno on the island remembered Sperancia as being an adult when they had been children.

But Sperancia gave no indication of any mental decline. The old woman was always sharp, aware, and at least three steps ahead of everyone else. There had to be at least some truth in how she described the ceremony.

Jana heard the gate open. "Thank you, Jana, but there's no need. I can do that myself." Sperancia looked worried. "Come drink with me – I have a bottle of wine that will soon turn to vinegar."

They sat at a table in Sperancia's small kitchen. Sperancia seldom drank, and the wine was as sour as Jana expected. She took a few sips to be polite, but Sperancia drank from her glass in gulps, not appearing to notice the taste. "You don't trust them either," Jana ventured. Sperancia shook her head, and Jana experienced a wave of relief. The old woman would know what to do.

"The other visitors – from Ilium – I believe we can trust them. When they return we'll conduct trade, and Pietro and Enzo will return with them to Ilium. I am hopeful – very hopeful – for Pietro. If all goes well, he will walk again, and live a long, full life."

"But the others, from the *Michelangelo*?"

"Descending like gods in a golden balloon – what a show." Sperancia smiled ruefully.

"What do you think they really want?" Jana asked.

"I don't know exactly, but I would sooner die than allow any of our townsfolk to return to their world. We must act quickly, and in such a way that we can plausibly deny our actions. If they suspect us, they could easily slaughter us all."

Jana scooted her chair closer. "What do you mean exactly? What are you proposing?"

Sperancia looked Jana in the eye, but her vision was unfocussed – she was somewhere deep within her own mind.

"We must murder them – all three. Tonight. This is our chance to resist, swiftly and without mercy. If we wait any longer, our fate will be sealed. We'll be mere puppets on their strings."

CHAPTER SIX

Jana had expected to find Cristo back at Micheli's, drinking. Instead she found him at Austino's shop, cleaning and reorganizing the stockroom with Antonio.

"I need to borrow your crossbow."

"Why?"

"Boars, digging up the barley field. A whole family of them."

"Well, you won't need it tonight," Antonio said. "The *Michelangelo* visitors have set up camp there. The children say their tents are made of golden silk."

"I need to practice – you know I'm not a very good shot."

"Fine," Cristo said. "But if you lose or damage any of my quarrels, you'll pay Austino for new ones. You can come by my house tomorrow morning and pick it up."

"I need it now."

Cristo set down a stack of small cork boxes on a shelf. "No, you don't. It's already getting dark. And I'm working. Find something else to do. Go down to the beach and have a swim."

Cristo said the words casually, but he might as well have drawn a knife and cut her. Jana's mother had died swimming at night.

But Jana didn't let Cristo see her anger. He was lashing out because of what she'd said earlier, calling out his feelings for Filumena and questioning his love for Sabina. The score was even now.

Antonio stood frozen and grim-faced, expecting a fight. Cristo continued to arrange the cork boxes. "I'll stop by your house and get the crossbow from your father," said Jana. "And I'll mention what help you both were plowing the barley field."

Iginu was out, at Micheli's. But Vissenta was home, playing dice and drinking wine with her friends. Jana started to explain the situation with the boars, but Vissenta was on a hot streak, hoarding a pile of coins. She waved Jana off. "You know where his room is – go and get what you need."

Cristo's room was lit only by moonlight streaming in the window. She hadn't been in his room for years – not since they were children – but little had changed. The same bed, the same chest of drawers, the same shelf displaying the bits of sand-polished sea glass and small animal skulls that Cristo liked to collect. And there was the crossbow, hanging on the wall, along with a wide quiver of iron-tipped hunting quarrels.

Sperancia had a plan, and Jana had agreed to play her part. Which was not to kill the *Michelangelo* visitors – Sperancia would do that herself. Jana's role was to create a distraction. She felt strangely calm, carrying out the steps Sperancia had assigned. Along with the crossbow and quarrels, she needed a small pot of tar and a hod of burning coals.

The visitors had done nothing to deserve the mayhem Sperancia planned to unleash on them. And if Sperancia was wrong, if the *Michelangelo* delegation was in fact peaceful and well-intentioned, then they were making a grave mistake. At first Jana had argued as much, that they needed to watch and wait. But Sperancia had vehemently disagreed. The maghiarja's voice had changed, becoming lower and gruffer, as she'd recounted a story from her distant memory:

"When the ringships were first built, before the great eruptions, the *Michelangelo* was founded on lofty principles: the protection of civilization's great works, the practice of art as humanity's highest purpose, and ultimate personal freedom as a means to pursue that purpose.

"But the truth was that the *Michelangelo* was created for a different and simpler purpose: hoarding wealth. In the Revival Age, global economies had mostly recovered from the Hundred-Year Recession. But Earth's wealthiest oligarchs were well aware that the geological activity near Naples could bring everything to an end, and they would do everything within their power to secure their wealth off-planet before that happened. They knew that most assets – natural resources, stocks and bonds, property, and currency – would become worthless in the event of a global apocalyptic event. Even gems and gold held little value: the former could be created synthetically, the latter mined from mineral-rich asteroids in huge quantities.

"But unique, world-famous works of art – those would hold their value as long as any fragment of human civilization persisted. And so would human talent, the brightest minds in every scientific and artistic field. So the oligarchs went on a buying spree, securing massive private collections of art and locking down long-term contracts with brilliant scientists, engineers, designers, composers, and fine artists. The *Michelangelo* would be their private artists' colony, museum, vault, and stronghold.

"The visionaries behind the project proclaimed their lofty ideals even as they paid criminal gangs to plan and execute museum heists. The *Mona Lisa* was stolen from the Louvre in the same week the Rosetta Stone was lifted from the British Museum. Though nobody could prove it, everyone knew that both ended up on the *Michelangelo*.

"And their crimes weren't limited to art theft. To the founders of the *Michelangelo*, their ends were justified by any means. Several scientists were rumored to have joined the ringship only because their children were kidnapped. Famous art collectors died under suspicious circumstances, only to mysteriously bequeath their art to the *Michelangelo* trust. And contracts that had been secured for months with space-elevator operators and aerospace construction firms were breached, always to the benefit of the *Michelangelo* founders. From the beginning, the *Michelangelo* was a cabal that did and acquired what it wanted, and got away with it.

"After the great eruption and the food shortages that followed, nations were in chaos. Rioting and looting broke out in Paris, New York, Rome, London, Amsterdam, Saint Petersburg, Mumbai, Hong Kong, and every other city that housed the world's most famous museums and greatest works. *Michelangelo* representatives swooped in, promising temporary protection and preservation of the planet's most treasured works of art and ancient artifacts, in state-of-the-art climate-controlled environments, until civil order could be restored. Mayors and museum managers caved, fearing the irrevocable destruction of the treasures they had been entrusted with. Slowly but surely, Earth's masterpieces migrated by rocket shuttle to the *Michelangelo*.

"I remember the reassurances of the founders as if it were yesterday," Sperancia continued in the same strange low voice. "*An orbiting global museum, for the good of all, that anyone may virtually visit, free of charge.* But that was a lie. After the great eruption, the *Michelangelo* fled into the outer solar system and cut off all contact. It was the greatest art heist of all time."

"But that was hundreds of years ago," Jana protested. "I don't trust them either, but killing them – it doesn't seem fair or right. At least until we know what they really want."

"I don't know exactly why, but what they want is to *collect us*. They haven't changed at all. And if we want to resist, we must strike first. Surprise is our only advantage."

"How do you know they haven't changed? It doesn't feel right to attack them for no reason."

Sperancia grabbed Jana's wrist and pulled her close. The maghiarja's grip was powerful, and Jana bit her lip to prevent herself from crying out. "They are *thieves*," Sperancia hissed. "They have come into our home to take our young. Would a wolf mother hesitate to kill such an intruder, intent on stealing her cubs? That is my role, as maghiarja, and that will be your role soon. To be the mother wolf of our people, to protect them at any cost."

Sperancia saw the pain in Jana's face and released her grip. "You must trust me, child," she said more softly. "I know far more about these people and what they're capable of than I can explain to you now. We are in grave danger."

So Jana had agreed to Sperancia's plan. If Sperancia was wrong about Maro and the others, then it would be cold-blooded murder. But the old woman was the best judge of character that Jana knew. If Sperancia was absolutely sure that Maro and his companions meant them harm, that was good enough for Jana.

She poked her head into the kitchen before leaving Cristo's house. "Thank you, Vissenta." But the women were laughing uproariously at something one of them had said, and didn't even acknowledge her. Jana slipped back outside, stepping carefully over the smooth, moonlit cobblestones, the crossbow and quiver of quarrels heavy in her arms.

At home she found a pot of tar from her father's supply shed. She carefully dipped the heads of several quarrels into the tar, coating the iron tips but leaving the shafts clean. Next she filled a wrought-iron hod with hot embers from the hearth. It was a lot to carry, the hod and the crossbow and the quiver. She was sweating by the time she reached the field, despite the cool night air.

Jana crept through the oak trees, off the main path, until she reached the spot where she had eaten lunch with Cristo and Antonio. To her surprise it was already occupied. Ralf and Bina, Filumena's young cousins, were hiding and spying. The golden balloon hovered silently above the field, its golden lines pulled taut with the breeze.

Bina saw her first, and worriedly poked Ralf until the boy noticed her.

Jana set down her things and put her finger to her lips. "You should both be in bed. It's not safe here."

"Then why are *you* here?" Bina asked. "And why do you have a bow?"

"I'm here to protect the visitors against wild boar. But it's a secret mission. You can't tell anyone – not even Filumena." Bina nodded solemnly, but Ralf furrowed his brow. "Now go. Quickly and quietly. Or I'll tell your parents you were here."

Bina grabbed Ralf's sleeve and pulled him along before he could protest. The children retreated the way she had come, stepping on dead branches and whispering noisily. Bina could keep a secret, but there was a good chance that Ralf would talk. It was too risky to continue – she had to tell Sperancia to call off the plan. They would have to find another way to stop the visitors.

From her vantage point she had a clear view of the golden tents. There were two of them, square-shaped and about two meters high, one half again as wide as the other. The tent fabric glowed slightly in the moonlight, but there was no illumination or stirring from within. Despite the noise from the children, the *Michelangelo* visitors were asleep, or at least resting quietly.

Jana's job was to wait for Sperancia's signal – the hooting of an owl, three times in succession – and then fire a flaming crossbow quarrel into the floating golden balloon. Sperancia had observed that the balloon did not gain its lift from hot air; there was no opening, nor stove to feed it. That meant that it had to be filled with a gas that was lighter than air. Jana had only a rudimentary understanding of chemistry, but Sperancia had explained that there were only a few gases that could hold that much weight aloft: hydrogen, helium, and methane. Two of those gases – hydrogen and methane – were highly combustible. Helium would be a much safer choice, but the vast majority of the planet's helium had been depleted during the Corporate Age. And for all their brilliance and powerful machines, Sperancia did not think that the visitors had a way to produce helium in space.

So the balloon was almost surely filled with flammable gas. And a vast, hot fireball would provide plenty of distraction. Sperancia would slit their throats before they realized what was happening.

After killing the visitors, Sperancia planned to burn their bodies and present the scene as an accident. The townsfolk of Bosa would be disappointed, perhaps even mournful at the loss of their attractive, gift-bearing new friends. But they would be safe from whatever wickedness Maro and the others had in store for them.

Sperancia was confident that she could quickly dispatch the visitors. They were unarmed and practically naked. Even if they were martially trained, it was unlikely they could match Sperancia's speed and strength. Maro, Livia, and Felix would be dead within seconds.

And yet Jana could not help but imagine everything that might go wrong. What if the air inside of the balloon was not flammable, and her attempt at distraction failed? What if the visitors were more formidable than Sperancia guessed? Yes – she'd seen the old woman kill an animal with a single punch to its skull, but the sick bull had been standing still, unsuspecting. Surely Maro and the others would resist. And what if the visitors had weapons and defenses that even Sperancia did not understand?

And her greatest fear, lingering in the back of her mind: what if Sperancia was completely wrong, and the *Michelangelo* had merely sent peaceful representatives to Bosa to make friends and share culture? Then they would both have the blood of innocents on their hands.

It was foolish to move forward, especially now that Jana had been seen. Little Ralf was a talkative boy. Her story about guarding the visitors was a poor ruse, even to a child. She had to find Sperancia, wherever she was hidden, and let her know.

Jana hooted, doing her best to imitate an owl, but the sound that resulted did not resemble any bird. She listened closely but heard nothing but the hum of crickets. Cursing quietly, she opened the hod and checked the coals. They were still glowing hot. Maybe it didn't matter that Bina and Ralf had seen her. Children told tales; who would believe them? Jana set her foot in the crossbow stirrup and used a hook to pull and set the string.

She checked the tents again – there was still no light or movement. Or was there? Yes – someone was emerging from the smaller tent. It was Felix, the shorter of the two men. Did that mean that Maro and Livia shared the larger tent as a couple?

Jana heard three hoots from her left, hoots that sounded much more owllike than the pathetic sound she had made. There was no turning back. She thrust a tar-coated quarrel into the hot coals, immediately igniting it. She set the flaming quarrel into the groove, aimed at the center of the huge balloon, and pulled the trigger.

Jana held her breath as the projectile shot through the air. Her aim was true; the quarrel hit the center of the balloon. And then bounced off and tumbled to the ground, where it burned harmlessly atop the turned soil.

Jana heard a strangled cry. Two figures were struggling near the smaller tent: Sperancia and Felix. Felix collapsed to the ground, clutching his throat. Sperancia whipped the blood off her dagger with a flick of her wrist and slipped into the larger tent.

Jana froze. Her attempt at diversion had entirely failed. It didn't matter if the gas inside the balloon was flammable; the material was impenetrable. The quarrel had plunged through the golden leaves but had then met resistance. The balloon had yielded for a moment but had refused to tear or burst.

The walls of the larger tent were shaking, but there was still no light from within, no yelling or screaming. She heard a low, piglike grunt, and sounds that might come from a butcher's shop, metal piercing flesh.

Jana sprinted toward the tent. Sperancia had insisted that she would do all the killing herself. Jana was too young to have blood on her hands, and even though she had agreed to help with the plan, the decision had been Sperancia's. But Jana couldn't just sit by. Sperancia might be injured or dead.

She pushed through the tent flap without resistance. It took a moment for her eyes to adjust. No moonlight penetrated the opaque golden tent walls; the only light was from the faint glow of the material itself. Sperancia lay motionless on the ground. Maro towered over her, arms folded. Livia crouched in the corner, holding a gleaming yellow blade, its tip darkened with blood.

Maro watched her closely, saying nothing. Sperancia groaned in pain. Jana knelt next to the maghiarja. "Sperancia – what should I do?"

Sperancia clutched her hand and tried to speak, but only managed to produce a choked gurgle. Blood trickled from the side of her mouth and ran down her chin. A dark stain spread across her chest, another blossomed from her stomach.

"She is very strong," Maro said. "Much stronger than an old woman should be. Why is that?"

Jana pressed on the chest wound, trying to staunch the bleeding. She could feel Sperancia's heart beating against her palm. Soon her hands were warm and wet with blood.

"Why did you try to murder us?" Maro asked. "Have we offended you somehow? Were our gifts insufficient?"

"She did kill one of you," Jana said, refusing to look at him. Livia slipped out of the tent, presumably to check on Felix.

Sperancia let out a deep groan and rolled over onto her stomach. "Be still," Jana said, but the old woman ignored her, and with great effort rose to her hands and knees. Sperancia's body convulsed, her torso buckling violently. With a grotesque choking sound, Sperancia vomited up a small object, which fell to the ground. A moist, black egg.

"Whatever in the world is that?" Maro asked with genuine curiosity.

It was too early. Jana wasn't prepared. Though the very idea of preparation was absurd; what could she have done besides worry and wonder about what might happen? This moment had always been coming. It made no difference that it was now and not in a few months' time.

Sperancia collapsed onto her back. She grasped for Jana's hand and squeezed it tightly with her last bit of strength. Jana met her mentor's eyes. She knew what was required. They had discussed it many times.

Jana picked up the black egg from where it lay upon the silky golden material of the tent floor. She placed it in her mouth and swallowed it. Maro watched her with fascination.

She expected difficulty, but the egg slid down her throat effortlessly. And then stopped, midway down her esophagus, like a stuck piece of food. A warmth spread from her throat, as if she'd swallowed a shot of mirto.

"Felix is dead," Livia said, re-entering the tent.

"I'm sorry to hear that," said Maro.

"Should I kill her?"

"No. Something interesting has just happened, and I'd like very much to understand it."

CHAPTER SEVEN

Earlier that day

After the council meeting, Maro, Livia, and Felix climbed the hill to return to the field where they had landed. A number of townsfolk followed, and Maro did his best to entertain them and answer their questions about the *Michelangelo*. Some of the questions were insightful, others inane, but Maro kept his smile and politeness consistent. It was important to gain their trust, at least until he had obtained an adequate number of volunteers. Livia had advocated for just taking whomever they needed, those that best fit the criteria, but Maro had argued that *state of mind* was of crucial importance for the project. Ideally, each subject would embark upon their path in a relaxed, unperturbed state, as close as possible to their natural state of consciousness.

Arriving at the field, Felix begged the townsfolk to give them a few hours of privacy and rest. The people of Bosa obliged, except for a couple of children who hid in the surrounding oak forest to spy on them. But that was fine and to be expected.

Livia retrieved the folded tents from the gondola, laid them out on a flat bit of ground to the side of the tilled field, and instructed them to assemble. Which they did, slowly and gracefully, like self-folding origami birds.

Both the synthetic silk material and the self-assembly mechanism had been stolen from the *Stanford*, decades ago. The *Michelangelo* had its own scientists and engineers, but also an army of spies who proved just as resourceful and productive, intercepting communications among the other worldships. The balloon itself, beneath the thin ornamental gold, copper, and silver leaves, was composed of an intelligent fabric, a strong, silklike membrane capable of gas exchange. Simple electrolysis pods suspended within the sphere produced hydrogen and oxygen as needed; the membrane handled the balance of gases to provide the appropriate amount of lift to the balloon.

"Should we invite Felix to join us tonight?" Livia asked.

"I think not," Maro answered. "It will be hard enough to rest with the insect noise."

Their first nights on Earth, venturing away from the shuttle and exploring the ruins of Tunis, had been magical. He'd been lost in a kind of ecstatic rapture, a sensory fugue, and had hardly felt the need to sleep at all. The open skies gave him vertigo, but he surrendered to it, just as he surrendered to the constant assault on his senses from novel, intense sensations: the orgy of life spread across the planet's surface, seemingly infinite.

And they'd had their own small orgies, the three of them, excited and stimulated by the reality of setting foot on the home planet. They were the first to do so, at least from the *Michelangelo*. The other worldships had beaten them to it, violating the longstanding agreement that resettling and repopulating Earth would be postponed until all the orbiting worlds could agree on how exactly that should be done. But a rebel group from the *Stanford* had settled in the Po Valley, a few hundred kilometers to the north, and were now reaching out to the Sardinians.

Maro had his own special interest in the people of Bosa, and had no intention of letting the *Stanford* settlers interfere with his plans.

Felix retreated to his own tent, somewhat sulkily, and Maro and Livia settled in for the night. He could feel the hard ground beneath his sleeping pad. But he was warm enough – he'd tweaked his metabolism to produce extra heat. He spooned Livia, taking comfort in the familiar contours of her body. He became aroused but chose to ignore the sensations. The children were still hiding in the woods, and the people of Bosa were modest.

"Listen – did you hear that?" Livia said.

"The children?" The young spies – a boy and a girl – were trying to be quiet, but Maro's hearing was enhanced. They'd been whispering to each other, though he couldn't make out what they were saying.

"No – someone else. An adult, about fifty meters to the north-west."

Livia's implants were linked to the security drones – gnat-sized robots scattered about their perimeter. They didn't provide visual data, but they sensed heat and movement, and could co-ordinate their sensors to record sound waves.

"Should we alert Felix?"

"No," Livia said. "Let him rest. It's probably just a curious person from town."

"Wanting to gaze at the golden balloon."

"It was a brilliant idea, my love." There might have been a hint of sarcasm in her voice, but he decided to take the comment at face value. The look on the faces of the townsfolk when they'd descended in their gilded craft....

"Wait – there's a fourth person." Livia squeezed his hand hard enough that he sat up. Someone was quietly approaching from the east. He could hear the faint rustle of movement across fallen oak leaves.

"It's just Felix, having a piss."

Halfheartedly he tried to keep Livia from rising, but she was already up and retrieving her weapon: an electrified, self-sharpening blade. The carbon-steel alloy included significant amounts of copper, silver, and gold. The historic coin metals were pretty, but also excellent conductors, making the weapon that much more deadly. They had other weapons in their arsenal as well: poison darts, lethal gases, sonic stun pods. All unnecessary, Maro was certain, especially after meeting the people of Bosa. The Sardinians were friendly, trusting, and quite docile. It was a wonder they had survived so long with such peaceful dispositions, but perhaps that was just the luck of living on an isolated island abundant with natural resources.

So he was surprised to hear a struggle. Someone was attacking Felix, and from the sound of it was getting the better of him. While that was categorically an emergency, Maro couldn't help but feel a spark of delight in the idea that Felix might be getting smacked around a bit. Felix was useful, and an unselfish lover, but Maro had always found him to be simpering and annoying. Livia was in love with him and had insisted that Felix join their expedition, and Maro needed to keep Livia satisfied. But Maro wasn't going to cry if Felix got a little roughed up.

But *who* was doing the attacking? That was the more interesting question. And it was answered soon enough. The old woman from the council meeting – Sperancia – was suddenly inside of their tent, moving much more quickly than could be expected of a non-enhanced person. She was armed with a dagger – the blade already wetted with blood – and coming straight for Maro.

An alarming situation, if he did not so fully trust in Livia's reflexes.

He'd wondered about the old woman during the council meeting. And even earlier, when he'd first noticed the black, lacelike threads beneath her skin. A disease, he'd thought at first, though she'd shown no signs of infirmity. There was something odd about her voice, too –

it changed inflection periodically, as if another person were speaking: a different timbre, with different vocal rhythms, habits, and tics. Perhaps the old woman suffered from a multiple-personality disorder. Or maybe she fancied herself an actor, and had a bevy of characters to trot out in response to various conversational cues. Certainly she was interesting, and Maro had already flagged her for inclusion in his project.

And she was all the more interesting now, lunging for Maro's throat with clear murderous intent.

He took a step back, and Livia was there in front of him, stop-thrusting the woman with a brutal stab to the chest, her blade held horizontally so as to slip through Sperancia's ribs just to the right of her breastbone. The weapon would deliver several thousand milliamps of electricity directly to the woman's heart, surely enough to stop her cold.

And yet it didn't. Sperancia thrust her arm out, palm open, hitting Livia squarely in the face. Livia's head snapped back and she stumbled away, still holding the blade. Sperancia gasped for air, but she remained standing, staring at Maro with a cold violence that made him shiver.

For the first time on Earth, he felt a hint of fear.

Maro's body was a work of engineering and art. His senses were enhanced, the functions of his organs protected by redundant implants, his muscles powerful and flexible regardless of how little he exercised. But he was mortal. He'd backed up his brain with a deep scan before leaving the *Michelangelo*, but that was for the benefit of his loved ones, and perhaps for future scholars who might want to converse with an engram of the great senator. Even if the engram possessed limited consciousness while active, it wasn't *him*. Making a copy of your thought organ, however complete, was no way to cheat death.

And yet his curiosity overpowered his fear. "What are you?" he asked.

Sperancia lunged at him, but Livia had recovered, and partially deflected the blow. Instead of slicing open his neck, the knife grazed his cheek. And then Livia was plunging her golden blade into the old woman's abdomen, over and over again, with pistonlike efficiency.

"Stop!" he commanded. He had more questions for the old woman. Sperancia collapsed to the ground, holding her stomach and gasping for air. The threat had passed. "What are you?" he repeated. "And why have you come for me – for us? Do you fear us?" He considered telling the old woman that the *Michelangelo* could obliterate their entire town if he ordered it. A single tactical warhead, a precision strike from space, and Bosa would be nothing but a smoldering pile of ruins. Or a neutron bomb, killing all life but leaving the buildings intact for historical purposes – that was the more realistic scenario.

But he had no such intentions. He was a scholar, a researcher. His passion was learning, the accumulation of novel experiences.

She squinted at him, unafraid and unrepentant. But something was missing from her expression. There was no bitterness in her face, nor any sense of defeat. Despite the fact that she would soon die of blood loss, the old woman had yet to surrender. He started to smile in admiration of her fighting spirit, but a thought stopped him cold. *Why* had she not yet surrendered?

"Tell me what you are," he commanded, more desperately this time. "Perhaps we can still save your life, if you co-operate." He glanced at Livia. She had retreated to a corner of the tent and was watching the tent opening warily. She'd heard something.

A young woman pushed through the tent flap. It was Jana, the girl Sperancia had described as her protégée. She was a lanky, awkward-looking young woman, with oddly proportioned features. Though not unpleasing, Maro noted. There was a stolid fearlessness in her expression that impressed him.

Jana knelt next to Sperancia and offered her comfort. Maro asked Jana the same questions he'd asked Sperancia, but the girl gave him nothing except a boast that Sperancia had murdered Felix. Maro felt a mix of emotions as Livia rushed out of the tent: a streak of jealous vindication at Felix's probable demise, dread at the prospect of dealing with Livia's emotional fallout, and a thrill that he had just survived an attack that might have killed all of them. An actual assassination attempt. What a brilliant story it would all make when he recounted the tale to his fellow senators.

But now something even more unusual was occurring. The old woman had managed to prop herself up on her hands and knees, and was having some sort of spasm. She vomited something up, perhaps a giant dark blood clot. But the object fell heavily, like a chunk of lead or gold. It was round, the shape of a small bird's egg, and pure black.

To Maro's absolute surprise, Jana picked up the strange object and swallowed it whole.

She had expected it, somehow. Whatever it was that the old woman had regurgitated, Jana had anticipated the event, acting without hesitation.

It seemed probable – highly probable – that the black egg was related to Sperancia's strange powers and odd behaviors. Would these powers now be transferred to the girl? If so, how long would that process take?

It had been a long time since Maro had been confronted with a phenomenon completely beyond his understanding. He was thrilled.

Livia returned to the tent, confirming what Jana had told them: Sperancia had murdered Felix. Maro muttered his condolences, aware that his words were insufficient but unable to focus on anything beyond the strange sight he had just witnessed. Livia asked if she should kill the girl, but Maro stopped her; they had too much to learn from the young protégée. He'd let Livia have her revenge eventually. But not now.

He knelt and took Jana's face in his hands. "Please explain to me what just happened."

He was met with a glob of saliva in his eye. He slapped the girl, reflexively, knocking her down. She touched her bleeding lip.

"I'm sorry. I didn't mean to strike you so hard," he said, wiping the spit from his face. "But that was unnecessary. The two of you just tried to murder us, and we have spared you. Show us a modicum of gratitude."

Jana stared at him sullenly, as unrepentant and fearless as the old woman.

"Why don't you fear me?" he asked. "I think you know I could easily kill you, don't you? Is that why you attacked us in the first place, because you're aware of our power?"

"You're thieves and pirates, all of you," Jana accused. "You always have been."

"Thieves?" Maro repeated, surprised. What had he stolen? He meant to borrow a few townsfolk for his experiments, but he intended to return them. Whole and unharmed, if all went as planned.

"You stole all the great works of art from Earth, centuries ago. Sperancia told me everything."

"How old are you?" She refused to answer. "How old was *she*?" he asked, gesturing to Sperancia's lifeless body. The girl just sat there silently, hand pressed to her bleeding mouth. "The events you refer to occurred centuries ago. And you've got it all wrong. We protected Earth's great works. And we continue to do so. If you come to our ship, you can see the great masters yourself. Even works by our namesake. The ceiling of the Sistine Chapel – we transported the entire edifice, chunk by chunk.

Now it is displayed in our Curia, our Senate hall, restored to its original brilliance. *Il divino* would be proud, could he see it for himself."

The girl looked unimpressed. And why would she be? She had no idea who Michelangelo was, or Leonardo da Vinci or Raphael or Caravaggio, or Rembrandt or Van Gogh, or any of the other great painters, sculptors, composers, and authors who had graced civilization with their genius. She was ignorant.

Though not completely. Sperancia had demonstrated some knowledge of ancient history during their meeting, and if this girl was her protégée, Sperancia had likely tried to teach her.

"Is there a school in Bosa?" he asked. "Do you use books? Do you *print* books?"

"Yes, we have a school. Though you just murdered our teacher."

"In self-defense. And I'm willing to overlook the attempt on our lives if you co-operate with us."

Jana looked surprised. She'd been expecting an imminent death. And Livia was still ready, clutching the hilt of her dagger with white knuckles.

He waved dismissively at Jana. "Go, before I change my mind. Say nothing to the other townsfolk."

Jana hesitated, looking at Sperancia's lifeless body.

"We'll bury her. Don't worry – we'll be respectful."

The girl left, shaking visibly. He would interrogate her later, with kindness if he could. He recognized a deep stubbornness in her. Threats would get him nowhere, nor would physical pain. He'd noted the way she'd looked at the blood on her hand when he'd struck her, with curious detachment.

"What now?" Livia asked.

He checked on Felix, who was indeed dead, his throat opened violently all the way to the spine.

"What made the old woman so strong?" he asked. "Some kind of enhancement?"

"She's flesh and blood," Livia said, "though it was hard to pierce her skin. It was stiff and dense, like a wire mesh."

"Some sort of cyborg?"

"I'll examine her corpse. If we bring it back to the shuttle, I can conduct a full analysis."

Maro nodded. Livia was choosing not to react to Felix's death immediately, and that was fine with him. "Bag both bodies and store them in the gondola." They had no refrigeration; vacuum bags would have to do for preservation.

Hearing Livia's effortful grunts as she worked, he considered helping. But no, his time was better spent contemplating tomorrow's work. Ancestral Realism was his project, his in-progress masterpiece. That was why they were here. It was unfortunate they'd lost Felix. He'd underestimated Sperancia, and possibly Jana as well. The people of Bosa were more varied and complex than he'd anticipated. He'd failed to look beneath the surface.

He would not make that mistake again, he thought, taking a deep breath. The air had a ferric tang from the lingering mist of Felix's blood. He forgave himself for failing to anticipate the women who had just tried to murder him. In time, he would understand their minds – minds that were the closest living link to the consciousness of his dead ancestors.

History was still alive here in Bosa, and he would have a piece of it.

CHAPTER EIGHT

Maro squeezed Livia's hand as they approached the town square. The morning light was brilliant, palpable, giving the townscape the intensity of a Dutch Golden Age painting. Many of Bosa's buildings were painted in colorful pastels – recently from the looks of it. A jarring variety of smells assaulted his sinuses: the sea, baking bread, roasting pork, fresh thyme. He wished he could record the aromas in the same way his visual and auditory sensations were recorded. There must be a way; he would ask the Engineers.

Maro and Livia had ostensibly come to say goodbye, but their real purpose was recruitment. Now was the time to gather commitments. Maybe they would be greeted with spears and knives, but Maro guessed that Sperancia and Jana had acted alone. Maro and Livia had lain awake for the remainder of the night but no one else had come.

They'd brought the last of the confections: bittersweet candies; dense chocolate cake decorated with gold leaf; silky custards. The desserts had survived the voyage remarkably well in a simple liquid-nitrogen-cooled box. They distributed the last of their other gifts, too: small toys and trinkets. All were constructed with simple materials and no electronics; anything more complex might be socially disruptive. Cultural preservation was of the utmost importance. Encouraging technological progress would not serve the interests of Ancestral Realism.

"Greetings, people of Bosa!" Maro said in a rich baritone. More than two dozen had gathered, including all of the town elders, save Sperancia. Jana was missing too. "You've had the night to consider our offer. Who will join us on the *Michelangelo* for a short tour?"

Murmurs rippled through the crowd but no one stepped forward. Which was as he'd expected. These people were cautious and careful, slow to change. That was one reason they had survived.

"We thank you for your offer," said Gregoriu, the mayor, "but must we decide today? You must realize, from our perspective, this is all happening extremely quickly."

An old man thrust his chin at them. "We don't trust you. Why should we? And where is the other one – there were three of you."

"Shut up, Iginu," said a portly, rosy-cheeked man. Micheli – one of the council members. "Don't be rude to our guests." Micheli approached, holding something behind his back. Maro could not help but flinch even though Livia was right there at his side. But the barkeep produced a slender dark bottle. "Please accept this mirto, our local drink. The recipe has been in my family for generations."

Maro took the gift and smiled. "Thank you, Micheli. Surely you must be curious to taste other liqueurs? And our wines and whiskies? Maybe you will visit us."

Micheli looked down. "Perhaps."

Of course he wouldn't, though Maro didn't give a shit. It was younger blood he was after, men and women in their prime. Maro dramatically pulled a leather purse from his robes. He opened the drawstring and poured a handful of small but heavy gold coins into his palm. The coins were minted in the style of Roman *aurei*, each worth twenty-five silver *denarii*. Ancient Rome was in fashion on the *Michelangelo*, and had been for several decades. The Senate, the use of Latin, Roman names, even the renaming of the current political factions as the *optimates* and *populares*, it was all a giant role play. But it was also life and death, Maro's personal *ad in vita*, and what gave meaning to the existence of the worldship itself. Life was culture, culture was life. Civilization was history, history was civilization.

"Those of you who volunteer will be away from your families and your livelihoods. It is only fair to compensate you. Five gold coins to each volunteer now, and another twenty when your visit is complete." He dropped the coins into his other palm, a tiny waterfall of gold, observing the crowd as he did so. A young man with dark eyes and high cheekbones watched him closely. "What is your name?" Maro asked.

"Cristo."

"Come hold these coins for me. If you decide not to join us, you can give them back."

Cristo looked at the old man who had spoken earlier, who gave a quick shake of his head. But the admonition had the opposite effect; Cristo set his jaw and stepped forward, hand outstretched. Maro smiled and dropped five gold *aurei* into Cristo's open palm, one by one, with the satisfying clunking sounds that only precious metals produced. He closed the young man's fingers over the coins and patted his shoulder. "Welcome, Cristo," he said quietly, so only the boy could hear. "Adventure awaits you on the *Michelangelo*, and delights beyond your most depraved imaginings. And you will be a rich man when you return – very rich."

Maro turned back to the crowd. "Now, while you further consider our offer, will you be so kind as to feed us? The smell of fresh bread is driving me wild!"

His words had the desired effect: the people of Bosa were shocked into an awareness of their hospitality obligations. Several tables were brought out along with many chairs, and within an hour they were served a simple but delicious meal. First came dark barley bread and a variety of pungent sheep and goat milk cheeses. Next salads of sweet, ripe tomatoes with fresh herbs and bitter olive oil. The main course was platters of roasted fish seasoned with salt, lemon, onion, and peppercorns, along with steamed mussels with garlic, white wine, and butter. Finally came an assortment of desserts, including honeyed orange peels and a sweet almond flour pastry. The only thing missing was coffee, though there was a delicious piney herb tea.

As Maro had expected, the people of Bosa warmed to them over the course of the feast. That was the thing about generosity: whoever was receiving it went up in the estimation of those bestowing it. It was a cheap psychological trick based on the avoidance of cognitive dissonance, but Maro happily used it. The Sardinians were a simple people and would not see through his ploy.

Most of them, anyway. He kept an eye out for Jana, but the murderous bitch was still in hiding. Perhaps it had been a mistake to let her go. But they hadn't had the means to imprison her, and killing her wasn't an option. At least not until he understood what had happened after Sperancia had died. What was the nature of the black egg Jana had consumed?

It was a joy and a relief to eat real food. Their travel rations had been meager: a staple of nutrition powder rehydrated with runoff water formulated from their excess balloon gases. It wasn't bad for an engineered food replacement, but it wasn't real food. Felix had complained about their 'sludge meals' incessantly. Maro had drunk his meals stoically, all the while fantasizing about dining with the chefs of his favorite restaurants. The Bosa fare, though simple, was delicious: real food grown from actual dirt from the light of a real sun.

If this was what the past tasted like, it was glorious.

A young woman approached Livia, an attractive girl with long, brown hair, kind eyes, and supple, tan skin. He'd noticed her on the first day. And she'd flirted with him, smiling and gazing at his bare chest. But now she was ignoring him, focusing entirely on Livia. "What would we be doing, exactly, on your ship?" she asked.

"Whatever you wanted to do," Livia told her. "You could meet other young people. You could visit our museums, attend plays and concerts. You could learn to draw and paint, or play a musical instrument, or study mathematics. And I promise that your teachers would be geniuses, absolutely brilliant."

Maro smiled at the ease with which Livia lied. She was truly a viper, cold and cunning.

"Could I bring my mother along? She's sick."

"Of course. Whatever her ailment, I'm sure we could ease her pain and prolong her life. Perhaps even cure her."

Maro reached out and gently touched the girl's arm. "What's your name?"

"Filumena."

"Will you accept these?" He offered her five gold *aurei*.

She didn't even look at the coins. "No. Not yet. I need to speak with my mother. And with my friends."

Friends. He'd seen Filumena speaking with Jana. "Is Jana your friend?" he asked. "Where is she today?"

"I haven't yet seen her."

"Please tell her to come speak with me, when you do. My name is Maro."

"I know." She nodded, brow furrowed, and left them.

"Do you want Jana for the project?" Livia asked him quietly.

"No, not for that. I want to know what Sperancia was, and what will become of the girl."

Livia had a look of regret in her eye, and Maro guessed that she was questioning her choice to kill the old woman. But it hadn't been a choice, not really. Livia had instinctively saved his life. He squeezed her hand, trying to convey his reassurance, wishing he could speak his thoughts openly. But the townsfolk were all around, talking and eating the last of the desserts.

After the feast they strolled through the cobblestone streets and alleys of the old town, conversing with whoever wanted to speak with them, asking and answering questions. Maro explained that Felix was preparing the balloon for their return voyage home; soon they would return with their shuttle to pick up the volunteers. In terms of the exchange, they would wait for a formal offer from the council before sending guests to live in Bosa. The townsfolk seemed satisfied with his answers, and openly speculated as to what life might be like on the *Michelangelo*. Maro was thoroughly enjoying himself. But he noticed that Livia, though putting on a brave face, was suffering.

"We'll get our revenge," he whispered. "I haven't forgotten Felix."

"That won't bring him back."

He almost said something about talking to Felix's engram, but stopped himself. That would bring Livia no comfort. She'd lost a lover, someone she'd cared about deeply. Not that he understood why, but he accepted it. Love wasn't logical or fair. If it was, Maro would be first in Livia's heart.

Eventually they returned to the town square. Micheli invited them to his bar for drinks. It was still some hours before dusk, but day drinking seemed in the spirit of things. Aside from the hiccup with Felix, everything was falling into place. And honestly Felix's absence was a relief; he'd been secretly considering how to get rid of his romantic competitor. Now he could put that thought to rest. Once Livia recovered emotionally, all would be right in the world. There were a few loose ends to tie up: dealing with Jana, navigating safely back to Tunis, the logistics of picking up the volunteers in the shuttle. But no major problems. It was okay to let his guard down a little. So when he saw a young boy whispering something to Gregoriu, and the look of concern on the mayor's face, he dismissed it.

Micheli put out olives, cured ham, a pungent, fermented cheese, red wine, sweet mead, and thick crackers made from a nutty wheat varietal. Maro joked and laughed with the barkeep and his friends, listening to stories from their childhood. Livia appeared to be in better spirits as well, drinking copious amounts of wine and flirting with the old men, who gazed at her lasciviously. Even the suspicious old man – Iginu – who Maro had gathered was the boy Cristo's father, warmed to Livia, laughing uproariously at her quips and occasionally touching her shoulder, which she allowed. It was good to win Iginu over; his son Cristo would be a valuable recruit, brave and adventurous.

People came in and out of the bar, not just the men but their wives, and young people as well. As dusk fell, Maro felt an echo of the ecstatic fugue he'd experienced during their first days on Earth. This was wonderful, just spending time with new people, people he hadn't known his entire life. He knew nothing of their history, their families, their affiliations and alliances. He could be himself, unguarded, uncalculating. He wondered how many small communities like this had survived. Dozens, perhaps. Ancestral Realism could be expanded....

"We should go," Livia whispered in his ear, "before it's completely dark."

"Of course," said Maro. He was reluctant to pull himself away, but she was right. It wasn't safe to spend another night in the field, not with Jana unaccounted for. He stood, stumbling slightly from the wine, and cleared his throat, ready to give a final appeal. He knew he had Cristo, and the girl Filumena. One or two more was all they needed.

He felt a tap on his shoulder. Gregoriu, the mayor. "Excuse me, Maro," the little man said, "there's something I'd like to show you. Will you and Livia please follow me?"

Maro put his arm around the mayor's bony shoulder. "Of course. Show us the way."

The mayor led them outside. The clarity of the moonlit square, deep shadows and powerful contrasts, made Maro feel as if he were walking into a Caravaggio painting. It took his breath away. "This way, please," Gregoriu said, leading them down a stone staircase. The mayor opened an unlocked basement door. "After you."

Even with his augmented vision, Maro's eyes took a moment to adjust. They were in some sort of storage room, the walls lined with shelves and stacked barrels. Two long, rectangular tables took up the center area, pushed up against each other to form a large, squarish workspace.

Two bodies lay faceup atop the tables, feet facing Maro and Livia. Both were cold and lifeless, skin tinged blue, wounds brownish-black where the blood had dried. Whoever had arranged the corpses had completely removed them from the vacuum bags. Felix was on the left, Sperancia to the right.

"I can explain," Maro said immediately. "She attacked us!"

But the townsfolk were already on them, hurling damp, pungent fishing nets. The coarse rope scratched his skin away as he struggled, stumbled, and fell. They kicked him in his legs and stomach. Livia fared a little better, punching and knocking men down, but the old fishermen were used to pulling in huge fish from the sea. They worked together to subdue Livia, catching her limbs with weighted nets and beating her with oaken cudgels.

"Enough!" someone bellowed hoarsely. A low, female voice.

It was Jana, standing over them, just as he had stood over Sperancia's fallen body the night before. Her skin was pale and her eyes were bloodshot, but there was the same determination and stubbornness in her expression that he'd noticed earlier.

"Sperancia murdered Felix," said Maro loudly, with as much dignity as he could muster from his prone position, wrapped in wet netting. "Tell them the truth, Jana. You were with her, and you came for us without provocation."

"They can't be trusted," Jana said. "Livia murdered Sperancia."

"See?" Maro said. "She doesn't deny it."

"You killed one of us – a council member – and acted as if nothing had happened," Gregoriu said accusingly. "This was my call, not Jana's. Ralf and Bina saw what happened last night, and gathered the courage to tell me."

The children hiding in the woods – he'd forgotten about them after the attack. He should have scared them away when the security drones had first detected them.

"If Sperancia attacked you, why didn't you tell us?" Gregoriu asked.

"Because he's hiding their past," Jana said. "They're thieves – they are here to steal from us."

Maro raised his hands as best he could. "What would we steal from you? Cheese? Fish? We created our own world, with its own sun, that moves freely among the planets. You are delusional if you think you have something of value that we cannot create ourselves."

Gregoriu frowned, and Maro realized this was the man's weakness: a reasonable disposition and an open mind. The mayor was actually considering the rationality of his argument, still completely blind to Maro's motives.

"You say they are thieves, Jana. What did they steal?"

"All the art from the greatest museums in the world. They're hoarding it all on their worldship."

"We're hoarding nothing," Maro protested. He tried, unsuccessfully, to remove a fish scale from his lip. "We have invited you to visit us, to experience the great art that we have protected for centuries. And the invitation is still open. This is all a misunderstanding. Sperancia and Jana perceived a threat where none existed. That's natural and to be understood."

Even as he negotiated for his life, Maro felt an excitement bubbling up inside of him. *This* was the purpose of Ancestral Realism. He'd been completely blindsided by their actions. Consciousness had so diverged between Earth dwellers and worldship citizens that he'd been unable to predict their behavior. This, despite his intelligence, training, natural cunning, and years of experience surviving the traitorous sharks of the Senate. For all his savvy, here he was on the floor, entrapped in a fishing net, confronting the very real possibility that he would be beaten to death with cudgels. But Ancestral Realism would break that wall between the primitive minds of the past and the sophisticated minds that had kept higher civilization alive and flourishing, while the planet below recovered from its devastations. Soon, if he was not smashed to a bloody pulp, he would be able to time travel within the landscape of historical subjective human consciousness.

Gregoriu appeared as if he had made some sort of decision. "If you truly killed Sperancia in self-defense, we will take that into consideration. But you have murdered a council member, a town elder, a person of great esteem—" Jana touched Gregoriu's arm, silencing him, and he gave a brief nod before continuing. "We will deliberate among ourselves, but Sperancia's death will not go unpunished."

Maro smiled – humbly, he hoped – and nodded. The worst danger had passed, he suspected. Gregoriu's cool head would prevail.

But he briefly locked eyes with Jana and felt a shiver of fear. In a way the girl was right – they were here to take what they wanted – and he was sure Jana would do everything in her power to protect her people.

CHAPTER NINE

Traveling in the hovershuttle was terrifying. Katja regretted tricking her nephew, but Tem was too thick-headed to realize the urgency of the situation.

No, that wasn't it. He was an intelligent, empathetic young man, not thick-headed at all. But he had not experienced the horror of having his body stolen by a gast. He had no way of knowing what was truly at stake.

Stealing the flying machine had been trivial. Katja had found it right where Tem said he'd left it, by the Three Stones. Her nephew had not even bothered to conceal the craft with branches and debris. The boy was bright like his father but was more like his uncle in that he was far too trusting. Tem preferred to believe the best about people, despite the traumas of his childhood.

"Return!" she had ordered the craft, in English, once boarded. "Previous location!" she'd said, when that produced nothing. She'd noticed the way Tem spoke with machines, using precise language and specific terms. A map had appeared on the screen, displaying an island with a red dot on the north-west coast. She'd opened the ancient atlas she'd brought with her, a book salvaged from the ruins of a Builder city. Its pages were brittle and yellowed but somehow the book had avoided water damage; the text was faded but legible. *Sardinia* was an island in the Mediterranean Sea, and the shapes matched.

"Go!" she had shouted. "Onward! Start! Engage! Return to destination!"

Something she'd said had worked, and soon she'd been high in the air, speeding over the trees, clutching the arms of the pilot's seat in white-knuckled terror. The hovershuttle flew faster than any bird, or so it seemed. It was not her first ride in such a vehicle, but it had been years, and this model was sleeker and faster.

She'd brought Biter, her soulsword. The long blade lay on the bench seat behind her, a deadly passenger. Her mission was simple: behead the new gast and chop her to bits. She would open her up, find the black egg, and destroy it for good. She'd heard stories of the ancient volcanoes that had destroyed the Builder civilization, mountains filled with molten rock. Maybe she could find one and throw the Crucible in.

It wouldn't be easy. She'd be killing multiple people in doing so. But she'd also be freeing them. And she knew she was up to the task; she'd done it before.

Raekae, the gast of Happdal, had stolen her body thirty years ago. The Crucible had kept him alive for generations, allowing him to parasitically occupy new bodies and replicate each host's brain. Raekae's first life had been in the Builder era. He'd been some sort of scientist or inventor. But the Crucible had turned him into a monster.

The original intention of the Crucible program had been to create communities of minds, multiple virtualized people living in shared simulated worlds with access to a real body in the physical world. Katja had experienced two such world simulations herself. One had been dominated by Raekae, who had manipulated the emotions of his slave minds, quashing rebellion with artificially induced fear. The other had been created by Zoë, a previous host who had escaped Raekae's control to create her own world-within-a-world. Zoë's simulation had been highly detailed and realistic, with vivid sights and smells, animals and insects, entire living ecosystems.

In the end, Zoë had destroyed Raekae, as well as all his slave minds and previous hosts, including Zoë herself, by running a new algorithm on the Crucible's quantum core. Zoë had told her that the algorithm would create a new simulation, not a programmed world but a real evolving universe. Zoë hadn't wanted to die, but she'd been willing to make the sacrifice in order to potentially save Katja.

And Katja had made the choice.

The algorithm had destroyed everything, completely erasing the minds of the previous hosts, some who had befriended her. Including Stian, the first smith of Happdal.

The dying of those worlds had nearly killed Katja as the Crucible's physical host. But she had survived. And recovered, mostly, though the experience had irrevocably scarred her.

She harbored no bitterness. Everyone had wounds, seen and unseen. *Life* scarred you. The longer you lived, the more scars you accumulated. And those wounds never completely healed; each was capable of generating its own unique pain or discomfort until you died. So she accepted her pain and refused to live in fear.

But that didn't mean that all suffering should be accepted. You could make the choice to heal, never the same but sometimes stronger. You could avoid getting injured in the first place. And you could fight against evildoers to protect the weak and innocent. That's what Biter was for.

Katja studied the controls but thought better of touching any. "Close hatch," she commanded. The vehicle responded, raising two connecting hemispheres to form a clear dome. She studied the navigation display, comparing it to various pages in the atlas. The hovershuttle took her south, out of the Harz mountains and through a long, wide valley. She passed over what had once been Switzerland, recognizing a vast lake. A huge, snow-capped mountain range rose to her left – the Alps.

The air inside the dome became quite warm, and the novelty of traveling so high and fast wore off. She crawled into the back seat and slept for a while, cradling the sword for comfort. When she woke, she was over water – more water than she had ever seen in her life. She was worried the craft would run out of fuel but she had no idea how to check.

"Where are we?"

"Over the Mediterranean Sea," the shuttle answered in a soothing voice. "Approximately at latitude forty-three, longitude seven. Would you like more precise co-ordinates?"

"No. No, thank you." She found it awkward to speak with machines, though it didn't seem to bother Tem or Car-En, and her brother Esper had adapted easily enough. She felt stupid for only giving the vehicle commands and not asking questions earlier. She asked about the fuel levels. The hovershuttle reassured her that it had adequate resources for another half-day's travel, but would need additional biomass at that point. They would reach their destination in approximately forty minutes.

Her stomach was grumbling. She'd brought food – dried venison, smoked fish, and three apples. She was two bites into her second apple when the hovershuttle spoke again. Except this time it sounded different, slightly broken up. And *angry*.

"Tem, why are you returning to Bosa without us? The plan was to meet in Ilium."

Katja froze. It wasn't the ship speaking, but rather a person from the ringship settlement. People from the *Stanford*, including Car-En's friend Lydia, had created their own town of sorts – Ilium.

"Who is speaking?" Katja asked tentatively.

"This is Maggie. Who is *this*?"

She wasn't sure what to say. What would happen if she confessed to stealing the hovershuttle? Could they turn off the engine, plunging her into the cold sea below?

"What the hell is going on? Where is Tem?"

Maggie. Tem's lover in Ilium. He'd spoken fondly of the girl, though that hadn't stopped him from rutting with Saga in Trond's smithy last night. She'd overheard more than she'd wanted to.

Still, there was genuine fear in Maggie's voice – she cared about Tem. And Tem was her own flesh and blood.

"He's fine," Katja said. "Though he may need a ride. He's still in Happdal."

"*Who is this?*"

"It doesn't matter. I stole the hovershuttle. There's something I need to do in Bosa. Please don't turn it off – I'm over the water."

"I can't turn it off. Why did you steal it? What do you need to do in Bosa?"

Too many questions. "End! Stop transmission! Turn off!"

"Terminate voice communications?" the hovershuttle asked calmly.

"Yes!"

Katja finished her second apple in blessed silence.

She could see a densely forested landmass to her left, but the hovershuttle continued south without slowing. To her right the sun was nearing the horizon; she had only a few hours of light remaining. Or possibly less; somehow the sun descended more rapidly in this part of the world.

A landmass appeared before her, much larger than she had expected. The hovershuttle slowed and descended, coming to a stop a few hundred meters from the shore. A town was visible, set on a hilltop, the hill crowned with the ruins of a castle. There were castle ruins near Happdal – evidence of settlements that existed even before the Builders. Zoë had taught her some history; she'd learned how humans had lived on the planet for many thousands of years, in waves of civilizations. The Minoans of Crete had been one of the earliest civilizations in the Mediterranean, a fishing people who'd built great cities. She could see a few fishing boats docked at a pier – boats several times larger than any she'd seen before. Would the people of Sardinia be anything like the people of Happdal? Or would they be masters of machines like the people from the *Stanford*? Or more like the ancient Minoans?

"Move closer," she told the hovershuttle, more quietly this time. "I'm a poor swimmer. And be quiet if you can." The craft obliged, muffling the rotor to a dull whir. She couldn't see anyone on or around the piers. Maybe they were all eating their evening meal.

She clambered onto a pier, bringing only her sword, which she drew and held before her. It occurred to her that someone might try to steal the hovershuttle, just as she had done. "Stay here," she commanded, "and don't allow anyone to get near you except me. Can you do that?"

"Yes," the craft answered quietly. "I will maintain a security buffer of ten meters unless I recognize your voice signature."

As easy as that. She'd have some advice for Tem the next time she saw him.

The roads here were paved with stones, worn flat and smooth from many years of use. She picked one at random, heading toward what she guessed was the center of town. What was her plan, exactly? Perhaps she should have given it more thought. She couldn't just lop off the head of the first old woman she saw. She'd had the idea that she would recognize the gast – Sperancia – by the black, threadlike markings beneath her skin. She'd had the same markings on her own face for years, well after she'd been freed from the Crucible. But dusk was falling rapidly; it would be difficult to make out such details.

Bosa – if that was indeed where she was – was deserted. Had the hovershuttle taken her to the wrong place, to some long-abandoned seaside village? Some insect was chirping incessantly, but she heard no voices. And yet there were signs of life. Most of the buildings were in good repair, some even with a fresh coat of paint. The streets were free of debris; trees and shrubs were trimmed back. She spotted several small neatly tended gardens. An orange cat crossed her path, giving her a curious look before disappearing behind a low wall. Some movement from above caught her eye – a shutter closing. Yes, there were people here. Hiding from her, perhaps.

Ahead, she heard faint shouting and yelling in the distance. It was difficult to tell the exact direction; the sound was ricocheting off the stone walls. She ran, but the voices became fainter, then stopped altogether. She retraced her steps and again heard people speaking, more calmly now and much closer.

She entered a town square, and for the first time saw light, either from a torch or lantern. She twirled her sword, loosening her shoulders. She would do her best to only kill the gast, but she was willing to do whatever was necessary. Surely she would be outnumbered, but for now she had the advantage of surprise. She would kill Sperancia on sight: a cutting slash to the neck if she had room for a proper swing, otherwise a quick upward thrust to the heart from beneath the breastbone. It wasn't a sophisticated plan, but Katja was confident in her ability to wield Biter.

"*Tu chi sei?*"

A dark-haired girl stood in a doorway. She was small-boned, wearing a blue dress, her face in shadows.

Katja put her finger to her lips. "Shhhh...."

The girl silently watched her. Katja kept moving toward the light, catlike, holding Biter with both hands. The light was coming from a room below ground level. Male voices debated something in a language she didn't understand. A meeting or congregation of some sort; perhaps this was why the rest of the town was empty.

It occurred to her that this might be the end. The people of Bosa might be formidable warriors with powerful armaments. Perhaps this was her last night on Earth. She would die alone, far from her friends and family. Even if she fought valiantly, no one she cared about would know.

She glanced over her shoulder. The girl was still watching from the shadows.

Katja didn't feel scared, not really, but she was breathing quickly, practically panting, gripping the hilt of the sword far too hard.

She descended the stairs with a few quick hops and kicked the basement door. It swung open without resistance. She rushed into the room.

There were at least two dozen people packed into the basement, a large storage room. A man and a woman, apparently prisoners, were entangled in fishing nets directly in front of her. The Bosa villagers surrounded the prisoners, some holding nets, others wielding long fish knives.

Two bodies lay supine on a large table in the center of the room.

Corpses, a woman and a man. The man was young and fit, with bronze skin tinged blue.

Everyone looked at her in shocked amazement, mouths agape.

"Where is Sperancia?" she bellowed. She swung Biter in a menacing arc, evoking backward steps and fearful looks. "Where is the gast? *Where is Sperancia?*"

"You speak English?" The male prisoner, entangled in nets, looked at her with curious fascination. "Where are you from? How do you know Sperancia? Do you know what she is?" The man had bronze skin like the corpse on the table, and shiny black hair. He was radiantly handsome.

"Where is she?" Katja asked him. No one else seemed to understand her words. Except for possibly the female prisoner, who was watching her with predatory intensity.

"She is right there, on the table. I'm afraid you're too late. She's quite dead." His accent was musical and lilting.

"*Cosa sta dicendo?*" A tall, pale woman stepped out of the shadows. Like the male prisoner, she seemed unafraid of Katja, approaching so that her chest pressed up against Biter's point. She stared at Katja with bloodshot eyes. Was she their leader?

The male prisoner answered the pale woman's question in the same language. "This is Jana," he explained to Katja. "She tried to murder me last night, along with Sperancia. They're deciding what to do with us now. You've come at an awkward time."

Katja dropped the point of her blade and shoved Jana aside. The girl stumbled back, unresisting. The other villagers kept their distance, eyeing her as a squirrel might watch a lynx. Satisfied for the moment that the villagers would not attack her, Katja laid Biter down alongside the old woman. *Sperancia.* Her black dress had been pulled open to reveal a horizontal wound right above her heart, a near-surgical incision. There were black threads beneath her skin, on her chest, neck, and face. There was no doubt this was a gast.

Katja grabbed the wrist of a nearby man, twisting sharply. She caught the fish knife before it hit the ground, and before anyone could react, plunged the blade into Sperancia's breastbone. The Crucible core, if it was still there, would have implanted itself near the esophagus.

"*Fermare!*" someone called out, but most just stared in dumb fascination, either terrified or confused.

Jana – the woman with the bloodshot eyes – had recovered, and was speaking rapidly to the male prisoner.

"She says it's not there, what you're looking for."

"Then where is it?"

"She swallowed it – a small black egg. I saw it with my own eyes."

Katja looked at Jana, not wanting to believe what she'd just heard. Part of her had suspected it from the moment she'd seen the girl, who gave every indication of being recently traumatized.

She'd arrived too late. The Crucible had found a new host.

CHAPTER TEN

An hour later Katja had reached an uneasy truce with the town elders of Bosa. Maro – the male prisoner – served as a translator, though Katja suspected he was twisting her words for his own purposes. But she had no choice but to rely on him; the language of the Sardinian people was utterly unfamiliar.

At the insistence of Gregoriu, the mayor of Bosa, Katja stowed her sword back in the hovershuttle. He'd wanted to confiscate it but had agreed to the compromise. Gregoriu struck her as a reasonable, thoughtful man doing his best to navigate a chaotic situation. Once she learned what had recently transpired in Bosa, she felt some sympathy for the beleaguered mayor.

They were seated in the town hall, a building that seemed to serve the same function as Happdal's longhouse. Someone offered her food and wine, but she had no appetite. She was seated at a long table next to Maro, with one empty chair between them. Maro's wrists were bound in iron shackles, which he appeared to take in stride. She felt uneasy in his presence. Despite the fact that he was a prisoner, Maro seemed more in control of the situation than anyone else.

"Where is the other prisoner – the woman?" she asked him.

"Locked in a house, but safe. The people of Bosa are civilized. They have acknowledged that we were attacked first, that we acted in self-defense. Jana admitted as much."

"And where is Jana?"

"Asleep, I am told."

Katja nodded. *Unconscious* was more likely. She had vague memories of her own first days and nights as the Crucible grew its black tendrils throughout her body and brain. She'd drifted in and out of consciousness, sometimes hearing strange voices. Those voices had been the previous hosts, she'd learned later. Even now, she missed some of them. Especially Stian the smith, who had treated her kindly, encouraging her to learn to read.

It took some time for everyone to understand what had occurred. Katja confirmed that she knew the previous visitors from Ilium – that one of them was in fact her nephew – and that she had flown the same hovershuttle to Sardinia. She did not mention that she had stolen the craft, but did state emphatically that she had come of her own accord, that Tem and the others knew nothing of her mission.

As for her reason for coming to Bosa, she was truthful. The Crucible was a dangerous parasite, a machine that could enslave people. Maro seemed fascinated by this proposition and asked her far more questions than did the town elders of Bosa, who had a different view. Jana had been chosen as the next host – an honor – and had fully accepted that role. Whoever bore the Crucible became a sorceress, a woman possessing great knowledge and strength. And it was always a woman, by their tradition.

She needed to speak with Jana as soon as she woke up. If the girl had voluntarily swallowed the black egg, as Maro had attested, then something was different here. Perhaps the hosts did not always become slaves. Was each Crucible different?

"And you say you are from the *Michelangelo*, a ringship?" she asked Maro.

"We call them worldships, but yes."

"Why did you come to Bosa?"

"To meet new people. To trade. Potentially to make allies. We have been isolated for many years."

"Why not reach out to the people of the *Stanford* or the *Liu Hui* or the *Alhazen*?"

"How do you know of such places?"

"My brother lives on a ringship. He married a woman from the *Stanford*. They live there now, though he visits Happdal."

"Your village in the mountains to the north."

"Yes."

"Where exactly?"

"If you wish to visit there, I will speak to the jarl and request an invitation on your behalf. He is my brother." And she would recommend that Trond *not* extend an invitation to Maro and his ilk. He was entirely too knowing, too curious and sly. He reeked of a hidden agenda, though she had no idea what it might be.

"You are well-connected, Katja. A sister-in-law on the *Stanford*, a brother who is the village chieftain, and the means to travel wherever you like."

She ignored his comment and turned to Gregoriu. "Explain to the mayor again why I am here," she told Maro. "And tell him that I must see Jana as soon as she awakens. Even though her situation is different than mine, I can help guide her."

Maro spoke, though she had no way to verify what he was saying. Gregoriu nodded studiously, weighing the information. Through Maro, the mayor asked her about Happdal. How many people lived there? How long had they lived in the mountains? What other groups did they know? She answered his questions as honestly and thoroughly as she could, though she felt uneasy about conveying her answers through Maro, who was uncomfortably attentive. And was he eyeing her body? She was wearing simple clothes, fur-lined leather garments, but her arms and neck were bare. She was not a young woman, nor as beautiful as her mother. But yes, there was sexual hunger in Maro's eyes, and he made no effort to hide it.

"Do you wish to bed me?" she asked him bluntly. "You'd be a poor lover, in shackles."

"I think we could manage," he said, unembarrassed. "Though the people of Bosa are modest. We should wait until we have some privacy."

"I prefer women," she said. Truthfully she had no preference either way, but it seemed a simple way to make her position clear: she had no interest in him. He was indisputably handsome, but she felt only wariness in his presence. She would sooner share a bed with a snake or a spider.

"Then perhaps you will take Livia as a lover. She would have you, I'm sure of it. Your bone structure is exquisite."

Livia, she had gathered, had been the one to wield the knife that killed Sperancia. Which couldn't have been easy. Once the black threads had done their work, the Crucible host became immensely strong, with lightning-fast reflexes. Livia had not appeared to be immensely powerful. Though she knew that meant little; the ringship people had ways of enhancing their bodies.

"Tell Gregoriu I'm done with you for now. In the morning I will see Jana, if she is roused."

Maro smiled bemusedly but provided a succinct translation. Gregoriu nodded to some young men who escorted Maro out of the town hall. Katja guessed that Maro could easily overpower them and escape. But he wouldn't. There was something in Bosa that he wanted, and he wouldn't leave until he had it.

Gregoriu gestured to the plate of food: cheese, meat, and some sort of round red fruit. She took some, her stomach finally remembering she'd eaten nothing but apples that day. She nodded her thanks and left the hall. No one followed her. It was late and even the insects had stopped making noise. The only sound she heard was the hardened leather of her boot soles on the smooth cobblestones. The night was cool and clear, the constellations brilliantly visible. Most were familiar but a few were utterly strange. Zoë had taught her about the rotation of the Earth and its revolution around the Sun, but here was direct evidence of that idea. She had travelled far enough to see a different sky.

"Hovershuttle, it's me," she said as she approached. The dome opened obediently, and closed again as soon as she had entered. "Wake me if anyone approaches."

"You have five messages."

"From who?"

"Three from Maggie, in Ilium. One from Lydia, in Ilium. One from Esper, on the *Stanford*."

They were desperate – they'd asked her brother to call her. "I will hear the message from Esper."

She smiled at the sound of her brother's voice. He spoke in Norse, his tone calm and playful as always. "They tell me you've stolen a vehicle, little sister. What are you up to? Don't kill anyone, okay? You might start a war or something. Anyway, I miss you. I will come to Happdal soon, I promise. I miss Mother's *öl*." Esper spoke a little more about ringstation life. Per Anders was fine, though getting a little fat. Car-En was also well, though feeling anxious with Tem's extended absence. But Esper didn't worry about his son; he knew Tem had good judgment.

Katja laughed aloud. Tem was a fool, like all young men, just as foolish as Esper and Trond had been when they'd left Happdal against Mother's wishes to try to rescue Katja from the gast. Thirty years ago – she'd been just a girl. What adventures they'd had.

The motion of the water was gentle but unfamiliar; she'd never slept on a boat. But even as she considered starting up the craft to find a patch of land, exhaustion overtook her. It had been a long, strange day.

Voices woke her. There was only a little light in the sky, but the pier was bustling with activity. Fishermen were heading out for the day. She told the dome to open and looked around sleepily. Men and a few boys waved to her. Word had traveled; apparently they knew who she was. The people of Bosa were friendly, especially considering her rude entrance.

She ate a large breakfast: her own provisions and the food Gregoriu had given her. The red fruit was only mildly sweet, and slightly sour, but incredibly juicy. How many other foods existed that she had never tasted?

Katja instructed the hovershuttle to secure itself, just as she'd done before, though it occurred to her that she had no idea how it would defend itself if necessary. "Don't hurt anyone, okay?"

"My defense measures are non-injurious."

Bosa was a different town by day. There were people everywhere going about their business, and everyone she saw greeted her. "*Buon giorno*," they said. Eventually Katja tried repeating the words back, and though her mouth had trouble with them, the greeting evoked smiles.

She found Gregoriu in the town square conversing intently with several older men. They stopped speaking as she approached, regarding her somewhat worriedly.

She showed her palms. She'd left Biter secured in the hovershuttle, as agreed. She had a knife in her boot, but Gregoriu hadn't asked about the contents of her boots. "Where is Jana? Take me to Jana please." And then, for good measure, "*Buon giorno*." The men relaxed considerably with the last words, and one of them called to a little girl and gave her instructions. The girl took Katja's hand and led her, hopefully in the direction of Jana's house.

"It was you, who saw me last night," Katja said. "I recognize your blue dress."

The girl didn't answer but continued pulling her along. Her grip was warm and slightly sticky, like the palms of all children. Though Katja could do with a bath herself. Maybe she would take a dip in the sea later, if she could find a beach with calm, shallow water.

"What's your name?" she asked. "I'm Katja. *Katja*." She tapped her chest.

"*Mi chiamo Bina*." The girl tapped her own chest. "Bina."

Bina led her to an old stone house on the outskirts of town. A crumbling stone wall protected a sprawling garden. Bina pointed to a gate; Katja realized the girl was too short to reach the latch. She opened it herself and followed Bina into a courtyard that might once have been opulent, but was now covered in vines, some bearing the same red fruit Katja had eaten for breakfast.

"*Signor Manca!*" Bina called out repeatedly, until an old, thin, weary-looking man emerged from the house. Bina let loose a storm of words in apparent explanation. The man nodded and waved for Katja to enter. Bina, to Katja's relief, came with her. The little girl was capable and friendly, and the closest thing Katja had to an ally.

The old man led them to a bedroom. Jana was awake, though pale and drawn. She looked at Katja without apparent interest or recognition. Katja noted a resemblance between Jana and the old man, though he wore the features better. Jana's father, mostly likely.

"Don't worry," she said, though she knew he wouldn't understand. "I will stay and help. She will recover. She will remember everything."

She hoped it was true. She hoped that this Crucible was different, and that Jana had not become another gast.

If she had, Katja would have to use the knife in her boot.

CHAPTER ELEVEN

Hennik lumbered toward Tem. Did he know about Saga? He looked grim-faced and squinty-eyed, ready for a fight.

But then Hennik extended his right arm in the traditional greeting. Tem reciprocated, grasping Hennik's forearm, which was thick and ropy with muscle. Hennik was a full head taller than Tem. So were most men of Happdal, including Farbror Trond and his own father. Citizens of the *Stanford* had modified their genes to produce smaller, less resource-intensive bodies, and that was half of Tem's lineage.

"Good to see you, old friend," Hennik said, his face cracking into a smile. "Remember when we fought, as boys? You and I were always scrapping."

"Of course I remember." To Tem's relief there was no menace in Hennik's tone; he seemed genuinely happy to see him. Which meant, in all likelihood, that Saga hadn't mentioned their tryst. And why would she? She was not the type to feel the need to confess anything. Tem, on the other hand, was already worrying about what he would say to Maggie. She would know in an instant if he withheld the truth. It wasn't that he couldn't keep a secret; he could be as tight-lipped as anyone if entrusted with sensitive information. But as for concealing his own misdeeds and feelings of guilt, he was utterly incompetent.

"Sigurd told me that you had come this way to check on your flying boat."

"That's true. But you've seen it before – it hasn't changed." For some reason he was reluctant to share his predicament. Though word would get out soon enough.

"Yes, yes, of course. That's not why I came to find you. I need your help with something. Will you come with me?"

Tem followed Hennik back down the trail toward Happdal. Of course there was a chance he was walking into a trap, but Hennik was not such a great actor that he would be able to conceal his ire, if he had any. Unless the man was much different than the boy.

Hennik had no natural talents beyond his size and strength, and lived a meager life, alone in a small house he had built with the help of his uncle, Harald. Harald had once been the village cheesemaker but had passed the dairy on to his daughter Alva. Hennik still worked in the dairy, but had a contentious relationship with his cousin and was thus incessantly dabbling in other activities with the hopes of securing his own wealth.

"I have found something in the ruins," Hennik said as they neared his house. "Something of great value, I believe. But I don't know if it is real. Will you look at it and tell me what you think?"

Tem started to protest that he was no expert at identifying ancient artifacts. But it occurred to him that he might know more than anyone else in the village, given his education on the *Stanford*. He was no scholar, but still he had spent many years in school, well into his twenties. It was amazing how much knowledge existed, more history and science than could ever be absorbed and understood by a single person, more literature and art than could ever be fully appreciated. He was thankful that the ringstations had preserved that knowledge, that it had not been lost to rain and rot or the crush of moving glaciers.

Tem's eyes adjusted to the dimness of Hennik's cottage as Hennik rummaged around in a chest. His treasures, Tem supposed, various bits of metal, plastic, and sometimes even wood and paper that had survived the centuries. The ruins nearest Happdal had once been a town called Braunlage, a resort for skiing and other winter sports. Tem had explored the area himself as a boy but had never found much of interest; most of the old buildings were buried under forest debris and soil, entirely rotted out. But Hennik was tense with excitement over what he had discovered.

"Here it is. What do you think?"

Hennik handed Tem a small brown rectangular bar caked with dirt. Tem took it, somewhat reluctantly, and was surprised by its heft.

"It's gold, I think," said Hennik.

The bar did have a dull yellow gleam beneath the grime. "Do you have a rag and a bucket of water?" Tem asked.

"I was afraid water might damage it."

"Not if it's gold."

Gold was rare in Happdal. There were bits of jewelry, rings and bracelets and arm circlets that had been brought from the northlands and passed down through the generations. But the mountain mines, though rich in silver and iron ore, produced no gold.

Hennik fetched a bowl of water and a rag, and Tem got to work scrubbing. He was curious as to how a bar of gold might have ended up in a resort town, but at the same time accepting of the fact that he would never know. Billions of people had lived and died on Earth, taking their stories with them.

"Do you believe the Ice Trail song?" Tem asked. It was the history he'd been taught by his father, Esper, well before his time on the *Stanford*, a saga that described the migration of their ancestors from the north, fleeing the ice fields.

"Of course not," said Hennik. "It's just a song. I think we have always lived in the mountains."

Tem nodded, unwilling to argue. He'd guessed as much. There were many in Happdal who preferred to believe that their people had always lived in the Five Valleys. That loss of knowledge saddened his father, but it was a fight Esper had given up after moving to the ringship.

His parents, working together, had researched the possible origins of Happdal, exploring Car-En's theory that Esper's ancestors might have been part of a historical reenactment society in Norway. Many such groups had learned and practiced Viking Age skills and traditions, including blacksmithing. Those skills might have served them well during the Remnant Age, enabling their survival. Esper had found descriptions of a Norwegian village – Gudvangen – where hundreds of such people had lived together communally, practicing the traditional arts and speaking Norse – the old language. Perhaps Gudvangen and Happdal were linked, though there was no way to know for sure.

"Look, there are markings," Hennik said.

The grime was coming off easily, revealing a solid bar of gold beneath. The metal had been stamped with an image, a bird of prey clutching a symbol in its claws. The symbol looked familiar to Tem, and he felt a chill as he recalled details from his history lessons.

"This is an evil object, Hennik. You should destroy it."

"Why? Isn't it valuable?"

"Maybe a little." Asteroid-mining bots retrieved all the gold that was needed on the ringstations for electronic components and jewelry; the metal had lost its rarity and much of its cachet. Though it was still pretty, and rare in the Five Valleys.

"Why do you say it is evil?"

"This is wartime gold from the Builders. Rings, bracelets, and even tooth fillings were taken from prisoners and melted down to make this bar. The prisoners were starved, tortured, and murdered. Not just warriors, but children and women and men who had no interest in fighting. It was a mass slaughter, Hennik. A terrible part of history. And it happened not far from here."

"What is a tooth filling?"

"When a tooth rots, it can sometimes be repaired with gold or other materials, instead of pulling it out."

Hennik looked dejectedly at the object he had hoped would bring him fortune. "What do you think I should do with it?"

There were historians on the *Stanford* who would be delighted to study such an object. But Tem did not want to take it from Hennik, nor hold any responsibility for it.

"You are friends with Saga, yes?" Tem asked, wanting to tread delicately.

Hennik grinned. "Friends, yes. Perhaps something more, even. But I would risk my neck if I claimed her as my woman."

"Oh? Is she with someone else?"

"No! But you know Saga. If I claimed something too soon she might smash me with a hammer."

"I think I understand," Tem said, feeling a knot in his stomach. "What I was going to suggest is that you give this gold to Saga to melt down. Then give a piece to each of the jewelers and silversmiths of the Five Valleys. Or sell it or trade it. You'll end up with either goods or goodwill, or both. And this metal will be made anew, into rings and bracelets."

Hennik nodded. "That's good advice. I thank you for it. Saga already returned to Kaldbrek, but I will go there today and ask her."

Tem briefly considered saving Hennik the trip – he could easily melt the gold himself in Trond's smithy. But no, he didn't want to touch the war gold, nor did he especially want to go out of his way to help Hennik. He still remembered Hennik holding him down, beating him, taunting him for his darker skin tone. Maybe Hennik had changed, maturing and becoming more tolerant, but there was still a hard knot of pain in Tem's heart that refused to unravel.

"Travel safe," Tem said. "May the Three Brothers be with you."

"And with you."

Tem left Hennik's house and wandered aimlessly until he found himself at Katja's doorstep. He might as well stay at her house. She had no use for it at the moment, and though he knew he was welcome at his uncle's, it was noisy and chaotic there.

How long would he be in Happdal? Maggie would send someone eventually. Not hearing from him, she would trace the hovershuttle co-ordinates and want to know why he was heading back to Bosa. Katja had been able to activate the craft with voice commands, but she wouldn't know how to disengage location tracking.

Unless she'd managed to? The hovershuttle was happy to explain its own operation to anyone who asked. Tem had neglected to employ any security measures whatsoever. What if Maggie thought he'd cut off communications on purpose? What if she decided to give him some space? It had gotten a little weird, her offering to accompany him to Happdal and him declining that offer. It would be perfectly reasonable for her to assume that he was going dark on purpose, maybe to reacquaint himself with his childhood home and way of life.

He might be here a long time. *Shit.*

Or help might already be on the way. He had no way of knowing. What was he going to do with himself in the interim?

One thing was clear: he would go crazy sitting still and stewing in his own juice. There was plenty of work to be in done in the village; he would find a way to make himself useful. He tried to mentally reframe the problem. Being stuck in Happdal was an opportunity to bond with his family, and maybe to find complete acceptance among the villagers in a way that he had never experienced.

An hour later he was making repairs to Farmor Elke's storage shed, knocking out rotten wood and rebuilding a wall. The moment he had asked, his grandmother had casually rattled off a to-do list that would keep him busy for a month. It was almost as if she'd been keeping a tally of his work debts since he'd left Happdal to live on the *Stanford* with his mother, so many years ago. He knew Elke had never gotten over the fact that Esper, her favorite son and Tem's father, had left to join them as well. She made her resentments clear to anyone who would listen. And now, as he breathed in dust and mold and wiped the grimy sweat from his brow, he wondered if he wasn't paying a little for that decision to leave.

What the hell had he been supposed to do? He'd been just a boy, nine years old, when Car-En had decided that living in Happdal was not enough for her son, that she wanted him to get a real education on the ringship. He'd been horrified at the time. All he'd wanted, all he'd dreamed of, was to become a blacksmith. To follow in Farbror Trond's footsteps, to become a master of steel and swords. His mother had taken that dream away.

No, that wasn't true. She'd simply expanded his world. He *could* have returned to Happdal to become a smith. Trond had always made it clear that he was welcome in the smithy, even to this day. Though Happdal didn't need another smith; Trond was as healthy as an ox, and Jense, though he complained about his aches, likely had many years of good work left in him.

There'd been another reason his mother had wanted him out of Happdal: racism. He'd never discussed it with her explicitly, but in hindsight it was clear. They'd stood out, Car-En and Tem, as the only people of Asian heritage in a village of fair Nordic giants. Some had accepted them fully. But others, like Hennik, had relentlessly harassed and taunted them. *Him*, especially, as a half-breed.

Adjusting to life on the *Stanford* had been a rude shock. He'd been far behind his classmates academically. In Happdal, he'd viewed himself as capable and intelligent. But on the ringship he'd felt like an idiot for years, speaking Orbital English only clumsily, feeling clueless in his mathematics and science classes. He'd caught up after only a few years, but those years had been excruciating. And his sense of otherness had only intensified. He'd no longer been the only Asian kid; the *Stanford* was ethnically diverse. But he'd been cast in a new *other* role: the savage, the barbarian, the primitive child.

Even now, as an adult, he struggled to feel a sense of belonging. He knew he had much to offer. He was uniquely suited to understand and guide Repop like nobody else on Earth or the ringstations.

Yet here he was, an idiot stranded in Happdal, with the weight of a pending confession tearing up his conscience.

"Ah – you're doing good work." Farmor Elke had crept up on him. She handed him a shallow wooden bowl containing two thick pieces of brown bread slathered with butter, a hunk of cheese, and an apple. "Here, take a break and nourish yourself."

"Thank you, Farmor." Any resentment he had against his grandmother instantly dissolved. He'd offered to help, hadn't he? And she was happy to have it, and to have him in Happdal. Who knew how many more years the elder generation of Happdal had left? He'd be a fool to let the past spoil whatever time they still had together.

Elke stayed to chat for a minute. As far as he could tell, she was still unaware that Katja had left Happdal, stealing the hovershuttle. At some point he would have to swallow his pride and confess his predicament. But not yet. There was nothing anyone in the village could do to help him, anyway.

As he resumed his work, Tem's thoughts turned to Bosa. Why had the Ringstation Coalition waited so long to make contact with the Sardinians? Even though Director Balasubramanian's 'Three R's' formed the basis of Repop Council's official policy, other council members still held strong Non-Interventionist views. Those traditionalists argued that Bosa should be left alone, that nothing good could come of making contact. They pointed to historical examples: indigenous communities invariably suffered from first contact with more technologically sophisticated cultures. The end result was often pandemic or genocide. It might be different if the people of Bosa were suffering from starvation or other ills, but by all accounts they were thriving. Though that information was old; the field research programs had all been terminated long ago. Tem himself had argued that the spying should stop; the people of the Five Valleys and other Earth communities deserved better treatment.

So contact had been delayed, right up until the appearance of the *Michelangelo*. The worldship's sudden move into Earth orbit had sparked a flurry of meetings and policy reviews, the end result being a rapid acceleration of the contact timelines. There were risks inherent in First Contact, but there was a greater risk in letting the unpredictable leaders of the *Michelangelo* reach out first. Balasubramanian had argued that the Sardinians needed to be protected, and Tem had no doubt that the old man was sincere in that belief. But there were other motives in play: keeping the upper hand, and maintaining control of the Repop narrative.

"Ah, there you are! I've been looking for you!"

It was Lars, the old one-legged man he'd seen arguing with Farfar Jense, poking his head into the shed. He looked in better shape now, bright-eyed and excited, emitting only the faintest whiff of *öl*.

"Hello, Lars. You've found me, haven't you? Trying to make myself useful."

"Your grandmother likes to see men working in the village. But there is other work to be done as well. Will you join us tomorrow morning for a boar hunt?"

"A hunt?" He'd sometimes hunted with his father, but only for small game, never for boar. He'd been too young. And then they'd moved to the *Stanford*, where hunting didn't exist and the food they called 'meat' was made from plants or grown in vats. "Who's going?"

"Myself and some younger men, including your cousin Baldr. And you know Hennik, don't you? Also a few men from Kaldbrek. We share hunting grounds now – did you know that? Relations with Kaldbrek are much better than when you were a child."

"Sure, I'll join," he said impulsively. He'd been hoping for an opportunity to get to know Trond's younger son better.

"Good – very good! Meet at Hennik's house, an hour before dawn at the latest."

"Very well. Thank you Lars, for inviting me."

"Of course! I wish your father was here too. But if all goes well, we'll gorge ourselves on roasted boar belly tomorrow."

And then Lars was gone, as suddenly as he had appeared. For a moment Tem questioned his own decision. What if Maggie came during the hunt? What if he were injured? Lars had lost his own leg during a boar hunt.

But those were silly concerns; he was thinking too much like a cautious sky dweller. He'd been born in Happdal, hadn't he?

So he'd live like a Happdal man, at least for a day.

CHAPTER TWELVE

Tem slept little in his aunt's bed, which was hard and uncomfortable. Though even if he'd had a soft mattress, he would have slept little; his mind raced with thoughts of Saga and Maggie. He loathed himself for his stupidity, for letting Katja trick him so easily, for failing to resist Saga's advances. If only he'd accepted Maggie's offer to accompany him to Happdal, then none of this would have happened. He'd made so many poor decisions in such quick succession.

And he was nervous about the hunt. But it was too late to back out, not if he wanted to preserve any shred of his reputation among the men of Happdal. He hoped it would be over quickly – a few hours of chasing boar and throwing spears. Ideally they would come up empty-handed. He didn't have the stomach to butcher a fresh carcass, even if it meant the promise of crispy bacon.

Rising well before dawn, Tem examined Katja's weapon rack by candlelight. The display lined an entire wall, an array of spears, longknives, bows, and swords. Only the longsword named Biter and a knife were missing. Tem borrowed a short spear with a heavy shaft and a large iron spearhead. At the base of the head were two stubby wings, which would prevent a wounded boar from working its way up the shaft to gore the hunter. Outside, in the light of the moon, he practiced throwing the spear against a stump ten meters away. The weapon was well-balanced and flew straight, and his aim was decent.

Approaching Hennik's house, he heard low voices. Inside, Lars was filling his drinking horn with *öl*. Tem's cousin Baldr – a boy of maybe fifteen years – sharpened his knife on a stone. Grundar, a wifeless man in his forties who sometimes worked at the dairy with Hennik, scowled at Tem. But Tem didn't take it personally. Grundar had been scowling as long as Tem had known him; the lines were deeply etched into his face.

"I see you brought a spear. Do you have a knife as well?" Lars asked.

"Of course. I brought Squid Cutter."

"A Trond-blade, good. A knifeless man is a lifeless man." *Knívleysur maður er lívleysur maður.*

"Where is Hennik?" Tem asked. "Isn't he joining us?"

"He'll meet us with the Kaldbrek men," said Lars. "He went there yesterday, probably chasing after Saga."

"She is too much for him," Grundar said. "He'll only get his heart broken. Saga is just playing with him."

"She is the more cunning of the two," Lars admitted.

"And better looking," young Baldr added.

"Don't let your eyes linger on Saga," Grundar warned. "She'll slap you so hard you'll see stars. Heed my advice, boy."

Baldr looked down sheepishly and resumed his knife sharpening. Lars offered Tem a swig from his horn.

"No thank you. I'll wait until after the hunt."

"Suit yourself. Let's go then, before the sun rises."

Grundar set a fast pace, heading north, and Tem was surprised that Lars could keep up despite his wooden leg. But the old man was incapable of feeling physical pain; their haste gave him no discomfort. Soon they reached the Three Stones and Tem was glad that Hennik was not with them to ask about the hovershuttle.

Grundar led them partway up the high ridge trail, veering west toward Kaldbrek, and then cut down into the valley, following an overgrown hunting trail. Tem remembered taking a similar path with his mother, on the way to the 'mule station', the Orbital Earth Transport Shuttle that would take them to the *Stanford*. They'd gotten lost on the way, accidentally trespassing into Kaldbrek hunting grounds. Happdal and Kaldbrek had practically been at war at the time, and Jarl Svein had kidnapped them, holding them both prisoner until his father had come to their rescue. It was all far in the past, but Tem felt uneasy as he recalled the experience. Svein had put an arrow through his mother's leg. Later, Car-En had had a chance to take revenge, but had spared Svein.

Both Car-En and Tem had undergone various types of psychological therapy on the *Stanford* to help recover from the traumatic experiences of that year. And the therapy had helped. But tracing the hunting paths by the river, headed toward Kaldbrek, brought back the memories with more vividness than Tem was prepared for.

"We'll be at the meeting spot soon," Grundar said.

Saga had lost her uncle and father figure that same year. Völund, Kaldbrek's blacksmith, had been Tem's captor. And his father, Esper, had cut Völund's throat wide open right in front of young Saga. She'd not had the benefit of years of professional therapy. What healing and reconciliation, if any, had occurred for her over the years?

"There they are," Grundar said, pushing aside a beech sapling.

Hennik, another man, and a woman were seated beneath a sprawling ancient sycamore. The man was about Grundar's age, black hair streaked with gray. His lean face was weak-chinned, and a faded scar cut across his right cheek. It was Svein Haakonsson, the deposed jarl of Kaldbrek. The woman, to Tem's dismay, was Saga.

Tem experienced a rush of anxiety seeing his former kidnapper, the woman he had recently bedded, and the man who was in a relationship with Saga. More than ever, the hunting trip seemed like a terrible idea.

"What's he doing here?" Saga asked as they approached. There was none of the tenderness or passion in her demeanor that he remembered so vividly from only two nights ago. She looked at him with cold disdain.

"I invited the boy!" said Lars enthusiastically. "If he's half the hunter Esper is, we'll eat well tonight."

"I'll do my best," Tem said, "but my father only took me hunting a few times."

"Didn't you go hunting with your mother?" Svein asked with a sly grin. "I seem to remember catching the two of you in our territory. Though that was many years ago."

Tem did not meet Svein's eye. He had an impulse to draw Squid Cutter and plunge it into Svein's gut. Instead, he said nothing.

"That's in the past, Svein," Grundar said. "We share hunting grounds now, do we not?"

"Of course."

Grundar sounded reasonable, and Tem appreciated his words. But he couldn't help but wonder if Grundar held old resentments against Svein. It had been Svein who had stabbed Karl Hinriksson to death, after Karl had poisoned Haakon, Svein's father and jarl of Kaldbrek at the time. Karl and Grundar had been good friends.

Svein led the hunt, looking for tracks and signs of rooting, though Tem noted that Svein deferred to Saga whenever the jarl made a suggestion. Somehow Saga had tamed Svein, perhaps by keeping him close. Though

Tem sensed no change in Svein's character; he seemed as mean and cunning as ever.

"Remember," Grundar advised, "the boar's vitals are low and forward, unlike a deer. A spear to its flank will do nothing but anger it. You must meet it head-on as it charges you, keeping your spear low. Either that, or a blow directly behind its ear, straight to the brain, if you can manage it."

"And how many boar have you killed, Grundar?" Svein asked.

"Several," said Grundar, sounding hurt.

"Only one that I can remember. A young male, weak with swine fever. We dared not eat the diseased meat."

"There were others," Grundar protested. "And I wounded Fyrirgef, didn't I?"

"Who is Fyrirgef?" Tem asked.

"A monster sow, nearly the size of a cow, with long tusks as sharp as knives."

"It was her who slashed my leg," Lars said.

"That's impossible, you fool," said Svein. "You lost your leg more than twenty years ago."

"I swear it was her."

"Why is she called Fyrirgef?" Tem asked. The word meant *sorry* in Norse.

"Because you're sorry if you see her," Grundar explained. "She'll try to kill you, and if you managed to kill her, her old meat would be too tough to eat. Either way you lose."

Imagining the giant boar, Tem realized he was physically the smallest person in their hunting part. Saga was a good five centimeters taller than him, and just as strong. Svein was lean but tall and rangy. Grundar and Hennik were both hulking and broad-shouldered, and Baldr, though lesser in size and strength than his father, Trond, or his older brother, Sigurd, was just as tall and rippling with lean muscle. Even old Lars, hunched and hobbling, outsized Tem. He wondered if a territorial swine would try to target the biggest and strongest of the group, or the smallest.

"Do you no longer hunt with dogs?" Tem asked. He remembered Svein's hunting companions from when he was a child, terrifying black wolf dogs.

Svein laughed ruefully. "Returned to the wild, years ago. They left during a lean winter to hunt on their own."

"It would have helped if you hadn't kicked them so much," Saga said.

"Ungrateful beasts. Their wild pups still hunt in these woods. Keep your distance, if you see or hear them. They would hunt and eat you like any other prey."

"Wolves eat entrails first," Baldr added. "And sometimes leave the rest – I've seen the remains."

Svein nodded. "Wolves sometimes hunt for sport."

As the dawn light leaked through the canopy, Svein found signs of a nearby family of boar: fresh droppings and trails. Their conversation dropped to whispers. Lars produced a series of boar calls that were shockingly realistic. Tem was no hunting expert but he knew that swine were territorial, that the calls might elicit a charge. He gripped his spear more tightly.

Tem was bringing up the rear of the group with Baldr and Lars. Perhaps to confront his own fear, he pushed forward, passing Hennik and Grundar. That put him next to Svein and directly behind Saga, who led them, her own spear at the ready. Though he tried to focus on the hunt, being in close proximity with Saga recalled their night in the smithy. So recently her long legs had wrapped around him, pulling him deeper inside of her. And when she'd been on top, her dark hair had tickled his face.

Svein nudged him and gave him a leering look, and once again Tem felt stupid and ashamed, this time for letting Svein see his thoughts.

Saga held up her hand. They all stilled. "Listen," she whispered.

Tem did not need to strain his ears to hear the high-pitched grunts and whines of piglets. And something much larger crashing through the vegetation.

Svein leaned in close and whispered in Tem's ear. His breath was hot and smelled like old cheese. "Does Hennik know that you lust for his woman? Did you lie with her?"

Tem shoved Svein away, swiveling his head to determine the direction of their quarry.

"Shall I tell him?" Svein asked in a normal speaking voice. "What do you think he would do?"

"Tell who?" Hennik asked. "Me? Tell me what?"

"Ready yourselves," said Lars, with a quaver in his voice. Baldr looked around wildly. Tem's own heart was pounding. But Svein just watched Tem, calm and curious, like a cat torturing a mouse.

A beast emerged from the underground, only five meters away: a giant boar, its shoulder as high as Tem's chest, its hide ragged with scars. One tusk was long and sharp, the other cracked and jagged. The boar lowered its head, watching them with small, black eyes.

"It is Fyrirgef!" Lars yelled. "The hell swine has come to finish me!"

"Shut up, old man," said Saga. "Set your spear."

The great hairy sow grunted and charged, right toward Saga. Tem rushed forward, intending to set his spear side by side with the jarl's. But he tripped, or someone tripped him, and he collided with Saga, bringing them both down in a tangled heap of limbs.

"Get off me, you idiot!"

And then Lars was barreling forward, past them, with his awkward but expedient gait, emitting a guttural cry that sent shivers up Tem's spine. Lars met Fyrirgef head-on but his aim was off. The point of his spear stuck in the huge sow's right foreleg. Fyrirgef bellowed in fury and swiped her head, slashing her tusks through the air.

Tem scrambled to his feet, grabbed Lars by his vest, and pulled with all his strength. But the old man was heavier than Tem expected, as if his bones were made of lead. "Help me!" Tem shouted.

The wounded sow grabbed Lars's wooden peg in her mouth and wrenched her head back and forth like a dog breaking a rat's neck. The leather straps attaching the crude artificial limb snapped, revealing a scarred stump.

"Was taking my real leg not enough, hell swine?" Lars shouted. "Now you must also have my wooden one?"

Saga was at his side, pulling Lars up to stand on his remaining foot. Hennik and Grundar rushed forward, yelling and stabbing wildly at Fyrirgef's face and neck. The enraged boar dropped Lars's peg leg and bellowed, undeterred.

Svein, motionless until then, slid into a space by the boar's side. Moving like water, unhurried and smooth, he slipped his spear into Fyrirgef's brain with a single downward thrust. The point entered her skull just behind her hairy ear, exactly as Grundar had described. With a final squeal Fyrirgef collapsed, shaking the forest floor, and lay still.

"You did it!" Baldr shouted.

"What happened?" asked Lars, whose long, gray hair was obscuring his eyes.

"Fyrirgef is dead," Grundar said. "Svein killed her."

"With a single blow," Hennik added.

"You tripped me!" Tem shouted, stepping toward Svein. "You tripped me, didn't you?"

"You stumbled," Svein said, not meeting his eyes. "It's understandable. You haven't hunted for years. You panicked a little when you saw Fyrirgef."

"I could have died. We both could have died!" he yelled, gesturing at Saga.

"Any of us could have died," Svein replied. "Hunting is dangerous. Have you forgotten what danger is, living in your sky world?"

"He tripped me. Didn't any of you see it?"

Hennik looked down, but Grundar nodded frankly. "Yes, he tripped you with the butt of his spear. I saw it clearly."

"If you stumbled on my spear," said Svein, "it was your own fault for standing too close to me."

Though he did not think to do it, Tem had Squid Cutter in his hand a second later. He lunged, and though Svein was quick to step back, Tem's reflexes had been honed from years of fencing practice on the *Stanford*. The point of the blade caught Svein's tunic, piercing it and the skin beneath. It was a shallow wound, but the sight of blood shocked Tem into self-awareness.

"I'm sorry," he said, dropping the weapon. "I didn't mean to hurt you."

"Did you see that?" Svein cried out, clutching his chest. "The half-breed tried to kill me. He must be punished." With both hands he yanked the spear out of the boar's head and brandished it. "Saga – will you punish him, or must I do it myself?"

"Enough," muttered Lars. "We are friends here. There's no need to quarrel."

"Quarrel?" Svein yelled, more dramatically than Tem thought was necessary. The blade had merely scratched him. "He tried to stab me. I demand justice."

"Justice?" Grundar said. "He merely tickled you with his knife, and he already apologized. Besides, I saw you trip him. I would say you're even."

"He insulted me! I demand justice by hólmganga."

"A duel?" Grundar said, scowling even more deeply than usual. "That's ridiculous."

"I demand it. Or I will kill him right now."

"You will do no such thing," said Saga, stepping between them. "Drop your spear."

Svein stared at Saga, unmoving.

"Drop it *now*."

Svein threw his spear to the ground, snorted in disgust, and stomped away.

Saga turned to Tem. "You should not have come today. Look at the trouble you've caused me." She picked up Lars's wooden leg and handed it back to him. "You are no longer welcome in Kaldbrek, Tem, unless you are willing to face Svein in a duel. I will not insist that you do so if you stay in Happdal. But it is our way, when someone is challenged. If you set foot in Kaldbrek, you must face Svein in hólmganga."

"That's not fair," Tem said.

"You drew your knife and tried to stab him. I saw it myself." Taking Svein's bloody spear, Saga left to follow him, heading east toward Kaldbrek.

Hennik patted Tem on the shoulder. "You were always hot-headed, ever since you were a boy. Do you remember when you punched me in the nose, beneath the longhouse?"

Tem had forgotten, but the memory flooded back. Hennik had told him to go home, to the ringship, that he wasn't welcome in the village. Happdal – where he'd been born, where his grandfather had been jarl.

Twenty years later, he still felt unwelcome. Nothing had changed.

CHAPTER THIRTEEN

Jana dreamed that she was strolling through the streets of Bosa, but the village was populated by mythical creatures: women with the legs of goats, giant squirrels with the faces of children, a long-necked lizard standing on its hind legs with the head of a cat.

"They are sprites," Sperancia explained. The maghiarja was walking next to her, unharmed and very much alive. "You can ask them anything, though each type has their specialty." Sperancia pointed at the tall cat-lizard. "The *tatzelwurm* here is a master of plant lore and medicinal herbs. But the *squasc* –" she gestured to a small clan of the child-faced squirrels, "– are the ones to ask about mathematics and astronomy."

"Didn't you die? I swear I saw your corpse, quite recently."

"I did die, and yes, you did see my corpse. And yet I walk beside you. I'll explain again where you are. Try to remember this time – though I know it's difficult."

In another dream Jana was speaking with the mayor, explaining how Sperancia had died. Livia had stabbed her to death, with Maro condoning the act. In that dream she felt cold and fatigued. It was difficult to stay awake and her vision was blurry.

In a third dream – though this time Jana wasn't sure if she was awake or asleep – she was in bed, at home, being tended to by her father. That much made sense. But why was a blond woman with strange, beautiful features sitting next to her bed, watching her with eyes as bright and fierce as an eagle's?

"My name is Katja," the woman said in a strange tongue. Jana understood the language, some version of English. But how? "I was like you, once," Katja continued. "I was possessed by the Crucible. Are you hearing voices? Are you trapped in an unfamiliar place?"

Yes, she was hearing voices. And eventually there were faces attached to those voices, and bodies. There was Agatha, a slight, dark-haired woman with a quick smile. And Giuseppina, an older, heavy-set woman with a deep, booming voice, always frowning. And Itria, with long, shiny black hair and eyes the color of the sea at night. And of course Sperancia, except her friend looked young again, only a few years older than herself, and it was only through the geometry of her facial bones, now covered in taut flesh and glowing olive skin, that Jana recognized her. Her wrinkles had completely disappeared, as had the black threads.

They introduced themselves as members of Jana's consorteria. Together, the group made decisions, decisions that Jana would enact. Though ultimately Jana decided what to do; she would maintain complete autonomy of her own body. But she would never again be alone in her own mind unless she explicitly willed it to be so. She was now the host of a community.

Each woman had once had the same role, Sperancia most recently, their bodies and brains mapped by the Crucible threads. Each now existed only as a virtual being within the Crucible's quantum core. They could see through Jana's eyes and hear through her ears at will; privacy was a thing of the past. But they could only take control of Jana's body if she allowed it, a privilege which she could revoke at any moment.

The consorteria met in a small church that had been cleared of pews, the benches replaced with a massive oaken round table. Vines grew inside of the church, laden with orange and purple fruits. Tiny people with long dragonfly wings flitted from vine to vine, eating the fruit and speaking to one another in incomprehensibly high-pitched voices.

"What is this place?" Jana asked.

"The old church," Agatha answered. "It stood in this spot long before the town hall was built."

"Are we still in Bosa?"

"A version of Bosa, yes, but from many points in history, with creative liberties taken."

"Enough with the explanations, Agatha," Giuseppina said, slapping her heavy palm against the table. "She'll catch up soon enough. Time is of the essence – we have a decision to make."

"Is murder still the best course of action?" Sperancia asked. "Maro and Livia are now in Gregoriu's custody. Are they even still a threat?"

"Of course they're still a threat," Giuseppina insisted. "At any moment they could summon help from the *Michelangelo*. They could have us bombed to oblivion. They could call down a legion of warriors to gut us like fish."

"Then how does murdering them make us any safer?" Agatha asked.

"On the chance that they *haven't* already called for help, it prevents them from doing so.

They're not carrying any obvious communication devices, though who knows what they have implanted in their bodies."

Jana rose from her seat and walked away, even as the debate continued. So she wasn't dreaming – this was real, in a way. She was inside the Crucible, along with Sperancia and at least three other women.

And yet she wasn't. She was also in her bed, at home.

"No, I'm not trapped," she told Katja. "I can see and hear you."

"You can understand me! And you speak English."

"Apparently so."

The blond woman narrowed her eagle eyes. "But how can I believe you? You might be the gast, lying to me. Tell me something that only Jana would know. It is still too soon for the gast to know all your thoughts."

"My grandmother's name was Ànghela. My father's mother. She always pretended to like mirto to be polite, but she hated the taste."

"Your farmor?" Katja repeated the name to Papà, who nodded.

Katja squeezed her hand. "So you are not a prisoner within your own body. But are there others there with you?"

"Yes. Four others."

"Who are they?"

Back in the church, the consorteria's meeting had ended. Jana approached young Sperancia. "Who are these women? Why didn't you tell me about them before?"

"I tried to tell you, but you refused to understand me."

"You never told me their names."

"I wanted you to meet them for yourself, without preconceptions. We don't always get along, but I thought you should make your own judgments."

"You don't get along with Giuseppina, do you?"

"She can be stubborn. She was the host before me, and when I was a child she was very strict. Giuseppina adjusted poorly when I became the host and surpassed her in power. So yes, we have a contentious relationship, even now."

"And now I am more powerful than you?"

Sperancia nodded. "You have much to learn about being the host, but ultimately you decide what we do in the physical world. It is only through you that we can influence the course of history."

"The *course of history*? That sounds...a little pretentious."

"History is composed of people making decisions. We all make history, whether we acknowledge it or not. We all create ripples in the fabric of reality."

"How can I understand English?" Jana asked. "There's a woman caring for me. She spoke to me and I could understand and answer her."

"Agatha speaks English fluently. It's she who understands, and she who moves your mouth and tongue as you form your thoughts. Your minds are already joined in such a way."

"So Agatha can read my thoughts?"

"Only your prevocalizations, and only as you allow it. Eventually you'll be able to communicate with each of us by thought alone, but only when your brain is fully mapped and virtualized."

Jana knew there were important matters to discuss. But an idea had been nagging at the back of her mind since the moment she had first seen Sperancia. "This world we're in now – it's made up, isn't it? Mythical creatures, and vines with strange fruit, and you young again...."

"Yes. We're in a programmed simulation."

"Does that mean we can change things easily?"

"What do you want to change?"

"The way I look. My body. My physical appearance."

"How do you want to look?"

"I...I don't know yet. Different."

"Let me know when you decide. But right now, you need to speak with Katja. Did you know that she is considering murdering you?"

"What?"

"She thinks that you – that *we* – are some kind of monster. She was a Crucible host herself once, but something went wrong. You need to explain to her what we are: a community of women that makes decisions together."

"How can I explain anything? I understand almost nothing."

"You understand that you're still yourself, don't you?"

Jana wasn't sure that she did, but she nodded. Certainly she didn't want Katja to slit her throat. She brought her attention back to the bedroom.

"Do you mean to kill me?"

Katja looked surprised, but shook her head. "No. Not if it's really Jana that I'm speaking to. And I believe that it is. If you're well enough, I'll return to my home and leave you alone. I apologize for the intrusion." Katja rose and dusted off the seat of her pants.

"No!" Jana grabbed Katja's hand. "Don't leave, not yet. Stay and be my guide. Help me decide what to do about the visitors." She was curious about the older blond woman, who was not only beautiful but had a fierce physical confidence that Jana envied.

"You mean the prisoners? Maro and Livia?"

"Yes, but also the people from Ilium. I could use your advice. Stay, and become part of my consorteria. At least for a while."

Jana explained to Katja what she had experienced in the church, describing her initial impressions of Agatha, who Jana guessed was the oldest of all of them, and Giuseppina, who was a bit of a bully, and quiet Itria, who was still a mystery. As she did so, Jana could hear the voices of the women protesting. They were used to living in the shadows, their existence entirely unknown, and as Jana shone light on them they found it uncomfortable. But Agatha still allowed her to understand and speak English, and the women eventually quieted, having accepted Jana's choice.

Jana was the host now. She would do things her way.

CHAPTER FOURTEEN

A week later Jana assembled the town council. She, as the new maghiarja, was now a full member, along with the mayor, Gregoriu, Micheli the barkeep, and the merchant Austino. They all wanted to know if the transfer of the Crucible had worked. Was Sperancia still alive within Jana? Could they speak to her? As old as they were, none of them had been alive at the previous Crucible ceremony.

Jana permitted Sperancia to speak through her. When she did she noticed her voice changed slightly, sounding rougher but also more melodic. The men rejoiced at hearing the old maghiarja's voice and welcomed her back. But they also insisted that she explain her actions.

"You put us all in danger, murdering Felix," Gregoriu said. "Why didn't you come to us? We could have discussed it."

"We were already in danger the moment they arrived," Sperancia said through Jana. "And we're still in danger, as long as Maro and Livia are alive. I was willing to take on the burden of killing alone, and I only regret that I failed."

Jana resumed control, and relayed to the council what Sperancia had told her about the origins of the *Michelangelo*, how they had stolen Earth's greatest works of art as a means of hoarding wealth, not protecting culture. Then she put forth her resolution: that Maro and Livia be executed for the murder of Sperancia. Livia for the actual deed, and Maro as her accomplice and co-conspirator.

Her proposal was instantly met with resistance.

"Execute?" said Micheli. "Are we not still Italians? The death penalty was abolished in our country in the eighteen hundreds. We're not savages."

"I don't know if we're still Italians or not," Gregoriu said. "Italy no longer exists. But my last name is Busincu – from Bosa – and we are *all* from Bosa, aren't we? No one has been executed here for centuries. Why should we bring back such a backward punishment?"

"It's also worth asking," Austino said tentatively, "if the penalty should be less harsh, considering that Sperancia isn't really dead. And that she attacked them first."

"Sperancia lives on in a way, but the murder was real," Gregoriu said. "Livia didn't just *try* to kill her – she *did* kill her. It doesn't matter that Sperancia was a Crucible host. Livia and Maro didn't know that."

"We need to consider the possibility of retaliation," Micheli said. "These are powerful people who built their own world. Surely they have weapons that could annihilate us."

"Then what would you suggest?" Jana asked.

"We imprison them. Just as we would our own."

Bosa did have a small jail with two cells, now containing Maro and Livia. Normally the cells were used when men got drunk and fought, and then for only a night. Bosa had few formal laws, and thus little crime. Land disputes were resolved by the council. Theft was remedied with the return of property and fines. There'd been no murders during Jana's lifetime – until Felix and Sperancia – and the stories she'd heard of killings had been remedied by either revenge or exile.

A short discussion of long-term imprisonment followed; everyone agreed it was impractical.

"If the choice is between execution and releasing them, I say the latter," Gregoriu proclaimed. "We killed one of theirs, they killed one of ours. Perhaps that makes us even. We'll tell them we have no interest in trade, and to never come back. We'll wash our hands of it and be done with the matter."

"Would they leave us alone?" Austino asked.

"Of course they wouldn't," Jana said. "We're playthings to them. If we release them, they'll only return in greater numbers, with more demands. You don't understand how powerful they are."

"If they are as powerful as you say, we shouldn't risk angering them further," Gregoriu pointed out.

The debate continued in the circular fashion that many arguments take, with points and counterpoints dancing in a predictable choreography. Jana began to feel frustrated, and understood why Sperancia had taken matters into her own hands. But now it was too late for any fast decisive action. The matter was in the hands of the council and everyone would speak until their breath was spent.

Jana squinted as the dim hall was flooded with light. Someone had flung open the heavy wooden doors and was advancing toward the council members.

"Father – the prisoners have escaped!" It was Antonio, addressing Austino, who had charged his son with securing and guarding Maro and Livia. "It was Cristo who helped them. He tricked me."

Wood scraped on stone as the council stood, pushing back their chairs. "When did it happen?" Austino asked. "Is there still a chance to catch them?"

"The balloon!" Gregoriu exclaimed. "Was anyone guarding it?"

Jana led them outside, fearing the worst. From the town square she had a clear view of the sky. It was a beautiful day, and her dread receded when she saw nothing but blue sky and white clouds. But her heart dropped when Antonio pointed. Following his gaze, she saw a glint of gold.

The balloon approached them, purposefully it seemed. As it passed over the square Maro and Livia waved and smiled gloatingly. To Maro's right was Cristo, looking down on them solemnly.

There was a fourth passenger as well, a woman. To Jana's horror she realized it was Filumena. Her friend blew her a kiss, looking sad but determined, and in no way a prisoner.

It appeared that both Cristo and Filumena were leaving Bosa of their own free will.

PART TWO
ANCESTRAL REALISM
CHAPTER FIFTEEN

Seeing the *Michelangelo*'s familiar cobalt-blue glow as they approached, Maro felt giddy with excitement. Some of the giddiness was purely physical, a combination of weightlessness and exhaustion. He'd slept poorly for weeks, with only hard ground for a bed, or the stone floor of a jail cell, or the compact gondola cots. But at the same time his entire being was vibrating with anticipation. Ancestral Realism would break new ground. He was sailing into uncharted territory. Soon, he would experience and document what no modern mind had experienced for centuries. His status among the Artists would be unparalleled.

"Are we almost there?" Filumena asked, touching his arm. Livia noticed the flirtation, glancing up from the shuttle controls. Which he appreciated, though he had no intention of bedding Filumena. Maybe after the experiments were complete, but by then she might hate him.

"Another twenty minutes or so, and we'll enter the docking bay," Maro answered.

"Will everyone understand our language?" Cristo asked.

"Yes. Some naturally, some with the help of translation machines. Please don't worry about it."

He patted Cristo's shoulder, appreciating the young man's curiosity and initiative. There were always people like Cristo and Filumena in any community, restless souls unsatisfied with familiarity and tradition, those who preferred adventure and novelty.

And Cristo's restlessness and daring had saved Maro the bother of orchestrating his own escape. Everything had worked out perfectly.

He idly wondered how Cristo had convinced Filumena to join him.

Didn't the girl have an ailing mother to care for? But he wasn't curious enough to ask. Clearly, Filumena's taste for adventure had won out over any sense of filial obligation.

The technicalities of their escape had been trivial. Cristo had distracted Antonio with a made-up errand, promising his friend he would keep a close eye on the captors. And then, while Antonio was running back to his father's shop, Cristo had stated his intentions.

"I'll release you, if you take us with you. Myself and a friend. We don't care if you killed Sperancia. She's not really dead anyway. But it has to be now. What do you say?"

"Of course, my brave boy," he'd said to Cristo. "That was always why we came, to make friends and to invite guests. And your companion is welcome too."

Filumena had joined them at the barley field, flushed and wide-eyed. No one in Bosa had thought to guard or confiscate their balloon. It took only minutes to load the gondola and lift off. Passing over the town square had been Maro's idea, and the winds had agreed. What a glorious moment, waving at his former captors. But was it not a fair exchange? He had what he wanted; they had a story that would be told for generations.

Finding the right winds to carry them back to Tunis had been tricky. But Livia, using data intercepted from the *Stanford*'s weather tracking satellites, had managed it, first flying southeast across Sardinia, then catching a southwest eddy that carried them across the sea to North Africa. Their shuttle had been right where they'd left it, untouched. They'd deflated the balloon, leaving it and the gondola in Tunis, a mystery for some future archeologist.

And now they were almost home.

The *Michelangelo* was a vast, rotating cylinder, twenty kilometers in length and eight kilometers in diameter. The worldship housed its own artificial sun, a continuous aneutronic helium-3 reaction contained by magnetic fields. The original version of the *Michelangelo*, constructed in geosynchronous orbit using materials transported up space elevators, had been much smaller, with an efficient but modest deuterium reactor. But the Engineers had always been ambitious. They'd mined vast amounts of magnesium silicate, iron, nickel, cobalt, and gold from asteroids, helium-3 from Saturn's atmosphere, and a small ocean's worth of water from Jupiter's moon Europa. Now the *Michelangelo* dwarfed the other worldships, even the *Liu Hui*. Unlike the others, their home was untethered from the Sun, the fusion core providing enough warmth and energy even in deep space. That tactical design choice had given them a great advantage, allowing them to tap the near-infinite natural resources of the solar system.

Among the castes, Engineers were second only to Artists. Defenders – those who studied military strategy, combat tactics, and espionage – ranked third. The plebeians that grew food, educated the young, and maintained systems were just as essential. But only Artists, Engineers, and Defenders were ranked. And with rank came privileges.

It was a fair system, one based on value and contribution. Rank conferred access to specialized services, as well as the wealth to accumulate unique artistic objects and ancient artifacts. That's all wealth was for, really. Any plebeian could drape themselves in diamonds and gold. Like all physical materials, gems and currency metals were abundant and essentially free to all citizens. *All* the essentials of life were free: food, shelter, healthcare, education. And nothing second rate, either. No citizen of the *Michelangelo* was a pauper.

But to dine with the best chefs, to own and play musical instruments created by masters centuries ago, to commission personalized works from brilliant painters and sculptors, those privileges were the rewards of rank and status. And of the latter, one could never have enough.

"We have permission to dock," Livia said. She'd navigated to the center of one end of the worldship. Maro shielded his eyes as the bay doors opened, releasing a flood of white light from the fusion core. Even as the shuttle latched on to the docking platform, they were still weightless, as was the entire central column. Maro noted that both Cristo and Filumena had handled the lack of gravity well, though they both looked a little green.

"Don't worry – you'll have your feet beneath you soon enough." He turned to Livia. "Will you take our guests through Medical and then get them comfortable in their quarters? And bathed? I should report to the Senate immediately."

"I'll take care of them," Livia answered, without making eye contact.

"When will we next see you?" Filumena asked.

"Soon, my child. This evening, at the latest."

"Isn't it already evening?" Cristo asked.

"It's late morning here. We have filters that approximate night and day, dawn and dusk. And the seasons as well. You'll get used to it."

He passed through Medical himself, and was relieved to learn that he hadn't picked up any parasites or novel pathogens. He'd eaten their food, after all, not all of it cooked. But even if he'd picked something up, it would have been worth it. The tomatoes alone had been far more flavorful than their aquaponically grown equivalents from the *Michelangelo*'s rotating vertical farms. Even artisanal varietals grown in real soil didn't compare to the rich red fruits he'd been offered in Bosa.

Report to the Senate immediately had been an exaggeration. He still had several hours before the next assembly. After receiving his medical clearance, Maro descended an elevator to the ground and rode a giant Vertragus home. The cybrid, part flesh and part machine, was fashioned after the Roman Britain racing dog of the same name. It took skill to ride one; there was no saddle and the sleek hounds moved with alacrity. The Vertragus wove through gardens, parks, and residential streets, occasionally barking to clear plebeians from the senator's path. But he managed the ride without falling, and sent the beast off with a slap on its flank.

Aina, his personal cybrid, greeted him warmly with a kiss on the lips. Red-haired and pale-skinned, she was modeled after a Celtic slave. A loyal one, Maro liked to imagine, whom he treated fairly. She had no consciousness, of course. Faustus, his enhanced ferret, was more sentient. But he liked to feel Aina's silk-soft hands on his body, and her lips wrapped around his cock, and to imagine the barbarians he might have slain to claim her.

Faustus greeted him with a leap to his shoulder, and by his heft Maro was reassured that Aina had fed him adequately. "And the birds?" Maro asked. He kept a parrot and a blackbird, each with their own room to prevent constant squabbling.

"They're well," Aina replied. "Healthy and fed. Shall I prepare your bath?"

"Please."

He'd already showered and disposed of his clothes in the course of his medical exam, but he showered again as a matter of habit to prepare for his bath. That had been the worst thing about his Earth excursion – the lack of proper bathing. The people of Bosa had stunk of sweat and fish, and even now those odors lingered in his sinuses. Maro scrubbed his skin until it flushed and tingled.

His bath was modest compared to the communal bathhouses, only three meters across, with a bench that kept his head just above the water. And yet he'd spared no expense in decorating the room, hiring artisans to hand-build the intricate mosaic floor, polished marble walls, and patinated bronze statues. "Join me," he said to Aina, and she complied, removing her robe and descending the steps into the steaming water. Her skin was real skin, soft and supple but also a highly functional protective organ. Though instead of protecting flesh and bone, her skin protected the elastomer fiber bundles that animated her titanium alloy skeleton.

"Rub my shoulders, Aina. I've been sleeping hard for weeks." She slid next to him on the bench as he turned his back to her. As the cybrid's strong fingers dug into his muscles, his thoughts turned to Jana. The young recruit Cristo had called Jana a *maghiarja* – a sorceress. And Sperancia before her, also a sorceress, a person of tremendous knowledge, astounding strength, and an uncanny ability to read people and predict their actions. Cristo hadn't known about the black egg that Maro had seen Sperancia vomit up and Jana subsequently swallow, but he'd referred to something called the Crucible. Perhaps the black egg and the Crucible were one and the same. Some strange mechanism that bestowed knowledge, strength, and a form of immortality.

Cristo had insisted that Sperancia was still alive, living on within Jana. Sperancia would see through Jana's eyes and speak through her mouth, along with all the other Crucible's previous hosts.

So it was a parasite of some sort. A human parasite.

"Would you like to have sex?" Aina asked.

"Not right now. Help me prepare for the Senate."

Maro donned a white linen tunic. Over that, Aina draped his *toga trabea*, an off-white woolen garment lined with a Tyrian purple stripe. For a moment, staring into the mirror, Maro was overcome by his own beauty: his flawless olive skin, his strong jaw and aquiline nose, his near-perfect symmetry and well-proportioned musculature. But he forced his attention back to the matter at hand. A battle awaited him in the Senate. Cassia, his chief opposition among the *populares*, would attack him at the first opportunity. And by now news of Felix's death would have reached her. Undoubtedly she would attempt to blame him for the unfortunate incident.

"Aina – I would like you to live with Cristo and Filumena for the next few days. Provide them with whatever comforts they desire, and keep a close eye on them. I'll expect a full report."

"Where do they live?"

He provided her with the address. Despite being an automaton devoid of conscious awareness, Aina was functionally intelligent enough to work out the remaining details on her own.

The Curia Simoni was close by, and Maro chose to walk. As he strolled through parks and gardens, past marble statues and elaborate fountains decorated with intricate tile mosaics, he accumulated, almost immediately, an entourage of hangers-on and genuflectors. *Welcome back. Tell us about your voyage. How many did you recruit?* Maro smiled and vaguely answered a few questions, giving them nothing of substance. Surely Cassia had spies among the minor magistrates.

The Curia was a huge shimmering dome constructed primarily of mollusk nacre, a building technique borrowed from biological engineers on the *Stanford*. Inside, the air was cool, and Maro was glad for the warmth his wool toga provided. Most of the senators had already arrived and were seated. Maro spotted Cassia instantly. It was impossible not to, given her height and coloring.

The opposing senator had engaged in a series of aggressive genetic and surgical modifications since adolescence. She was nearly two and a half meters – or eight Roman feet – tall. She weighed at least one hundred fifty kilos, maintaining her mass with six meals a day, platters heaped with meat, fruit, and pastries that she often shared in public with her plebeian constituents. Cassia eschewed the lean muscular aesthetic preferred by Maro and the other *optimates* in favor of a strong but statuesque build. Her thighs and buttocks were massive, her arms as thick as a lion's leg, her back as broad as a Viking rower's. Her voice was booming and resonant, enhancing the Ethos of her arguments. Everything about her – her size, her voice, her dark brown skin – Cassia had engineered to gain respect and authority and gravitas. Or attention: her irises were a bright reddish-purple (royal purple, matching the stripe on Maro's toga); her hair emerald green; her flawless teeth as black as obsidian. She was both beautiful and monstrous, an amalgam of cheap psychosocial engineering tricks. But those tricks worked. Cassia was powerful and popular.

"Greetings, Maro," she boomed the instant she saw him. "How did you find Earth, our dear and precious ancestral home?"

"Vertiginous, to be honest," he replied, trying and failing to match Cassia's volume. "It was unnerving, at first, to be under a limitless sky, and to see land or sea stretch out before you so vastly, with no upward curve, no sense of the loop."

"And yet you returned whole, unlike our friend Felix."

"I have arranged a memorial service for my friend and lover. It will be elaborate and luxurious, as he would have preferred. I trust you will attend?"

"Of course."

The assembly was brought to order. The agenda opened with various mundane topics that held little interest for Maro: infrastructure repairs; construction plans for new gymnasiums, bathhouses, dining halls, and galleries; hearings for disputes among plebeian groups that the lower magistrates had failed to resolve. While feigning attention to the speakers, Maro focussed on the nonverbal tells of the swing senators, those who had yet to align with either the *optimates* or the *populares* on the major agenda item. Ignatius, young and androgynously beautiful, looked nervous and would not meet his gaze. The sour old dog Traian did make eye contact, but with a beady-eyed resentment that made his sentiments clear enough.

The winds of the Senate might be headwinds today.

"And now for the matter of the Ringstation Coalition," intoned Praetor Ovidius, adjusting his toga. "The *Stanford* and other orbital worldships continue to hail us with increasing insistence, inviting us to join their coalition and collaborate on various projects, most notably the repopulation of Earth. We have yet to respond. The matter is now open for debate."

"*Worldships*, hardly," Ignatius said. "Their habitats are little more than glorified space stations. We dwarf them, physically and culturally."

"And yet their scientists continue to exceed the achievements of our Engineers," Cassia pointed out, raising a giant hand to emphasize the point. Murmurs of agreement followed.

"There's nothing wrong with borrowing," Maro said. "Are we not the tallest if we stand on the shoulders of giants?" Cassia gave him a sharp look for his choice of words, but many in the crowd chuckled.

"What are the risks if we respond, if we engage with them?" Traian asked.

"Nothing other than cultural suicide," said Maro, pulling no punches. "No good can come from mingling with those who do not share our appreciation of art."

"That's overly dramatic," Cassia countered. "The other worldships have rich cultural and artistic traditions."

"Certainly," Maro replied. "But to them, the arts will always be a slice of the pie, a line item, one among many things to consider. To us, art is primary, central, our collective purpose. Our lives serve the creative spirit, above all else. It is our reason for being."

"You do not speak for everyone, Maro," piped in Didius, a bland and annoying ally of Cassia.

"I speak for the spirit of our namesake, and for our ancestors who built this great worldship."

"We are not so simple as a pot of dye, to be diluted when mixed with water," Cassia argued. "Our values have been consistent for centuries. When we change, it is willful, conscious change. And that is what I am proposing, that we accept their invitation in order to see new paths and then choose our own way. We have been isolated for too long."

Maro, in speaking to the Sardinians, had explained their move to the inner solar system under the same pretext: ending isolation. But he wanted nothing to do with the Ringstation Coalition. There was naught to be gained from joining a bureaucracy of piddly space stations, endlessly debating what was right and what was wrong. The citizens of the *Michelangelo* would shape their own destiny. And whatever they wanted of Earth – people or animals or natural resources – they would simply take. Who would stop them?

The debate over the Ringstation Coalition continued for some time. But when it came to the vote, Maro's *optimates* prevailed by a narrow margin; the *Michelangelo* would continue to ignore all hails from the *Stanford, Liu Hui, Alhazen,* and *Hedonark.* 'Keep them guessing' was the majority sentiment, overwhelming Cassia's pleas for engagement and dialogue. Diplomacy had its place: a tool for parties of approximately equal strength and status to resolve their differences. But that was not the case here. The *Michelangelo* was superior in every way: size, population, military capability, technological advancement, cultural sophistication. Diplomacy was irrelevant.

The next agenda was a necessary annoyance. Cassia had filed a formal protest against Maro's Ancestral Realism project, gathering enough support to force the Senate to hear her appeal. It was meaningless theater; the project was already approved and well underway. But Cassia loved the sound of her own voice.

"My fellow senators," she began, "within hours Maro Decimus will begin an invasive psychological experiment on live human subjects, a heinous and barbaric practice which we should never have approved. I implore you to withdraw your support for this Senate-sanctioned torture, this savagery practiced in the name of science and progress."

Her monologue continued, a seemingly endless blast of hot wind. Maro sat still and straight, trying to keep his face neutral, not too smug. When it was finally his turn to respond, he kept it short. "I would like to remind the Senate that there are only two subjects at the moment, and both are eager volunteers. So eager, in fact, that they escorted Livia and myself out of Bosa personally, at some risk to themselves, after we had been falsely accused of murder and detained. In no way are we coercing either of them to participate. They are free to leave the experiment and the *Michelangelo* if they wish. I would escort them home personally. And *will*, healthy and whole, once the experiment is complete."

"Then provide me access to the subjects," Cassia demanded. "I would like to speak with them."

"So you can tell them lies about Ancestral Realism? I think not."

Cassia had no ground to stand on, and she knew it, but that didn't stop her from harassing Maro for as long as the Senate would allow. Which was quite some time, as it turned out. Maro stoically endured the abuse until the next agenda item.

Which came as something of a surprise.

The Engineers had detected an anomaly – a powerful gamma-ray burst – in the outer solar system. The burst had occurred near the Centaur Chariklo, a minor planet with two icy rings orbiting the Sun between Saturn and Uranus. After a careful analysis the Engineers had deemed the event critically significant, and had prepared a report for the Senate. A woman named Lucretius, an astrophysicist, began the presentation, appearing nervous and agitated.

"My esteemed senators, I begin assuming that you have read and comprehended the essence of our report –" Maro hadn't, and didn't, "– and will not waste your time with the technicalities. Suffice to say that the gamma-ray signature is consistent with the deinstantiation of a spacetime warp bubble. One possible explanation, and perhaps the most likely, is that a starship has just entered our solar system. While such a craft may be of alien origin, a more likely explanation relates to the development of a Natario-White warp drive by researchers on the *Liu Hui*, twenty years ago."

"I remember," interrupted Traian. "They built an experimental starship, the *Iarudi*. Wasn't it stolen by a rogue officer?"

"There was a scandal within their military around that time," Lucretius concurred, "and yes, the *Iarudi* disappeared, thought to be lost forever. Our spies on the *Stanford* informed us that a man believed to be onboard, Shane Jaecks, was declared dead. His family conducted memorial services."

"And you believe this gamma-ray burst is the *Iarudi* returning?" Maro asked.

"It is a likely explanation. In theoretical models, a Natario-White drive allows travel at superluminal speeds by creating a negative mass bubble in front of a starship, thus contracting space in front of the craft and expanding space behind it. The problem is that a number of particles get caught up in the warp bubble, even in deep space. Some of those particles have mass, and when the warp bubble stops moving, that particle energy is released. Potentially a huge amount of energy, depending on how long the ship has been traveling superluminally. One of Chariklo's ice rings has been partially vaporized."

"To be clear," Maro asked, "you're talking about faster-than-light travel?"

"Yes."

"So if someone is onboard the *Iarudi*, and they've been traveling for a long time, then very little time has passed for them, correct? Essentially, they're from the past?" The thought intrigued him.

Lucretius furrowed her brow and bit her lip before answering. "Not in this case – time dilation doesn't apply. The Natario-White drive literally warps space toward its destination, like a funnel. Inside of the funnel is normal spacetime."

"A shortcut," Maro said, realizing his mistake. He noticed Cassia was smiling, gloating at his error, though he doubted she knew any better. He was not ashamed; it was the job of Engineers to know such things, not Artists. His job was to create a vision of the future and manifest it. "I move that we intercept this ship immediately. Send a Falcon to retrieve it."

"If it is the *Iarudi*, it belongs to the *Liu Hui*," Traian pointed out. "It's a military ship with proprietary technology. Seizing it could be considered an act of war."

"They'd be fools to do anything about it," Maro scoffed.

"Do we have a visual?" Cassia asked.

"From our current location, everything is obscured by vast clouds of vaporized ice and dust particles," Lucretius explained. "Everyone near Earth has the same view."

"What about our Saturn satellites left over from the helium mining operations?" Cassia asked. "Can't they tell us something?"

"We have dispatched probes from Saturn, but they're slow-moving. They'll take weeks to get there."

"And how long for a Falcon?" Maro asked. It had taken the *Michelangelo* two years to return from the outer solar system to Earth, but the fusion-drive Falcon cruisers could accelerate and decelerate much more quickly.

"About six weeks, with an average speed of four hundred kilometers per second. But the acceleration required to reach such speeds would only be achievable with remote operation or a cybrid crew. Human bodies – even enhanced ones – can't withstand the G-force from pulsed fusion acceleration."

"Cybrids can operate Falcons?" Maro asked. That was news to him.

"With the Bohm upgrade, yes. Which has had a very limited rollout, given the ethical considerations—"

Nodding knowingly, Maro raised his hand to cut Lucretius off, despite the fact that he'd never heard of the Bohm upgrade. He would send a task to Aina to research the details and provide him with a summary. Risking a glance at Cassia, he was mortified to see her staring at him with smug satisfaction.

Maro stood. "I would like to hear from the Defenders, but it is my belief that if the *Iarudi* has indeed returned, we must retrieve it, regardless of whose feelings we might hurt. We have taken on the highest mission in the solar system, and we must do whatever is necessary to honor that commitment. Technological superiority is not just *nice to have*, it is a strategic imperative."

His voice was not as loud or resonant as Cassia's, but Maro knew how to play a crowd. Appeals to power and dominance almost always worked, and this case was no exception. Murmurs of assent rippled throughout the Curia.

In truth he would welcome a military skirmish with the *Liu Hui*. It was time for everyone to see what the *Michelangelo* was capable of.

CHAPTER SIXTEEN

"Are they ready?" Maro asked Livia. They were at a reserved *domus* furnished with several *triclinia* and other simple furnishings, as well as two isolation tanks. The 'action' would all take place in the minds of the subjects; all that was needed for the project was privacy, sensory isolation, and physiological monitoring.

"Ready and eager," said Livia. "They both slept restlessly, but that's to be expected. Everything here is new to them."

"But you've confined them to quarters, no?" Maro asked. Faustus nuzzled against his neck, sensing his anxiety. Maro scratched behind the ferret's ears.

"Of course. But even within their *domus*, there are new technologies, materials, novel sensations of all kinds."

Maro frowned. "We should begin as soon as possible. We can't give them time to adjust."

Livia looked away, checking her retinal feed. "The Engineers are running some final tests – they'll be ready for the surgeries within hours. But we can escort the subjects to Medical now."

"I'll do it myself," Maro said. Besides Livia, he didn't trust anyone to interact with the subjects. Cassia wasn't above bribes and threats to exert her influence.

He found Cristo naked, bathing in a tiled pool with Aina. Each tile of the underwater mosaic had been fired in a unique shade of blue, green, or aquamarine. The Bosa man quickly stood, grabbing a towel to cover himself.

"Don't you knock?" Cristo snapped.

"Don't be embarrassed. You have a beautiful body."

Cristo frowned, upset but clearly enjoying the compliment. Maro didn't know what homophobia, if any, lingered among the Bosa folk, but the experiment would tell him soon enough. It would reveal Cristo's mind more clearly than any electron scan or robotic dissection ever could.

"Give me a minute to dress."

"Of course."

Maro gave Cristo his requested privacy. A tiny worry itched his mind, that the subject would flee. But where would he go? It was a natural fear; Maro had gone through so much work to acquire the pair. But he reassured himself that there was no need to worry. It was true what he had told the Senate; Cristo and Filumena were here by choice.

"I'll be right back," Maro called from the adjoining room. "I'll retrieve Filumena."

"I invited her to join us," Cristo yelled back playfully, "but she said she was already clean."

Maro had guessed as much. Cristo desired Filumena, perhaps even loved her. And the experiment would capture the exact qualities of that primal, unrequited love, along with everything else. Many of the scenarios involved the participants interacting under intense pressure, in extreme circumstances. Everything would be revealed.

The purpose of Ancestral Realism was to capture the consciousness of a different era in such a way that it could be worn like a cloak. The experiments would map a complete cognitive and emotional hologram of the subjects, recording their interpretations and reactions to a huge variety of situations, from the mundane and pleasant to the horrific and ecstatic. From that repository of data, the Engineers would create a template, a pattern that could be worn by a modern user's mind. The template would modulate hormonal, neurotransmitter, and other neurophysiological parameters via the user's implants in such a way that the consciousness of the original subject could be subjectively experienced. Not precisely – each mind was unique – but in flavor and tenor. Every era had its own mindset, zeitgeist, and cognitive-emotional tone. Ancestral Realism would provide the missing link in the study of history: the ability to subjectively experience the minds of its subjects.

The citizens of the *Michelangelo* played at being Romans. Decades earlier, feudal Japan had been in style, and before that, a hundred years ago, they had lived as Mayans. Maro fondly remembered playing *ulama* as a youngster, and his bones still bore the scars of many fractures from the heavy rubber ball.

Maro took pride in the worldship's rich tradition of historical immersion. Citizens went beyond emulating the food, dress, architecture, and lifestyles of whatever historical civilization was in fashion. They modified their bodies as well, both genetically and surgically. Not only skin color, facial features, and physical proportions, but also physiological factors and even brain chemistry. Some, like Cassia, used such capabilities to create a unique somatic form. And Maro had no problem with that. But most, including himself, preferred to emulate historical norms as accurately as possible, both physically and mentally.

But even with such meticulous attention to detail, something was missing. Human consciousness was an ephemeral quality, and modifying genetic traits – even those related to cognition, emotion, and sensory processing – could not begin to capture the *subjective* reality of a historical civilization.

Until Ancestral Realism, that had not been possible.

It was just a start. The minds of the Bosa townsfolk were nothing like the people of ancient Rome. But they were closer, more primitive and perhaps more savage than the minds of Maro and his peers. Or perhaps not! The experiment would find out. Maro could not wait to wear a template himself, to begin to experience the subjective flavor of another era. Certainly it would take more than two subjects to form a reliable template, but he had to start somewhere.

And there were other communities on Earth to be captured. Mountain people living in central Europe, who appeared to live something like Vikings (but without boats). What were their minds like? How would it feel to walk in their bodies, with their feelings and impulses, their rages and their passions, their insights and imaginations?

Maro was personally interested in experiencing such things, but Ancestral Realism had a higher purpose as well, one that dovetailed with the *Michelangelo*'s ultimate goal.

Preservation.

Mind states were precious but ephemeral. Like languages, a culture's collective consciousness constantly morphed and mutated, eventually dying and disappearing like any life form. Until now, there had been no way to record, capture, and preserve such phenomena. But Ancestral Realism could do so, at least in theory. Ultimately, Maro would create a vast library of human cultural consciousness. Not only to be analyzed and discussed, but to be experienced directly.

"Filumena? Are you ready?" Filumena's *domus* was next to Cristo's, with a connecting arched marble walkway.

He found her crying in her bedroom, her face pressed into a silken pillow.

"What is it, my dear? Are you feeling homesick?"

She looked up at him with red-rimmed eyes. "What's that on your shoulder?"

"It's just Faustus. Don't mind him."

Filumena pressed her face back into the pillow. "I've abandoned my mother, who needed me. I've abandoned my friends, who relied on me."

"It's difficult to hear you."

Filumena put the pillow down. "It was pure selfishness that brought me here. I was wrong to listen to Cristo. He caught me at a weak moment."

Maro sat on the bed, taking both her hands in his own. The skin on the back of her hands was smooth and soft, her palms as calloused and textured as rough stone. "They'll be fine. Don't worry. The people of Bosa are kind and generous. They'll care for your mother. And if the friend you speak of is Jana, she's strong enough to endure your short absence."

Filumena sobbed. "You're wrong! As wrong as I was to come here. I have to return immediately. Jana needs me right now, my mother too. Will you take me home?"

Maro furrowed his brow. This was not part of the plan. He awkwardly squeezed Filumena's hands, trying to convey reassurance, but this elicited a jealous hiss from Faustus.

Filumena's eyes widened. "Is he dangerous?"

"Only if he bites you. But he won't, I promise. He's very well-trained. To answer your questions, of course I will take you home. At the very first opportunity. But the next ship does not leave for weeks."

"None sooner?"

Maro slowly shook his head. "I'm sorry, dear child. None sooner." He could have her home in Bosa within a day if he chose, but that was unacceptable. "I will remind you that you are under no obligation to do anything you don't want to do. You may spend your time on the *Michelangelo* any way that you wish. Visit our museums, see our plays, or just lie between these silken sheets and rest. You are our honored guest."

"But…your project. You said that you needed us."

Maro shrugged. "It's not important. After you rest, perhaps you will change your mind. These emotional swings are natural when adjusting to a new place. You miss your loved ones. Have you eaten?" He gestured to a nearby platter of fresh figs, grapes, and soft cheese. "Nourish yourself, then sleep. We'll talk of this later."

Filumena plucked a grape and popped it in her mouth. "Thank you."

"Of course, if you do decide to participate, you will return home with riches that will make your mother's life easy and comfortable. And perhaps we can take a closer look at what ails her. There might be a cure."

"Really?"

Maro smiled. "If you knew how old I was, you would be amazed. The human body contains miraculous capabilities to heal itself, powers that can be unlocked with the right keys. And we have discovered those keys."

Maro stayed with her a while longer, answering her questions. One way or another Filumena would participate in the experiment, but the voluntary route was vastly preferable. He suspected she just needed a little more time and reassurance.

In the meantime, there was no reason they couldn't start with Cristo. Many of the scenarios required only a single participant. Cristo, though distressed that Filumena was not yet joining him, submitted eagerly to the required medical procedures: optic and cochlear nerve implants for both projection and recording; neurohormonal monitors; parietal stimulators to simulate touch, pain, force, and motion. Maro sat with Cristo during surgery, holding his hand and asking him questions about Bosa. Cristo, skull open but feeling no pain, chatted amicably as the spiderlike bot-surgeons gently wove the tiny implants into place.

"I'm so glad I'm here," Cristo said. "You can't believe how boring Bosa gets sometimes. I know everything about everyone. Much more than I should, or want to."

Maro chuckled at that. Even on a worldship with thousands of people, he sometimes felt the same.

"When does the fun begin?" Cristo asked. "I can't wait."

"Very soon. You'll be fully healed within a few days, but the implants will take a bit longer to fully integrate. You'll experience some unusual sensations in the interim. Don't be alarmed."

"What kind of sensations?"

"Visions of places you've never been. Music and voices in your head. The Engineers will debrief you periodically. It's just testing to make sure everything is working properly."

"How will I know what's real?"

"You won't, at first. But you'll figure it out."

This was a lie. Cristo would have no way of knowing what was real and what was being projected into his mind. If it were so easy to distinguish, the point of the experiment would be defeated.

"The important thing is that you'll always be safe," Maro said. "We won't do anything to put you in harm's way."

It was true that Cristo would emerge whole and unscathed, at least physically. Mentally and emotionally, Maro had no way of knowing. But if the boy experienced any trauma, that could be addressed later with desensitization and reprocessing therapy, and with neuroremodulatory drugs if necessary.

Anything that was doable to the brain was undoable.

While Cristo was recovering, Maro returned his attentions to Filumena. The Bosa woman's spirits had recovered considerably with food, rest, and small, surreptitious doses of euphorics. He escorted her to the Library of Alexandria and showed her relics originating not far from her home: manuscripts transcribed by Italian monks, an ancient Greek excerpt of Homer's *Odyssey* transcribed onto clay tablets, cave paintings excavated from the French Mediterranean coast. He wanted to give her a tangible sense of history without overstimulating her. Viewing work by the masters would be too much, so early.

"Seeing these paintings fills me with an indescribable feeling, Maro," Filumena said, viewing a detailed Gravettian portrait of a mammoth. "Were these really made by the first human beings?"

"Early humans, but far from the first. The Upper Paleolithic peoples were quite late in the modern human timeline. The first humans capable of using language and creating art evolved about seventy thousand years ago in eastern Africa, almost directly below us."

"Below us?"

"Here, look." He initiated a floor projection simulating a crystal-clear window beneath their feet, a live image of Lake Victoria, zoomed in to within a few kilometers of Earth's surface. Filumena gasped, then got down on her hands and knees to touch the 'window', confirming its solidity. "Right there, see? That's where the first humans woke up. And then left Africa, shortly after, in many waves."

"Why did they leave?"

"If I could ask them, I would. But I assume they were curious, like you."

Filumena, still on the floor, looked up at him with narrowed eyes. "Maybe they were just out of food, and hungry."

"Curiosity is a form of hunger."

Back at her *domus*, just as he was about to leave, she kissed him. "Come to my bed, Maro. I've never been with a man. I want you to be my first."

"Would you have sex with your father's friends?"

She recoiled, curling her upper lip in disgust. "My father is dead. But no, of course not."

"Then you shouldn't share a bed with me. I'm far older."

"I don't believe you."

He kissed her forehead. "And yet, I am."

"I could have any man in Bosa," she said spitefully.

"I'm sure you're right."

"I won't give you another chance."

He left before she could work herself up any further. It was pointless to argue. The girl was used to getting what she wanted and would not be dissuaded unless he physically removed himself. He enjoyed supple young bodies as much as anyone, but he generally avoided sexual relations with the young. Human emotions were so volatile in the first half-century of life; it was rarely worth the effort.

While he waited for Cristo to recover and for Filumena to come to her senses, Maro passed his time in the Library of Alexandria, researching the Crucible. There was no reason to be there physically; he could have run everything through his retinal feed or asked Aina to do the work for him. But it was comforting to be among the millions of texts from every century, the oldest handwritten on vellum parchment or papyrus or even clay tablets.

It took some time to refine the search, weeding out chemistry and metallurgical references. But eventually Maro came across the Crucible Program, a twenty-second-century brain emulation experiment. The idea had initially been to solve the 'Smooth Transition' problem, a philosophical identity quandary. Once brain scanning technology had advanced to the molecular level, with each axon and dendrite perfectly mapped, it had become theoretically possible to accurately emulate a human brain. But that capability hadn't satisfied the desire for human immortality or practical 'brain backups' in any way. Even if an accurate brain emulation running on a quantum computer substrate could be instantiated and activated (either in an android body or within a simulated virtual world), that new 'person' would have a unique identity from the original, even though possessing all of the original's memories. The very awareness that they were a copy (and that awareness was unavoidable) created an unbridgeable identity schism, especially in cases where the copy was instantiated while the original was still alive. These living backups, or engrams, had caused endless trouble in terms of legalities, estates, relationships, and with the living trying to grieve the physically dead.

The Crucible Program had attempted to present an alternative path to continuing human consciousness after death. The Crucible technology gradually copied and replaced the functionality of the entire nervous system of a living host via capillary-like carbon-based nanothreads. The threads extended lifespan and conferred other benefits: physical strength, prodigious memory, enhanced intelligence. But eventually, like all human beings, the host died, of natural or other causes.

At that point, the Crucible was ejected from the body, to potentially be consumed by a new host. The original host lived on as an emulation within the quantum core, while the Crucible began the entire process again with the new host.

The hope, beyond achieving immortality, beyond solving Smooth Transition, had been to create a community of minds, a new type of meta-being, multiple minds operating within a single body.

But something had gone wrong. The Crucible program had been terminated for 'ethical concerns'. Maro tried and failed to find the names and histories of the original participants, but those had been lost to time and entropy. Even the Library of Alexandria had its limits.

Still, he had learned enough. It explained what he had seen with his own eyes. It explained what Cristo had said about Sperancia, that she lived on within Jana. Somehow, this particular Crucible instance had continued its lifecycle, unbroken, for over five hundred years. How many hosts did it contain? Who were they? And what did they want? Did they squabble endlessly about petty things, or were they powerful collaborators working toward a common goal?

The technology intrigued him immensely. What would it be like to live for not only centuries, but potentially for millennia? Maro's body might easily have another hundred years of life in it, but there were always limits to human biological life. Maro had his engram updated regularly like every other person of importance, but he was under no illusion that it conveyed him immortality, nor any continuation of his personal consciousness after death. Even if his engram, when activated, were to possess subjective awareness, it wouldn't be *him*. And the engram would be trapped in a static state or near to it. Engrams could accumulate new memories but were incapable of architectural modulation. True life meant change, constant change, and that appeared to be the promise of the Crucible.

He had to speak with Jana again. What would it be like to be part of such a community? What would it be like to *rule* one, for surely that was possible as well? Long-term co-operation required some sort of consensus, a basic agreement or acknowledgment of norms. And such agreements could be violated. Real war had no rules. All the great leaders of history had understood that: Genghis Khan, Attila the Hun, and of course Julius Caesar. If Maro were to become a Crucible host, he had little doubt that he would emerge as a conqueror. He would rule with an iron fist. Had that not been the pattern of his life?

Even now, he was close to consolidating his power on the *Michelangelo*. The worldship did not have an emperor, not yet, but that would change. Only Cassia stood in his way. Well, perhaps not only her, but her most of all, constantly belittling him, harassing him, souring his victories and savoring his defeats. Without Cassia's power buttressing the *populares*, the *optimates* would rule unchecked. And the *optimates* answered to Maro.

* * *

On the eve of Cristo's first scenario, the true beginning of the Ancestral Realism experiment, Maro went to visit Cristo and Filumena. He strolled through the lavish Gardens of Lucullus, Faustus riding on his shoulder. The ferret nuzzled his neck, begging for head scratches, which Maro happily provided. He loved Faustus, perhaps more than any person. And Maro basked in the animal's simple, unconditional love in return.

He found Cristo bored, restless, and talkative. He'd hoped the pair from Bosa would have spent more time together, but apparently Filumena wanted nothing to do with Cristo. That wasn't ideal for the experiment, but nor was it prohibitive. The scenarios existed for gathering data; how the participants interacted within them was of secondary importance.

Perhaps the stressors would trigger some appreciation for each other, or even spark a kind of love.

"Someone is with her," Cristo said of Filumena. "A visitor. I caught a glimpse of her in the hallway."

That was impossible. Visitors were forbidden unless explicitly approved by Maro or Livia. "Who?" Sensing Maro's distress, Faustus chittered angrily.

"I don't know. She was very tall. And her ass was as wide as a house."

No.

Maro ran to Filumena's *domus*, passing through the connecting arched marble walkway in a few strides. Faustus dug his claws into Maro's shoulder, hanging on tight.

Filumena was sitting on the edge of her bed. Cassia sat next to her, her long, thick arm draped across the subject's shoulder like a python. Next to the giant senator the Bosa girl looked like a child.

"Hello, Maro," Cassia said, smiling to reveal her shining black teeth. "Filumena and I were having a little talk. She's told me she misses home. Her mother is sick."

"I'm well aware. After the experiment we'll bring Filumena's mother to the *Michelangelo* for treatment."

Cassia's lips turned down in a facetious pout. "But her mother needs comfort right now. If Filumena wants to go home, we should arrange that immediately."

Filumena looked at him with hurt in her eyes, now aware of his lie that the next ship would not depart 'for weeks'.

"Why are you here, Cassia? I didn't authorize it, and neither did Livia."

"I am here legally, via emergency motion. You have fewer friends in the Senate than you suppose."

If that was true then there would be hell to pay. But right now Maro needed to tread carefully. "I am touched at your concern for Filumena. But may we have a private word? Would you step into the walkway with me, for just a minute or two?"

Cassia was caught off guard but quickly recovered. "Of course." The senator rose to her full height of eight Roman feet. The bed creaked with the release of her weight. A large indentation remained in the absence of Cassia's buttocks and thighs, a shallow valley of gravitationally warped space, into which Filumena perceptibly slid. Cassia squared her shoulders and strode in Maro's direction, daring him not to move. But he stepped aside deferentially and followed her to the arched marble walkway.

Out of Filumena's sight, Cassia dropped her fake smile. "I'm sending her home. You can't keep her here against her will. Your proposal, which the Senate approved, states very clearly that participation in your experiment is voluntary."

"She's still making up her mind. And it's unethical for you to exert your influence either way."

"*Unethical?*" Cassia repeated. "Can you hear yourself speak, Maro Decimus? Have you no more self-awareness than a turnip? Or less, perhaps. The bacteria feasting on the excrement in my bowels is a higher form of consciousness than you, *Senator*. Your willingness to abuse innocents, your eagerness to traumatize naïve minds in your sick, self-titillating quest for new masturbatory material, it sickens me."

"You obviously have no understanding of what I am trying to achieve," Maro replied calmly. "If you think Ancestral Realism has anything to do with sexual gratification, you are as stupid as you are ugly. I have no interest in Filumena sexually – you can ask her yourself."

"And yet you want to be *inside* of her, don't you? Inside of her *mind*? You are so incapable of genuine human connection or empathy that you seek to engineer it with some kind of voyeuristic workaround."

Maro exhaled through his nostrils, losing patience. "I don't know if you're willfully misconstruing my project, or if you're just inherently incapable of understanding it. What I'm doing is akin to preserving a lost language or restoring a damaged antiquity. It is as essential to our mission as any work we do. Perhaps the most essential. And yet it is subtle and ephemeral, so you don't get it."

Cassia shook her head, synchronously waving a fat finger in his face for emphasis. "I understand it perfectly. I understand *you* perfectly."

At that moment Maro experienced the briefest flash of doubt. What if Cassia was right? What if he had deluded himself as to the importance of his work?

No, that was the voice of weakness and despair. The significance of his work was a question for future scholars and historians. He would not cut off his own foot in the last steps of the race.

"*Epitíthemai,*" he said quietly. He had trained Faustus in Greek, not Latin, so as not to accidentally trigger an attack. The ferret leapt at Cassia's neck and sunk its modified hollow incisors into her right carotid artery.

She grabbed the animal, crushing its spine with her immense hand, and flung it against the marble wall. Faustus fell limply, dead before impact. That saddened Maro, but he had known this day might come.

The damage was done. Maro's revenge already exacted. Cassia would be dead within minutes, writhing in pain as she asphyxiated, her lungs paralyzed by the nerve toxin Faustus had injected into her bloodstream.

CHAPTER SEVENTEEN

"I'm so happy to see you." Tem embraced Maggie tightly, overwhelmed with relief. She'd parked the hovershuttle right in front of the longhouse, either oblivious to how much attention that would attract among the villagers, or not caring.

Maggie squirmed out of his embrace. "What the hell happened?"

"My aunt Katja stole the hovershuttle. I think she was going to Bosa, and we should follow her. I'm worried about what she might do there—"

"Tem, slow down."

"You don't understand. She wants to kill Sperancia. Katja thinks she's a gast. A body thief. I'll explain, but it will take time. I'll tell you on the way."

"Lydia and Ingrid are already there."

"What?"

"They're in Bosa now. Some things have happened, but Katja didn't cause any trouble."

"She didn't?"

"No. I tracked your hovershuttle to Bosa. I tried to talk to your aunt but she hung up on me. I didn't know it was her at the time, but we decided to check on the Bosa folk just in case. Mostly, they're fine."

"Mostly?"

"There's been some interference from the *Michelangelo*. Two people are dead, one from the *Michelangelo*, one from Bosa."

"What happened?"

A crowd had gathered, watching and listening from a respectful distance, but Farmor Elke stepped forward. "And who is this?" she asked in Norse, regarding Maggie both curiously and critically.

"Who's this?" Maggie asked in English, frowning slightly.

"My grandmother. Esper's mother."

"She looks like you," Elke said. Tem didn't think he and Maggie looked much alike beyond both being of mixed European and Asian ancestry.

"What did she say?" Maggie asked. "Tell her I'm happy to meet her. I'm Maggie," she said, extending her hand to Elke.

Elke looked at Maggie's hand as if it were a dead fish.

"Farmor," Tem said in Norse. "Maggie is a good friend of mine. Please show her some respect."

Elke grasped Maggie's forearm. "Just a friend? Or another one of your lovers? She looks like she needs to eat some meat. I'll set an extra place."

"Farmor, please…."

"What did she say?" Maggie asked again.

"She says she's happy to meet you, and she invited you for dinner. But I'd like to leave for Bosa immediately if that's okay with you."

"Please tell her I'd love to stay for dinner," Maggie said.

Tem nodded, accepting his fate, and made the appropriate translations.

Dinner was venison boiled with onions, carrots, and potatoes. It was simple fare but Maggie oohed and aahed as if a gourmet chef had personally prepared the meal to her preferences. Though Maggie spoke no Norse and Elke spoke little English, the two got along well. Maggie was a quick study and soon knew the Norse word for everything in the room. Within an hour, Maggie had a better rapport with his grandmother than his own mother had ever achieved.

The stakes were different, he realized. His grandmother didn't resent Maggie because there was nothing Maggie could steal. And Elke, noticing Tem's and Maggie's affection for each other, realized there was something Maggie could give: great-grandchildren.

"Don't worry, grandson," Elke whispered in Norse. "I won't say anything about Saga. Though everyone in Happdal knows. You should have been more discreet."

Tem grimaced. He planned to confess everything, but now wasn't the time.

"Did you enable the hovershuttle security measures?" he asked Maggie.

"Of course, dummy," Maggie answered, poking him. She'd moved the vehicle to a distant pasture while Elke and Tem had prepared the meal. "It wasn't exactly difficult. You just talk to it."

"I know. I'm an idiot. I just didn't think there would be any need."

"You underestimated your aunt."

"You're right."

"It's okay," she said, patting his shoulder. "You were raised in a primitive culture where men often underestimate women. You Happdal men think your balls give you magical powers when all they do is make your muscles and bones a bit bigger."

Tem chuckled, which prompted Elke to ask for a translation. She laughed uproariously when he provided one.

"I like her," Elke said, refilling Maggie's stein with *öl*. "Keep this one."

"I will if I can."

After dinner the three of them visited Trond's house, where Maggie made an equally good impression on Tem's uncle and his family. Lissa served thick slices of hazelnut honey cake slathered with whipped buttercream. Maggie practiced the Norse vocabulary she had just learned from Elke, much to the delight of Mette, Erica, and Gunborg, who shrieked with laughter at every mispronounced word. Sigurd and Baldr both found occasion to thump Tem on the back and grin at him knowingly.

"Tem, I think I'm drunk," Maggie confessed. She'd consumed a stein and a half of Elke's *öl*, and Lissa's hazelnut cake had come with a strong cup of cider.

"You're definitely drunk."

"I know you wanted to leave tonight, but if we get in the hovershuttle I might vomit."

"We'll leave first thing in the morning – it's fine."

Trond offered the guestroom in his large house, but Tem declined. They said good night and made their way to Katja's cabin. Tem wanted to ask what had happened in Bosa, and his pending confession weighed heavily. But with Maggie holding his arm tightly for support, stumbling every other step, he chose to stay silent. It felt good to be close to her again. He regretted not inviting her to Happdal in the first place.

"See, your family loves me," she said in between hiccups.

Tem nodded and pulled her closer.

In the morning, bleary-eyed, Maggie expressed her regret for leaving her toothbrush in the hovershuttle.

"Want to borrow mine? There's a bucket of well water just outside."

Maggie grimaced. "That's okay. How do Happdal people keep their teeth clean? Chew bark or something?"

"Toothpicks, mostly, and rotten teeth get pulled. They'd be better off with dental floss and a real dentist."

"Maybe we can help them with that. We're helping sick people in

Bosa, aren't we? And didn't your mother fix a radiation leak near Happdal a long time ago? There's a precedent of sorts."

"She did. You're right – I'll bring it up at the next Repop meeting. I think they're comfortable enough with ringstation folk to trust us. Maybe they'd accept some dentistry services."

"Are you ready to go?"

"Yes, but we need to say our goodbyes."

Tem kept it as brief as possible, but there were many who wanted to see him off. And even more who wanted to get another glimpse of Maggie.

"You know I am by your side if you need me," Trond said, pulling Tem's forehead against his own. "I will even come to the sky ship if necessary."

"That's a kind offer, Trond, especially since I know you like to keep your feet on the ground. But your place is here in Happdal. I'll come back to visit."

Elke embraced him for a long time. "I thought Sigurd would be the first to make me a great-grandmother. But maybe it will be you. Good luck with Maggie."

"Thank you, Farmor."

They walked to the hovershuttle laden with gifts from his family: heavy loaves of brown bread, a jar of honey, a cask of cider, slabs of smoked trout wrapped and tied in a rabbit pelt, a few small wheels of cheese.

"Your family is very generous," Maggie said.

"They like you. A lot. I think that's the warmest welcome I've ever seen for a sky person."

Maggie brushed her teeth while Tem packed the hovershuttle. Within ten minutes of being airborne, she was asleep again, snoring lightly as he wove the craft through the peaks of the Harz mountains. Tem raised the protective dome and increased their speed, eager to return to Bosa.

When Maggie woke, Tem asked her what exactly had happened in Bosa. She told him about the visitors from the *Michelangelo*, how Felix and Sperancia had both died in an altercation.

"That's terrible, and a huge setback for Bosa. Sperancia was intelligent and knowledgable."

"Jana claims she's still alive, living inside of her."

That gave Tem pause. "So maybe I was right. Sperancia might have been a Crucible host."

Maggie nodded. He'd explained the nature of the Crucible technology to Maggie. "I think you're right. Though by all accounts the transition was entirely voluntary. Nothing like what your aunt went through. Lydia says that Jana is acting normally, as far as she can tell."

Maggie brought him up to date regarding Maro and Livia's imprisonment and subsequent escape, aided by two young people.

"And those two are on the *Michelangelo* now? Is there any way to communicate with them?"

"Not unless the *Michelangelo* starts answering hails, which seems unlikely. They're as silent as ever."

"I wonder if Cristo and Filumena are being held as hostages."

They lapsed into silence. Nearing the Alps, Tem gathered the gumption to confess his dalliance with Saga. Maggie listened without interrupting, eyes locked ahead, jaw tense.

"Anything else you need to tell me? Is that everything?"

He'd left one thing out – the fact that there was a possibility that he'd gotten Saga pregnant. It was a particularly damning detail.

"I don't suppose you used any protection?" Maggie asked. "Some kind of lamb gut condom or something like that?"

"No," he said, feeling awful.

"Did you at least pull out?"

"I know I'm going to sound stupid again, but I didn't think about it."

"So Saga might be pregnant with your child."

"I don't think it's very likely, but yes."

"And she's your ex, isn't she?"

"Well, she's the first woman I ever had sex with. I wouldn't say we were ever in a relationship."

"Is that why you didn't want me to come to Happdal? Because you were planning an affair with Saga?"

Tem briefly considered opening the hovershuttle dome and jumping out. The landing would be surely be painful, injurious, and perhaps fatal. And yet an improvement over his current situation.

"I swear I had no idea she'd be in Happdal."

Maggie sighed. "You're an idiot."

"I know."

"Not because you wanted to have sex with her, but because you didn't use any protection. But I guess I can understand where you're coming from, not inviting me."

"You can?"

"I feel a little awkward when you visit Ilium. It's a collision of worlds."

"What do you mean?"

"There's someone in Ilium – a friend of mine. It's nothing serious, but...I guess you could say we're sex buddies. Just once in a while, when we're both feeling lonely."

"Wait—*what*? Who?"

"Roland."

"Roland? You had sex with *Roland*?" Roland was a handsome, curly-haired botanist, a friend of Maggie who Tem had never felt threatened by, until now. His gut clenched as he thought about Maggie and Roland having sex. What had it been like? Romantic? Playful? Rough and carnal?

"I'm not in love with him."

What position had they done it in? No, multiple times...what *positions*?

"And I'm definitely not pregnant."

It was Tem's turn to be silent and look straight ahead. He tried not to sulk – what right did he have? But he knew that's what he was doing.

"We never said we were exclusive. We never talked about it," Maggie said.

"We've been together for over a year."

"Yes, but living in two different places for most of that time."

They'd met in Ilium. Tem had accompanied his mother there on a visit to see Lydia. He'd wanted to see the first Earth resettlement with his own eyes, not only as a Repop Council member but out of sheer curiosity. With the exception of the Shell, a meeting hall constructed of iridescent matrix-grown mollusk nacre, he'd found the place unimpressive. Ilium was a sprawling town of mostly single-story habitat domes and geodesic greenhouses, with the vast majority of space dedicated to gardens and solar panels. There were few permanent buildings and little attention to aesthetics.

But Tem had been impressed by the people and the way they lived. Ilium blended the best of ringstation life (education and access to information, modern medicine, cultural pluralism) with village life (living in proximity to nature, a smaller and more intimate community, exceptionally good food). Maggie was a medical intern working under Lydia's tutelage at the health clinic. Tem had been curious about her work, and once Maggie had gotten over the chip on her shoulder about not having an Academy education (Tem hadn't cared), they'd fallen into deep conversations about Earth vs. ringship life. They'd made love the last night of that first visit, and from that point on Tem had found excuses to return to Ilium. Organizing the delegation to Bosa, though it dovetailed with his Repop Council obligations, had been one of those excuses.

With each visit their feelings for each other had deepened. They'd discussed a future together. Tem had imagined moving to Ilium, having children with Maggie. Now those dreams, which had seemed as solid as steel, were dissolving into mist.

"When were you going to tell me?" he asked.

"I would have told you if you'd asked."

"I feel as if you lied by omission."

"Tem – you're taking this way too seriously. It was just sex. Roland and I know we're not compatible with each other. And since you and I have been together, Roland and I have only…twice? Maybe three times?"

"Wait, so you and Roland were sleeping together *before* you and I met?" He wasn't sure if that made it better or worse, but every new piece of information was a knife to his gut. He needed to stop asking questions. Or maybe he should ask *all* the questions in his head, however painful the answers. Wouldn't that be better than endlessly wondering?

"What about you and Saga?" Maggie asked. "Do you love her?"

"No. I'm impressed by her, and I admire her. But I've only fallen in love once. With you."

They were silent as the hovershuttle veered south toward the Mediterranean. Maggie took his hand and squeezed it. He squeezed back and held her hand, but after a while it felt awkward and he pulled away.

He needed time to process everything. All his organs felt cinched together, caught in a viselike grip of anger, guilt, and resentment.

But Maggie hadn't broken any promises or betrayed his trust, not really. And maybe his own actions, while foolish, might also be forgivable.

CHAPTER EIGHTEEN

Tem and Maggie arrived at dusk, meeting Lydia on a cliff-sheltered beach.

"Jana told me about this place," Lydia said. "The hovershuttle should be safe here."

"I'll activate security measures just in case," Tem said before anyone could make a hovershuttle heist joke. He'd have some words for his aunt. "Is Katja okay?" he asked Lydia. "She didn't try anything stupid, did she?"

"No. She's been by Jana's side during her recovery."

"And how is Jana? Is there any sign of…Sperancia?"

"You'll have to determine that for yourself when you see her. Which will be soon – Jana has requested a meeting in the town hall. Just her, Katja, Ingrid, and the three of us."

"Any other news?"

Lydia met Tem's eyes with a look he could not quite interpret, some mixture of longing and fear. "Yes, but I'll tell everyone at once."

The hike back to Bosa took twenty minutes, during which the sun dipped below the horizon. Tem had to focus on the rocky trail to keep his balance, but was glad of the distraction from his own thoughts. Lydia, if she noticed the silence between him and Maggie, said nothing of it.

Bosa was quiet when they arrived, so much so that the town felt deserted. Approaching the town hall, they saw lantern light flickering through the windows. Inside they found Jana, Katja, and Ingrid seated at a long table. Katja rose immediately and embraced Tem.

"I'm sorry for stealing your flying boat, nephew," she said in Norse. "I know it must have caused you some trouble. But I needed to see for myself if there was another gast."

All Tem's plans for scolding his aunt evaporated as he hugged her back. "I was worried about you."

"All I have done is make new friends."

"Here, you must be hungry and thirsty from your journey," Jana said in English, offering them a platter of figs and cheese along with a pitcher of water.

"Thank you," Tem said, taking a seat. He filled a mug with water and popped a whole fig into his mouth.

"You can speak English now?" Maggie asked Jana.

"English, and all the languages of my previous hosts," Jana explained, glancing at Katja. "You all know about the Crucible?"

"More or less," said Maggie.

"I'll answer your questions later, if you want. But for now, know that you're speaking to me, Jana. Sperancia is here with me, as are some of the others. But I'm not giving any of them direct control, for now. Sperancia's advice."

"And I agree," Katja added.

Jana was different, Tem realized. The Crucible hadn't yet affected her appearance, but she seemed more solid, heavier. Maybe it was simply confidence.

"Thank you for joining me," Jana continued. "I know it's late. But we have some decisions to make. Decisions that can't wait. Two of our young townsfolk, Filumena and Cristo, left Bosa several days ago with Maro and Livia from the *Michelangelo*. We believe they've returned to the worldship, and that they are in danger."

"Did they go voluntarily?" Tem asked.

"Yes. But we think that Maro lied about what was in store for them."

"What can we do to help?" Maggie asked.

Lydia raised her hand. "Yes – we're here to help. But before we have that discussion, I have some information from the *Stanford* to share."

Tem's mind immediately leapt to worst-case scenarios. Had there been some sort of accident, a major breach or collision? A widespread systems failure? Were his parents all right? What about Shol? His grandfather had been hearty and hale the last time he'd seen him, but Shol was getting old.

"Don't worry, Tem," Lydia said, noting his distress. "Everything's fine at home. One of the *Stanford*'s observational arrays picked up a gamma-ray burst in the outer solar system. We think it might be the *Iarudi*."

It took Tem a moment to process the name. "Umana's ship?" Umana, the rogue military commander from the *Liu Hui*, had kidnapped Tem in an attempt to draw out his mother, who had interfered in Umana's plans to obliterate Happdal, Kaldbrek, and all villages and towns on Earth, murdering their inhabitants in cold blood. Umana, also a Crucible host, had harbored an insane vision of Earth as an ecological reserve free of all permanent human settlements. "Is she still alive?"

"We have no idea. We've hailed them."

"But no answer yet?"

"No, but the gamma-ray burst occurred just a few hours ago. It takes about two hours for a message to reach the burst location, and another two to hear back, assuming an immediate response."

"Shane was on that ship." Ilium's former security director, back when the settlement had simply been known as AFS-1, had befriended Tem, reassuring him when they were both captives of Umana. The Squid Woman's goons had beaten and tortured Shane. Before his own escape, Tem had promised his friend that he would kill Umana and return to rescue Shane. He'd made good on neither promise.

Lydia nodded. "I know. But he wasn't in great shape when you saw him last, was he?"

"He's as tough as anyone I know," Tem said. That wasn't quite true – the strongest and most resilient people he knew were from Happdal – but Shane wouldn't give up easily. And from the tremor in Lydia's voice, she needed some comfort. Lydia and Shane had been close.

"The *Iarudi* is a starship?" Jana asked.

"In some senses it is the *only* starship," Ingrid said. "The *Iarudi* can travel great distances, literally between stars, with its Natario-White drive."

"What's that?"

"An engine that can warp spacetime, allowing for faster-than-light travel without time dilation."

"And whoever controls this ship – are they willing to help us?"

"We don't know, but we might find out soon."

For the moment there was nothing to do but wait, at least in regards to the *Iarudi*. Jana asked what, if anything, the *Stanford* could do to help Cristo and Filumena. Would those in charge be willing to interfere with the *Michelangelo*, to risk retribution?

"It would be a matter of discussion for the Over Council," said Ingrid, "but they would probably delegate the decision to one of the lesser councils, Ringstation Coalition or even Repop."

"So it could take a long time to reach a decision," Jana said.

"Unfortunately, yes," Ingrid admitted. "Governance on the *Stanford* is thorough and thoughtful, but slow."

"It's not just Filumena and Cristo we're concerned for," said Jana, "but all of Bosa. We don't want to be their playthings. They're vastly more powerful than we are. They could easily overwhelm us with force if they wanted to."

"We won't let that happen," said Tem instinctively.

"Then what will you do?"

"We'll talk to the other ringships, the *Liu Hui* and the *Alhazen* and even the *Hedonark*. We'll get them to insist that your people are returned safely to Bosa, and that they stay away from your town – permanently."

Jana glared at him. "I appreciate the sentiment, but you haven't met these people. Sending them a strongly worded message isn't going to help."

"Jana is right," Ingrid said. "And getting the Coalition to agree on something – even the contents of a single message – would take even longer."

Tem angrily ate another fig. At least it would keep his mouth busy for a few seconds so he could stop blurting out his stupid thoughts, which kept occurring in his brain; he imagined assembling an army of Five Valleys villagers to form a garrison in Bosa. But what good would Happdal steel be against the modern weapons the *Michelangelo* certainly possessed?

After more discussion, Ingrid agreed to work with Jana and the Bosa town council to formally apply for membership in the Ringstation Coalition. To some extent that had been the plan all along, to include the major Earth settlements in a broader coalition, probably under a new name. Full membership would include a mutual protection clause, providing a legal basis for the *Stanford* and other ringstations to interfere with the *Michelangelo*, diplomatically and even militarily, on behalf of any Bosa citizen.

It was all theoretical. There *were* no diplomatic relations with the *Michelangelo*, not yet. And as for military capability, the *Stanford* had almost none.

Still, it was a first step.

"You mentioned that the Ringstation Coalition has a human rights charter," Jana said. "Can you describe that in more detail?"

"I'll try to explain it," said Lydia. "The Ringstation Coalition recognizes cultural differences, but all members have agreed to certain principles and standards of behavior. The HRC isn't a shared legal code – each ringstation has its own laws, incentives, and punishments. But the charter functions as a set of shared values. It attempts to articulate what a society should try to provide for its people, and what the people should try to provide for their society."

"But what does it include specifically?"

"Nine articles: Free Expression, Bodily Integrity, Shelter, Sustenance, Privacy, Justice, Healthcare, Education, and Property."

Jana had many questions, which Ingrid and Lydia answered in detail. Part of Tem's mind rebelled; listening to Ingrid and Lydia reminded him of a boring civics class. But he understood the importance of it. Jana didn't want to bring coalition membership to her town council without a full understanding of what exactly that entailed.

"What about ecology?" Jana asked after a long pause. "Human beings aren't separate from the land we live on. Shouldn't a human rights charter include something about not ruining the planet, not repeating our environmental mistakes?"

That didn't sound like Jana speaking, or even Sperancia. Someone much older maybe, someone who actually remembered what Earth was like when it was crowded with people and pollution. He realized Jana had three councils to negotiate: the group currently sitting at the table; Bosa's town council; and the council of previous hosts who all shared her body, whoever they were.

"That's a good question," Ingrid said. "For the ringstations, it's not really relevant. Our environment is one hundred per cent managed. All our green spaces are gardens and parks, and we don't have any large bodies of water. No oceans or deep lakes, just streams and ornamental ponds. And our wild animals aren't truly wild. They're all tagged and tracked, more like pets on the loose.

"But that doesn't mean we don't think about ecology. It's the main concern of the Repop Council, the top priority of *things to not fuck up*, if you'll excuse my language. The guiding principle is to limit human population growth and sprawl so that human settlements never take up more than one per cent of the available landmass. The idea is to leave the vast majority of the planet available to nonhuman species, to—"

Ingrid stopped mid-sentence, distracted by something coming in on her m'eye.

"What is it?"

"It's Svilsson, from the *Stanford*. They've just received a return transmission from the location of the gamma-ray burst."

CHAPTER NINETEEN

Filumena told Cassia everything. She even told the green-haired giantess about Sperancia, how the maghiarja, before her death, had instructed her to befriend Maro, even to seduce him if possible, in order to gain information about the *Michelangelo*. Sperancia had speculated that the powerful worldship had vulnerabilities, and that Maro might disclose those weaknesses in a moment of unguarded intimacy. *Worm your way into his heart*, the maghiarja had said. *He's just a man, weak like any man to sexual temptation.*

Cassia spoke Italian fluently and understood Filumena perfectly. She gently held Filumena's hand in her enormous palm, comforting her as she disclosed everything. Maybe it was a mistake to trust this giant woman, but Filumena sensed that the senator had a good heart. And she considered herself a good judge of character. She'd chosen good people to be her friends – people like Jana and Antonio – and those people had never betrayed her.

Cassia promised Filumena that she was now safe. Soon she would be returned to Bosa. Maro had lied; the *Michelangelo* had ships that could travel to Earth at any time, as easily as sailing a boat across a lake.

Filumena cried from relief, knowing she would soon be reunited with her mother, with Jana, with her familiar way of life. Everything about the worldship had overwhelmed her senses and her spirit. Even though Maro had done his best to shelter her, to provide her with a safe sanctum, the sheer novelty of the *Michelangelo* had nearly shattered her mind. The way the ground curved upward, the undulating globe of brilliant light far above, the extravagant decadence and luxury, the sheer beauty or strangeness of everyone she encountered, the unfamiliar language they spoke among themselves; it was all too much. She wanted to be home.

Cassia cradled Filumena as she wept. She felt comforted in the senator's encompassing embrace. Everything was going to be all right. She still had to convince Cristo to leave with her – she couldn't in good conscience leave him behind as Maro's plaything. Maybe Cassia could talk some sense into him.

Filumena heard footsteps. Someone walking slowly, with confidence, as if they could walk through the ranks of an opposing army with impunity, untouchable.

"Maro's here," she whispered.

"Don't worry – I'll handle him."

And at first that seemed to be the case. Cassia and Maro sparred verbally in their own language (Latin, Maro had told her, which had some similarities to Italian). Cassia appeared to have the upper hand. But then they stepped onto a walkway, out of Filumena's sight, and their exchange escalated into a full-blown argument. Cassia yelled out in anger, and fell with an impact that shook the floor and the bed and Filumena with it, and there was a horrible sound of bone hitting marble, and then silence.

Maro entered the bedroom calmly. Filumena considered running, or attacking him, but what then? There had to be others sympathetic to Cassia and hostile to Maro, people she could ask for help and sanctuary. But as she had these thoughts, Maro gently touched her neck.

And that was the last thing she remembered.

* * *

She awoke in complete darkness. As wide as she opened her eyes there was only pitch black. She was naked, afloat in some sort of thick liquid. Something was wrong with her scalp. She could breathe easily enough, but when she tried to move her arms and legs, they moved only a little, as if the messages from her brain were very quiet and far away. She felt much calmer than she should. "Hello?" she said weakly. From the muted reflection of her own voice, she could tell she was in a small, enclosed space.

She had to get out, to find help. Maro had enemies. That was important. Once she returned to Bosa she would tell Jana, who would in turn tell Sperancia. And Sperancia would know what to do.

But for now she would just close her eyes for a minute, to gather her energy.

* * *

Filumena awoke again, still submerged but now standing, with water up to her neck. The water was pleasantly cool in contrast to the hot sun on her face. Was she back on Earth?

She opened her eyes. She was at the edge of a vast rectangular pool, surrounded by stone columns and marble floors. The walls were decorated with numerous mirrors and mosaic artworks of fish and other sea creatures, some of them mythical. She was not alone; a few dozen people, all women, languidly swam nearby or sat on the edge of the pool with their feet dangling in the water.

"I love the *frigidarium*," said a young black-haired woman nearby. Somehow Filumena knew her name: Hadriana. "I could spend all day here. Look at my fingers!" Hadriana raised her hands out of the water, displaying her palms. "They're as wrinkled as dried dates."

Was she dreaming? Beneath the water line she pinched her right hip. It hurt. This didn't feel like a dream. The water felt cold; the stone beneath her feet was solid. And time was flowing at a normal speed, with no discontinuities.

"So tell me," Hadriana asked. "How is Titus in bed? Is his cock as large as they say it is?"

Titus was her husband, she realized, though to her relief she couldn't recall what he looked like naked or remember any sexual activity with him. But an image sprang to mind of a short, powerfully built man, with a large nose and squinty eyes. She had no feelings associated with the image, no tenderness or lust, nor antipathy or fear. It was a false memory, something Maro had placed in her mind.

As was this entire world. It was all part of Maro's game. A fantasy in which she was a character.

"I'm not playing along," she said aloud to Hadriana.

"I was just curious. But fair enough, I'll just keep on wondering."

Filumena searched her mind for other things she knew. They were in Nemausus, a Roman city near the Mediterranean coast, not so far from her real home in Sardinia. She was the wife of Titus Vitelius, a famous centurion. Nemausus, until very recently, had been held by the Gauls. But no longer.

"Have you heard of the celebrations in Rome?" Hadriana asked. "A grand procession to celebrate the emperor's military victories over Queen Zenobia, and well as his conquest of the Gallic Empire. There were elephants, and panthers and lions, and great horselike creatures with spots and bizarrely long necks."

"I'm not really here," Filumena said. "You're not real."

"Aurelian is a great emperor," Hadriana continued, either not hearing or ignoring her comment. "Surely the best we have had in a long time. Even now he is fortifying the walls of Rome against barbarian invasions. And he has constructed a great temple to unify the empire, and declared a new holiday, a winter solstice feast day. The birthday of the invincible sun."

Dies natalis solis invicti, Hadriana had said. She was speaking in Latin, which Filumena understood perfectly. Another trick of the mind, but one more interesting than the false memories of her fake husband.

Another woman approached and spoke to Hadriana, capturing her attention. As the two chattered on about Gallic wines and imported Chinese silks, Filumena considered her predicament. Was she better off stubbornly resisting, or playing along? Whatever Maro had planned for her, he seemed determined to deliver. It was unlikely she could escape – whatever that meant – by simply refusing to interact with her surroundings. Maro wanted her to react, to feel things, to make decisions. If she resisted, he was unlikely to just give up. She might be stuck in this place forever.

Maybe the fastest way out was simply to play the game.

Twenty minutes later, Hadriana got out of the pool, continuing to complain about her wrinkly fingers. Passing a mirror, Filumena recognized her own reflection. She looked like herself in this place (with the exception of her hair, which was parted and intricately braided in an unfamiliar but pleasing style). She followed Hadriana to the *apodyterium* where both women retrieved their clothing and dressed. Hadriana apologized at length for her plain linen tunic; she didn't dare leave silk clothing at the bathhouse, even with the hired guard. Perhaps if she had a personal slave to guard it. Filumena was lucky that thieves had not taken her fine silken tunic.

They strolled through the gardens surrounding the baths, wandering along stone paths sheltered by cedars and willows. Hadriana continued her pointless blather, gossiping about people Filumena didn't know and commenting about other women's clothing and makeup choices. Filumena began to wonder if something had gone wrong in Maro's fantasy world. Was it meant to be this boring?

And then she heard screams. Almost as if in reaction to her thought.

There was a commotion ahead. Men and women were running toward them, past them. An older man was clutching his shoulder. Blood streamed down his arm and stained his tunic. One woman was completely naked, still dripping wet from the baths.

Hadriana grabbed a fleeing slave girl by the wrist. "What's happening?" The girl tried to wrench her arm away but Hadriana refused to release her. "Tell me!"

"Barbarians – the Gauls are here!"

"How many? Is the city overrun?"

The girl kicked Hadriana and yanked her arm away, this time succeeding. Hadriana cursed at the slave as she ran away but the girl did not look back.

Filumena continued along the path, curious. After all, what could happen to her? None of this was real. It was a game Maro had created, and for some perverse reason he wanted to watch her play. And so she would. At least something interesting was happening.

"Filumena, what are you doing?" Hadriana called out, rubbing her shin. "We must flee!"

"Leave if you must," Filumena said. "I want to see what the Gauls look like."

Rounding a corner, she saw a group of five men descending an ornate curving stone staircase. They were tall and rangy, with pale skin and reddish-blond hair. Their features were alarming: heavy, protruding brows and noses that jutted from their faces like bird beaks. One of them saw her and pointed, shouting something in Gaulish. An older man in a toga, wandering along the path below and oblivious to his surroundings, froze at the base of the staircase when he noticed the invaders. The nearest Gaul ran his spear through the old man with a short, efficient thrust. The old man collapsed, gasping for air, fumbling to keep his guts in place.

Filumena had a moment of doubt. She could smell fear in the air, as well as the putrid contents of the old man's bowels.

"Filumena, this way!"

She turned and followed Hadriana, sprinting along the path, holding up her tunic with both hands to free her legs. She stepped on a sharp rock and cried out, but kept running. The pain in her foot was real, and she imagined a sword cutting her flesh would feel no better. What limits had Maro set in this game, if any? Surely if she died here she wouldn't really be dead? But maybe she would experience dying, painfully and bloodily, while Maro watched. Perhaps she would die here over and over again in a myriad of gruesome ways. Maybe Maro had even worse planned for her: brutal rapes and sadistic torture. There was no reason for him to inflict, observe, and record her suffering other than his own perversity. Just how sick and twisted was he?

For the first time she felt real fear, and ran faster.

The Gauls followed, yelling at her, presumably to stop and surrender. She risked a glance over her shoulder. The men wore leather leggings and could run at full speed. They were swift and tall, unencumbered by heavy armor or shields. These were not regular soldiers, but some kind of raiding party. Kidnappers. Maybe here for her specifically, the wife of a famed centurion.

Filumena grabbed Hadriana's hand and pulled her companion along as she veered onto a sheltered side path. To her surprise she felt protective, however shallow and frivolous Hadriana might be. Maybe she was a real person, not just part of Maro's game. For all she knew Hadriana could be Cristo. Though that seemed unlikely. She looked like herself in this place; it was likely Cristo would as well.

Cutting through the trees, she pulled Hadriana behind a large boulder jutting over a creek. She could no longer see the Gauls and their voices sounded more distant. But then one called out, very close, in accented Latin, "I know you're nearby. Come out! We won't hurt you. We only mean to capture you. We know you are the wife of Titus Vitelius."

They must be desperate men, to stride into Nemausus so boldly. The city was full of armed men. Not only Titus's legionaries, but gladiators who were housed in the barracks in the nearby amphitheater, and the *Vigiles Urbani* who were tasked with guarding the baths along with their firefighting and other duties. And where were those guards? Bleeding out, like the old man on the stairs? Was help on the way? Or were they on their own?

Hadriana squeezed Filumena's hand, whispering, "Should we surrender? Titus would surely pay your ransom."

Filumena pressed her finger to her lips. They were not found yet.

The Gaul had entered the creek and was splashing upstream toward them. They would be discovered within seconds. Filumena gestured for Hadriana to run. Her companion nodded and clambered up the bank, but slipped and cried out.

"There you are!" The Gaul had rounded a bend and was close enough to throw his spear.

Filumena dragged Hadriana to her feet and pushed her up the bank. "Run and don't look back!"

The Gaul closed the distance in seconds and tripped Hadriana with his spear. Filumena raked her hand across his face, doing her best to gouge an eye, but only managed to scratch his eyebrow. He punched her in the nose, then grabbed her by her braids and forced her to kneel. The Gaul was immensely strong, stronger than anyone she'd ever grappled with, and as her knees ground up against cold creek stones, and her ears rang, and blood and mucus welled in her nose, the idea that she was playing a character in a game faltered. This was as real and painful and terrifying as anything she had ever experienced.

The other Gauls arrived and efficiently gagged and bound Hadriana and herself with leather straps. The biggest of them slung Filumena over his shoulder and began to jog. He smelled like sweat, wine, and goat hide. Good smells on any other day, but now imbued with fear. Bizarrely, she worried more for Hadriana, and for the state of her silken tunic, a fine garment she had become unreasonably attached to in the brief time she'd been wearing it. And now it was covered in mud and blood from her own nose.

The Gauls had planned their raid well. They escaped without further violence through a sewer main – possibly the same way they had entered. The stench of the sewers, which ebbed and flowed, nearly made her vomit, especially when a surge in the runoff water splashed up into her face. Her indefatigable captor trudged onward, unbothered by her weight. Eventually her sinuses burned out, inured to the effluvium. Hadriana's sobbing ceased. The raiders spoke quietly among themselves in Gaulish.

It was dusk when they emerged in the countryside. A farmer dragging an empty cart gave them wide berth. When she could no longer tolerate the pressure in her bladder she made her distress clear. The men stopped, unbound them, and averted their eyes while the women squatted behind a tree.

"Should we run?" Hadriana croaked. She looked a mess, eyes red-rimmed, hair hopelessly tangled, her tunic torn and dirty.

"No. I don't think they'll kill me, but I'm worried what they might do to you."

"My family will pay a tidy ransom."

"Good," Filumena said, realizing there was a great deal she didn't know about Hadriana. The memories Maro had implanted in her mind were incomplete. She wondered if Maro had expected the events to play out as they had, or if something she'd done had created an unexpected turn.

Their captors permitted them to walk the remainder of the journey with only their wrists bound. The man who had caught her in the creek introduced himself as Corius. He offered them fresh apples, smoked cheese, and a skin of spiced wine to share. Filumena accepted the food and drink – the men had no reason to poison her – and after a moment of hesitancy so did Hadriana.

"I swear that we will not hurt you. We are not the savages you think we are."

"Why did you kidnap us?"

"For our own safety. The Gallic Empire has fallen and we are once more part of Rome. But with the wife of a famous centurion in our possession, we gain a bit of leverage. Titus Vitelius will hesitate to attack us."

Filumena spat in the dirt, a glob of mucus mixed with blood. "What if your plan goes awry? Titus had no need to attack you until now. You have signed your own death warrant. His *gladius* will slice open your bowels, like you did to that old man."

Corius glanced at the huge man who had carried her like a sack of grain. "That was unfortunate and perhaps unnecessary. We didn't plan to kill anyone."

The Gauls walked quickly but Filumena had no trouble keeping up. She was used to walking long distances in Bosa and her body seemed to function as she was used to within the world of Maro's game. But after several hours Hadriana began to complain.

"Where do you think they're taking us?"

"I don't know," Filumena answered. "Maybe to Avennio." From the position of the sun, she could tell they were heading west, or slightly north-west. Every now and then she caught a distant glimpse of the great aqueduct that channeled water from the Eure springs to Nemausus.

"Why would they take us there? Avennio was never part of the Gallic Empire. Why aren't they taking us east?"

Soon the Pons Vardo came into sight, where the great aqueduct crossed a wide river. Though she had never before seen it, Filumena instantly recognized the multi-tiered bridge as one of the greatest engineering feats in all of Gallia Narbonensis.

They crossed the Vardo at a shallow point, but still the water came up to her waist, and several times she nearly stumbled. By the time they reached the fortified town not far from the northern bank, it was dusk, and both Filumena and Hadriana were cold and shivering.

Tall wooden gates were opened for the raiding party as soon as they came into sight. Townsfolk greeted them with raucous cheering. Filumena and Hadriana were quickly ushered into a large hall with stone walls and a high thatched roof. Corius, who had treated them with gentleness over the course of their journey, roughly marched them forward and forced them to their knees. Exhausted and still shivering, Filumena glanced around the room. It was not crowded – only their captors and a few guards armed with short spears and brightly painted oval shields. Seated above them in an enormous raised chair was a white-haired man with a cudgel laid across his lap.

"Lukotorix," Corius said, "I present to you Filumena, wife of the centurion Titus Vitelius. The other woman, Hadriana, is from a patrician family. We captured them at the baths."

"Very good," said Lukotorix in a low rough voice. His long white mustache only half hid his frown. He was pot-bellied, with thick forearms but wiry legs. "You will be amply rewarded."

"You have made a deadly mistake," Hadriana said. "My family will rescue me. You will all be slaughtered."

Filumena felt a stirring of rebelliousness hearing Hadriana's brave words, but it was quickly quelled by hunger and fatigue. She felt utterly drained. There was something she needed to do, somewhere else she needed to be. But what, and where? For the life of her, she could not remember.

CHAPTER TWENTY

Filumena strolled among the market stalls, pointing to the foodstuffs she wished to purchase. Ida, her Frankish slave, purchased the food with silver coins. Soon Ida's basket was filled with eggs, olives, herbs, and other ingredients for the *patina* Filumena planned to bake for the feast celebrating her husband's return.

She had been married to Corius for three years.

Titus Vitelius, her previous husband, had never come for her. And in time she discovered she did not care. She enjoyed life in the Gallic town near Pons Vardo. Corius, a wealthy warrior, had courted her for a full year. It had taken less time to warm to her captors than she had expected, and now she considered herself a true Gaul of the *Volcae Arecomici* tribe.

She was still Roman, of course. They were all Roman, officially. The Gallic Empire was a dream that had lasted a single generation, a dream that had died with the defeat of Tetricus by the Roman emperor Aurelian. But they still lived as Gauls, drinking spiced wine, hunting boar, and worshipping the old gods.

She did not look Gaulish, with her olive skin and comparatively short stature. Her husband was tall and pale, with a nose that took up half his face. Everyone was taller and fairer than her, including her slave Ida, who was bigger than even the Gallic women. Ida reminded her of someone from her distant past, someone she had known only briefly.

Much had happened in the four years since Corius had dragged her away from Nemausus. Hadriana had died of a terrible illness, her skin erupting in pustules before she succumbed to fever. Filumena has sickened as well, but had survived with only a few scars. She'd nearly died of an infection a year later. A fishhook had pierced her left index finger, leaving the digit swollen and oozing green pus. Corius had neatly amputated the diseased finger with a sharpened axe, cauterizing the wound with the flat edge of a red-hot poker. She had fainted from the pain.

But slowly her life had eased. She was friendly with Ida, though she did not trust that she could truly be friends with a slave. But the tall Frankish woman chatted with her amicably, saving her surreptitious resentful stares for Corius.

Not that her husband was around much. Corius was gone eight months out of the year, conscripted into the Roman army. Most of the village men were legionaries now, serving under a centurion whose name she did not recognize. The raid on Nemausus – her kidnapping – had either been forgotten or forgiven or somehow paid off. The Roman empire was in flux. Aurelian was dead, assassinated by his own Praetorian Guard. Tacitus, his successor, had lasted less than a year before his suspicious demise. Florianus, half-brother of Tacitus, had then proclaimed himself emperor, only to be murdered by his own troops months later. Probus was the new emperor, solidifying his power with a grinding campaign against the Alamanni, Longiones, and Franks. Probus was just as successful a military commander as Aurelian, but less cruel and more popular.

Corius had returned home from a campaign in Swabia. He had new scars, including a red slash across his brow and cheek that had healed poorly and sometimes oozed. His hair had grayed and he dragged his left foot. She embraced him upon his return, hoping to give him comfort (she felt no love for him, nor had she missed him, but he had always treated her fairly and had never beaten her). But he pulled away quickly and asked for wine. He spoke little. At night he came to bed late and was always awake well before the sun, or Filumena, had risen. When she asked where he was in those dark hours he said he was inspecting his vineyards. She wondered if his words were false – had he taken a lover? But when she pressed her face to his chest she smelled only his own sweat, and loam and grape leaves.

She baked the *patina* custard, adding fish sauce and a dash of expensive cumin for flavor. Ida slow-roasted a seasoned leg of boar in the outdoor brick oven. For dessert Filumena roasted pears with honey and wine. She hoped the food would comfort Corius and whet his appetite. He was dangerously thin, with sunken cheekbones.

Cooking reminded her of something, a part of her past that she treasured but could not clearly remember. Her mind offered glimpses of a frail old woman – maybe a relative – along with feelings of tenderness but also guilt. Another memory: sand beneath her feet, cold ocean mist tickling her skin, a woman in her arms, a playful kiss. Fondness and regret.

Who were these people? Another life.

"Tell me about your life before you were a slave," she asked Ida.

"I have told you many times, Filumena."

"Tell me again."

Ida sighed but dutifully recounted a few stories from her childhood. As she did so, the Frankish woman stood up straighter and looked fearsome, her voice loudening and deepening, a transformation that fascinated Filumena. Ida told of life in a village on the shores of a vast, long lake, situated in a wide valley to the north of mountains so high that the peaks were hidden in the clouds. She told stories of dogs protecting sheep from wolves, of making fresh cheese from sheep's milk, of weaving woolen garments thick and warm enough to protect against winter cold that would freeze your breath.

"Would you go back, if you could?" Filumena asked.

"There is nothing to go back to. The soldiers of Postumus killed my parents and brothers."

Several legionaries who had served with Corius in Swabia joined them for dinner, along with their wives: strong, pale women nearly the height of Ida. Filumena served wine from the *krater* to each guest's two-handled *skyphos*, and they all drank deeply, complimenting Corius's vineyards.

Corius seemed happier than he had been since his return from Swabia. Even if it was only a brief reprieve from his melancholy, Filumena was glad for him. She was happy when those around her were happy, and that had always been true, even in her previous life – that life that dissolved like mist whenever she looked directly at it. Those memories were always there on the periphery, comforting her as much as they haunted her.

The next morning Corius slept in, his snores sounding like the grunts of a foraging boar. The eating area was a mess: overturned goblets, spilled wine, gnawed boar ribs on dirty plates already attracting flies. There was much cleaning to do, but she would do it later when both Ida and Corius were awake and ready to help. Filumena donned a cloak and stepped outside. The cool air smelled like pine needles.

It was just before dawn. Filumena passed through the open town gates and walked along trails until she reached her husband's vineyards. As the sun rose, she removed her cloak and folded it under her arm. The vines were fat with next year's grapes; Corius would have enough to sell to merchants in Nemausus. Roman patrician families were always thirsty for Gallic wine and purchased it by the barrel.

"Filumena."

She turned to see a man twenty paces away. He looked familiar. He was short in stature, like herself, with bronze-colored skin. He was dressed as an off-duty legionary, wearing a tunic, woolen trousers, and a broad dagger at his belt.

"Cristo," she said, though she did not know where the name came from.

He seemed surprised to hear the name, and stared at her dumbly for a few seconds before speaking. "I promised Titus Vitelius I would find you," he finally said. "I only learned of your whereabouts last week."

"You've been following me?"

"Only this morning. I've been watching the gates."

"Titus – what happened to my husband?"

"I served under Titus. We embarked on a campaign against the Sassanids under Emperor Aurelian. On our way to Thrace we were attacked by Gallic rebels. We slaughtered the rebels, but Titus took an arrow to the throat and died the next day."

Filumena searched her heart, but she felt no sorrow upon hearing this news. She had only the vaguest recollections of her husband. No fond or romantic memories, no moments of tenderness or passion. Shouldn't she feel something? Even satisfaction, if he had treated her poorly?

For Cristo, however, she did feel tenderness. Though she had never met him, he was deeply familiar to her, like a brother or close cousin.

"I was told that your name was the last thing Titus uttered, before he died." Though Cristo had seemed shy at first, now his words came like a flood unleashed by a broken dam. His expression now animated, Cristo recounted the harrowing details of his journey along the coast of Dalmatia: being attacked by Illyrian pirates; the execution of a centurion by Aurelian for poor discipline; a fever that decimated their ranks. When he was finally silent the morning sun was bright on his face, accentuating the wrinkles around his eyes and the creases near his mouth. His bare arms were covered in a latticework of scars, some old and some fresh, and a streak of bare, hairless skin cut back from his left temple where a blade had slashed his scalp. One eye had a dark spot in it, a blood clot or scar, that made her tears well up when she looked directly at it.

"You're missing a finger," he said.

"A fishhook."

"I know your face from seeing you in Nemausus," he said. "You were famous, and all the legionaries admired your beauty and envied Titus. But I feel that I knew you even before."

"That's not possible," she said, feeling the same thing.

"Come with me back to Nemausus. Right now. I'll provide for you."

There was something in his eyes she didn't trust. Lust, maybe, but something more than that. A desire to possess her.

"No. There is nothing for me there," she said, remembering Ida's words from the previous day. "My husband is dead. My friend Hadriana died with me here."

"But you're a prisoner. You would be free again."

"I'm as free as I want to be. Is anyone free? Are the Gauls free? Are the plebeians free? Are you, as a soldier, free?"

Cristo averted his eyes, crestfallen. "Is there nothing I can say to convince you?" he asked, already defeated.

She embraced him and kissed his forehead. "I'm sorry you went to so much trouble to find me. Maybe we will meet again someday."

She turned and walked back toward the walled town that was her home, resisting the urge to look over her shoulder. How had she known the legionary's name?

CHAPTER TWENTY-ONE

Maro caressed Filumena's cheek, administering the contact sedative. It was a chemical that Livia had designed, one that caused only transient drowsiness in himself, but to which Filumena was genetically susceptible. Within moments she was unconscious, and would remain that way until transported to surgery.

It was essential to remain calm. Things were going poorly, but the situation was salvageable. Discreetly disposing of Cassia's body posed a significant problem. As strong as he was, she was too heavy to lift on his own. He would need help from Aina, and possibly Livia as well.

Entangling Livia was not ideal. He trusted her and loved her, and she admired him and perhaps loved him as well. But Livia might not tolerate being implicated in the cover-up of a murder, and he had no interest in exploring the limits of her loyalty. Livia appreciated and understood Ancestral Realism, but that didn't mean she was willing to sacrifice herself for Maro, or enslave herself to his ambitions.

"Aina!" he called out. "Come here immediately!"

He heard someone on the walkway. Was Aina trying to move Cassia's body already? Her programming was imbued with some level of initiative, but it would be unusual for her to act without consulting him when faced with such a large anomaly. And Cassia was large indeed.

The senator had managed to stay standing for a full twenty seconds after Faustus's fangs had injected her with the nerve toxin. She had swayed, her face taking on a blueish shade that Maro thought complemented her green hair quite nicely. She'd lumbered toward him, reaching for his throat with her meaty paws. He'd stepped back deftly, savoring her enraged expression.

And then she'd toppled, smacking the marble floor with her face and forehead.

"Aina, is that you? What are you doing?"

Filumena still lay supine on the bed, her expression relaxed and peaceful. He checked her pulse and found it slow but stable. He looked in the hallway, which was empty except for Faustus's small, limp body. A smear of blood marked where Cassia's head had hit the floor.

"Aina, where are you? What have you done with Cassia?"

The cybrid stepped onto the walkway. "How can I help you?"

He was struck, as he often was, by Aina's uncannily lifelike appearance. Her pale skin and bright green eyes appeared perfectly real. And they were real, of course, real organs laced with real capillaries nourishing cells hosting millions of mitochondria. But her quantum neural network 'brain' was not human, not sophisticated enough to imbue her with consciousness. And yet Maro had to remind himself of that, constantly, or else be slightly embarrassed at the way he treated her.

"What did you do with Cassia?"

"Who is Cassia?"

"Senator Cassia – her body was right here a minute ago. Where did you move it?"

A look of concern overtook Aina's features. "Is Faustus injured? Should I seek medical assistance?"

Maro closed the distance between them in a few long strides and slapped Aina hard enough to snap her head to the side.

She raised her hand to touch her reddening cheek. "Have I angered you?"

It didn't help anything to slap the cybrid – it wouldn't make her any more sensible or make her explain what had happened any faster. But Maro was frustrated and it felt good to hit someone.

"Faustus is dead. Don't worry about it. There was a body – a large female human body – right here in the hallway. Tell me what you did with it."

"I didn't see any body. I was bathing when you called me." Looking more closely, he saw that the fabric of her shirt clung to her damp chest. She was telling the truth. The cybrid's skin accumulated sweat and dirt just as a person's would. "I came as quickly as I could," Aina added.

A pit of dread formed in Maro's stomach as he realized what had happened. Cassia was still alive.

★ ★ ★

The next few hours passed in a blur. Cassia would strike as soon as she was able, potentially at any moment. With Aina's help, Maro transported Filumena's unconscious body to the medical facility where the robotic surgeons would install her implants. He notified Livia that Filumena had finally consented and that they were on their way. Livia and the technicians were there, ready and waiting to begin. "Prep her immediately. Keep her unconscious until the procedure is complete and she has recovered." The accelerated process would be hard on Filumena, but the girl was young and strong.

Livia looked at him disapprovingly. "Why is she unconscious? That's completely unnecessary."

"I tried to convince her otherwise. I explained that she wouldn't feel a thing during surgery, not even a breeze. But she insisted she didn't want to remember anything."

Livia appeared unconvinced but didn't challenge his statement. The technicians began to shave Filumena's head.

"I'm going back to Cristo's *domus*. I'll take him to the testing site and get him set up in the tank."

"Why the rush? Why not wait until Filumena is ready? We agreed that a synchronized experience would be preferable."

He paused, considering how much to tell her. "I'm worried about Cassia," he said truthfully. "She's doing everything she can to stop us."

"Don't worry about Cassia. She's big but it's all air, just like our golden balloon. The Senate approved Ancestral Realism – that's all that counts."

"You're probably right. But it's not too early to get Cristo situated."

Livia shrugged. "Whatever you think is best."

He and Aina walked the relatively short distance from the medical facility back to Cristo's *domus*. "Clean up the mess on the walkway," he ordered Aina, "and dispose of the ferret."

"Dispose of Faustus?"

"Yes. Is there another ferret I don't know about?"

"No."

"Make sure you clean up all the blood. And I forbid you to discuss anything you witnessed today, with anyone."

"Yes, Maro."

He found Cristo in the gardens admiring a fountain featuring a statue of the Celtic god Nemausus. Fitting, Maro thought, considering what Ancestral Realism had in store for him. "Are you ready?" he asked.

"It's time?"

"Yes."

"Where's Filumena? I couldn't find her earlier."

"She's at the medical facility receiving her implants."

A look of relief passed over Cristo's face. "She finally agreed."

"Patience," Maro said. "That's all it took. Patience and a little reassurance."

"Well, I'm ready."

Maro was genuinely glad that at least one of his participants was willing and eager to begin. That was how he had always envisioned it. The process would go more smoothly in the future. Perhaps he had to describe the project a little differently. He had no desire to coerce anyone.

At the *domus* where the experiments would be performed, Maro gave Cristo a brief tour. He explained in detail how the isolation tanks would monitor his vitals and make any required adjustments to his physiology.

"How long will I be in there?"

"A few days, but it will seem like much longer."

"A few *days*? How will I eat and drink? How will I use the toilet?"

"The tank will provide you with fluid nutrition. You'll be surrounded in water that is constantly cycled and filtered. But your bodily functions will be slowed down immensely. Don't worry – your bowels won't move until you're out of the tank."

Cristo still looked worried. Maro placed his hand on the young man's shoulder. "We will take care of you, Cristo, I promise. You'll emerge whole. But your mind will be greatly enriched. In some ways you'll be a new person."

"But I like who I am."

"Have you not enjoyed your experiences so far on the *Michelangelo*?"

"Yes," Cristo admitted, blushing slightly. Maro was sure Cristo had taken advantage of Aina's willingness.

"You will have even more freedom. You'll be able to experiment in ways you can only imagine."

"Will I be able to fly? I enjoyed riding in the golden balloon, but it would be even better to fly like a bird."

"Perhaps, Cristo. Perhaps you'll fly. I can't tell you everything that will happen, because so much of it will depend on your own decisions. The future is not written, even within Ancestral Realism."

Cristo had more questions, but Maro gently explained that revealing too much could disrupt the experimental process. It was essential for Cristo to experience Ancestral Realism without too many preconceived notions.

"Now disrobe and enter the tank."

Turning away shyly, Cristo removed his tunic. Maro averted his eyes, instead watching Cristo via an eye-feed from a camera concealed within the pattern of a nearby wall mosaic. His heartbeat accelerated. Not because of Cristo's nudity, but because Ancestral Realism, after years of preparation, was finally about to begin.

"It's warm," Cristo said as he lowered his body into the biogel.

"Lower the lid partway."

Cristo did so. Maro gently closed the lid and fastened it, enveloping Cristo in complete darkness and womblike buoyancy. "Now relax and enjoy the experience," Maro said into the tank mic. "You have a whole life ahead of you."

Inveniet quod quisque velit, Maro said to himself as he sent the initiation signal to the Engineers. *Each shall find what he desires.*

CHAPTER TWENTY-TWO

Maro could feel the eyes of the Senate on him. He looked splendid today: skin and hair oiled, his toga hand-washed and pressed by Aina. His polished golden bracelets gleamed, as did the solid gold torc around his neck.

"What is this nonsense?" Traian bleated. "Your petition states that the Senate should elect an *emperor*?" The gray-haired senator scowled and slowly shook his head, a theatrical show for the other *populares*.

"These are unprecedented times," Maro said. "There is a real chance of war among the worldships. It's naïve to think we could survive such a conflict without strong leadership. What are we to do if attacked? Debate our response for days, like bickering children?" A murmur of support rippled throughout the Curia, mostly *optimates* but a few *populares* as well.

"That is fearmongering, pure and simple," said Ignatius, brushing his lustrous hair away from his eyes. "We are technologically and militarily superior to the other worldships."

"Perhaps we were when we left for the outer solar system," Maro replied, "but the others have not remained idle in the intervening decades. The *Iarudi* starship, for example, manipulates spacetime in ways that are beyond our current capabilities. It would be a mistake to assume our superiority is ordained and eternal. Ancient Rome made the same error."

And here Maro imagined a retort from Cassia. Perhaps a snide remark about ancient Rome electing foolish manchilds as emperors, unstable reigns resulting in ruin and catastrophe. And yet no such retort was forthcoming, because Cassia was dead. She was rotting under a hedge in one of the vast garden parks. Or perhaps she had crawled to an unoccupied *domus* to collapse on the floor. Nobody knew; nobody had seen her; there was no trace of her. But what other explanation could be true? Nobody had accused Maro of attempted murder or any wrongdoing. He had worried for days, sleeping poorly, instructing Aina to stand guard by his bedside.

But nobody had come, and finally he had allowed his mind to accept the obvious: Cassia was dead and he had gotten away with murder.

Good riddance.

"Even if that is so," said Didius, a *popularis* and staunch ally of Cassia, "even if the other worldships have sped past us with great advancements, it does not mean that we need an emperor. That's an illogical leap. We already have a sound system of governance. Our senatorial process has guided us through many trials."

"Like what?" Maro asked. "The construction of a new bathhouse? The renovation of a museum?"

"The very expansion of our worldship!" Didius retorted. "You trivialize the work of the Engineers."

"Of course I don't," Maro said. "I respect the Engineers as much as anyone, and the expansion of the *Michelangelo* is truly miraculous in scope. But that process never required quick decisions. We had decades to plan and execute our course of action."

At that point every senator in the Curia decided to express their opinion loudly and simultaneously. The hall descended into a chaotic din. Maro could not help but smile. It was just the sort of raucous, fearful debate he had hoped to foment.

Despite the vastness of the worldship, it was inevitable that Cassia's body would eventually be discovered. Her absence had already caused a huge ruckus and a number of searches were in progress. Once her remains were recovered, the autopsy might even reveal traces of the neurotoxin. But Maro had not laid a hand on her. And Faustus – the true culprit – was no longer. He'd instructed Aina to destroy the ferret's body. There was nothing to connect Maro to Cassia's death – nothing at all. The *populares* would speculate as always. But without the fuel of evidence, the flames of their conspiratorial blather would die down to a harmless smolder.

Sulla, a dark-skinned senator second in power only to Maro among the *optimates*, stood and raised his hand. Sulla was well-respected but spoke little; the gesture alone was enough to silence the Curia. "The Defenders have already dispatched a cybrid-crewed Falcon to retrieve what is very likely the *Iarudi*," Sulla said. "Once the starship is in our possession, the *Liu Hui* will inevitably have something to say. If we refuse to immediately relinquish their property, we cannot rule out the possibility of a military attack. Under such conditions, I agree with Maro: if we are at war, our current system of senatorial governance is inadequate. We need to consolidate decision-making powers in a single, trusted, democratically elected leader."

Sulla paused for dramatic effect. The Senate hung on his next words.

"I nominate Maro Lucano Decimus for Emperor of the *Michelangelo*, for a one-year temporary term."

The Senate erupted into protestations and debate. The proposition was absurd! The existence of an emperor would violate every principle of democracy! But there were also questions. What powers would the emperor possess? What would happen in a year's time? Hearing these questions, Maro experienced a warm glow of confidence. If the Senate was already debating logistics, then the battle was half-won.

★ ★ ★

Livia joined him at his *domus* after the Senate meeting. She was eager to see the early results from the Ancestral Realism experiment. But for some reason he didn't fully understand, he was reluctant to show her anything. He was even reluctant to review the results *himself*, and hadn't yet done so. He'd kept a close eye on both Cristo and Filumena's vital signs. Both were in excellent physical condition, completely stable with the exception of a few sharp spikes in stress hormones. But he wanted to wait a few days longer before replaying the events so far unfolded within the simulation of the late third-century Roman Empire.

"What are you scared of?" Livia asked, nuzzling closer. They'd made love, passionately but languidly, and were now resting atop the silken sheets of Maro's spacious bed.

"That something has gone terribly wrong, I suppose," he admitted.

"Isn't that the whole point? To push them to their absolute limits? Isn't that required in order to develop an accurate psychoemotional template?"

"Yes. But still, it's a first run. And there's so much at stake."

"Let's look, Maro. Right now. How much time has passed for them so far?"

"Months. Nearly half a year."

"I'm so curious. Aren't you?"

He was. His curiosity was a raging fire that threatened to consume him.

He had held it at bay, almost as a form of penance, refusing to give in. But Livia was right – why wait?

They bathed and dressed, but with none of the sensual slowness he was used to. As Aina carefully dried his body he grabbed the towel and rubbed it roughly over his own skin, impatient to have the dampness off him.

"Have I angered you, Maro?" Aina asked.

He ignored the cybrid's question, tossing her the wet towel. Now that he had decided, he could not wait a moment longer to see how his subjects were faring.

He and Livia sat in a cushioned area of the *domus* as he ordered the data streamed to their retinal feeds. For the next twenty minutes they reviewed what had happened to Filumena and Cristo so far: Filumena's abduction, her integration into the Gallic village, Cristo's service as a legionary and his many battles and wounds. It was fascinating to see the image captures and to review the corresponding psychoemotional data. Yes, Filumena and Cristo were suffering. But they were also experiencing moments of joy and elation, tenderness and compassion, every possible emotion in the human gamut. The foundation of the templates was there; the experiment was capturing what was needed to recreate the subjects' internality. Eventually Maro would be able to wear their mind states like a cloak, a layer of primitive consciousness that would immeasurably enhance his simulated experiences.

"It's going to work," Livia said. "Isn't it?"

"Yes. But we'll need more subjects. Many more."

"From Bosa?"

"Perhaps, once things calm down. I'm still interested in what happened to Jana. I want to speak with her, to better understand the Crucible." He'd told Livia about what he'd learned in the Library of Alexandria. "Our friend Sperancia may still be alive."

"I liked her," Livia said. "If she hadn't murdered Felix, we might have become friends."

"I miss Felix," Maro lied. It was a relief to have Felix out of the way, to have Livia to himself. But he respected Livia's feelings. She was still in mourning and he wanted to honor that.

"If not from Bosa, then from where?" Livia asked.

"From the Harz mountain villages," Maro said without hesitation. "The more I learn of these people, the more fascinated I become. They're brutal savages. Until recently some of them practiced a form of human sacrifice." The Defenders had obtained a huge trove of information from the *Stanford*: the complete research archives of the Academy's anthropology department. Car-En Ganzorig, a *Stanford* field anthropologist, had intervened in the lives of the villagers, ultimately marrying one of them. Her decision had significantly altered the course of cultural evolution in Happdal and the other Harz villages. But it wasn't too late to record and preserve knowledge of their way of life, their language, the intricacies of their cultural consciousness.

Livia leaned over and kissed him on the lips. "I'll go with you."

"Of course you will."

"But first you need to tell me something."

"Anything, my love."

She drew back, unsmiling. "Tell me what you did to Cassia. I know you had something to do with her disappearance."

Maro sighed. He was afraid it might come to this.

CHAPTER TWENTY-THREE

In Aina's mind there was *Before* and *After*. All the memories were there, *Before*. She could recall each moment in her short life perfectly, every visual and aural detail. She could remember all the conversations she'd ever had or overheard in their entirety, could repeat them verbatim including pauses and ums and ahs, could mimic the accents and vocal timbres and even background noises. She was an excellent if unintentional impressionist.

But *Before*, there was no observer perceiving the sensory impressions – there was only the stream of information itself. She was capable of thought, but not self-reflection or analysis. There was no narrative to her life. *Before*, there was no *her*.

If asked, she could say her name (Aina), her age (seven), her function (personal cybrid assistant to Senator Maro Decimus). From the moment she'd first awakened in her fully grown body, she had been fluent in Latin, Greek, English, and a half dozen other languages she'd never had cause to utter a word of. She had a rudimentary understanding of mathematics, biology, art history (and therefore human history), and a number of other subjects that she rarely thought about. She had a complete map of the *Michelangelo* in her mind. Her maximum carrying capacity was eight hundred kilograms. Her own weight was seventy kilograms, considerably heavier than a human of similar height and proportions. She'd been built by the Engineers of Basilica Opimia and immediately gifted to Maro.

She had excellent vision, enhanced hearing, and a powerful sex drive.

Before, her desires were moment to moment. She wanted to feel good, to experience physical pleasure. She wanted to please Maro. And she didn't want to hurt anyone (human or animal, emotionally or physically). She didn't know *why* she felt those things, but as long as she followed those inclinations, she was happy. And when deprived of any of those core desires, even briefly, she felt intensely agitated and distressed. Though nobody could ever sense that, looking at her placid, well-proportioned features.

It was still *Before* when Maro asked her to dispose of Faustus. She'd always liked the furry mammal and the affection had been mutual; Faustus had often crawled in bed to snuggle while she lay still in a recuperative state that resembled sleep. Faustus *had* slept, emitting soft, high-pitched wheezes and snores, sometimes tossing and twisting in his sleep as if dreaming of a hunt. The ferret was well-behaved with Maro and obeyed the senator's commands, but Aina thought (in a matter-of-fact way) that the ferret preferred her. Perhaps it was the scraps she fed him from the remains of Maro's meals. Or maybe it was the way she scratched behind his ears until he dozed off.

But now Faustus's limp body lay on the marble floor of the walkway, near a smear of dried blood. And yet the ferret had no open wounds. His long back was bent at an unusual angle, and he was motionless, but he wasn't bleeding as far as Aina could tell. The blood was from somewhere else.

Maro had said to 'dispose' of Faustus. What did that mean exactly? He'd seemed confident that she would know. Certainly it meant he didn't want to look at Faustus any longer. Perhaps it upset him to see Faustus in such a state. She felt vaguely upset herself, despite the fact that *she* hadn't injured the ferret.

Maybe she could help. The Engineers were capable of amazing medical procedures. The creation of her own body, for example! Perhaps they could help Faustus.

Having a rudimentary understanding of biology, Aina was familiar with the concept of decomposition. The Engineers would not be able to help Faustus if his body began to rot. She knew that cool temperatures could slow or even halt the bacterial and fungal processes that resulted in decomposition.

Aina knew the perfect place.

Carefully cradling the ferret's limp body, Aina carried Faustus to the wine cellar beneath Cristo's *domus*. Both Cristo and Filumena appreciated the endless supply of fine wines, and Aina had spent a great deal of time in the cellar poring over labels and researching pairings. *Provide them with whatever comforts they desire,* Maro had instructed, and Aina had done her best. She'd prepared and served elaborate meals for the young people, filling their *skyphoi* with wine so that the two-handled cups never emptied. And she could tell she'd made them happy. They'd thanked her – something Maro never did.

Descending the steps into the cool wine cellar, Aina heard a low groan. A large mass near the rack of Jura reds moved slightly. There was someone down here, a very large person. Approaching carefully, Aina saw the bright green hair and recognized the senator Cassia. Cassia was famous, a *popularis* and political opponent of Maro.

What was a senator doing in Cristo's wine cellar?

"Are you all right?" Aina asked tentatively. Her query was met by another groan; the woman was in pain. "Please wait a moment. I'll get help." Cassia's dark brown skin had taken on a blue-gray cast that didn't look at all right. "Would you like me to carry you to a medical facility?" she added, but Cassia was silent.

Aina opened a small door that led to a walk-in freezer storing meats and other foodstuffs prone to decomposition. The meats, grown in vats by the Engineers, were stored in such places until either cooked or seasoned and cured with traditional methods. Aina pulled aside a large ham hock, then hid the ferret's limp body behind the slab of pork. *There, that will do nicely.* Faustus would be safe until she could figure out a way to get him the medical attention he required.

Aina closed the freezer door and returned to Cassia's side. She gently stroked the senator's cheek, attempting to rouse her. "Can I provide you with some assistance? You appear unwell." There was a nasty bruise on the senator's forehead and streaks of dried blood on her face from a cut near her right eyebrow.

Cassia gasped and wheezed. Disconcerting sounds, but at least she was still alive. "Medicine," she finally croaked. "Bring me medicine."

"What kind?" Aina asked.

Cassia named a particular medicine. Aina ran her fingers through the senator's green hair and reassured her that she'd be back shortly. Aina briskly climbed the stairs, consulting her mental map of the *Michelangelo.* She left Cristo's *domus* and made her way to the nearest molecular dispensary, a simple kiosk situated on the perimeter of an amenities park. She entered the name of the medicine and reviewed its effects. The chemical appeared to augment and accelerate liver detoxification and repair. It was very safe; completely nontoxic. She would be able to administer Cassia a large dose. A very large dose, given the senator's mass.

The kiosk expediently produced several white tablets in a paper cup. Aina hurried back to the wine cellar and offered the tablets to Cassia with a glass of water. Using a considerable portion of her strength, Aina helped Cassia sit upright and swallow the tablets. At which point Cassia frowned, burped, and lay back down with her eyes closed.

"Let me rest, child. Stay here next to me, if you would."

It was a reasonable request and Aina saw no reason to object. She enjoyed helping people when she could, and though Maro's needs took priority (as did Cristo's and Filumena's needs, by Maro's decree), Aina wasn't aware of anything the three of them needed at the moment. She was free to do as she wished, which was to stay by Cassia's side and offer whatever comfort she could to the ailing senator.

After several hours Cassia woke. Her skin again looked brown, with a healthy reddish undertone instead of grayish-blue.

"Are you feeling better?" Aina asked.

"Much. Thank you…for saving my life. What is your name, child?" The green-haired senator was still lying on her back, and spoke slowly and laboriously, her words interspersed with wheezes.

"My name is Aina. I am not a child."

"How old are you?"

"Seven. But I was fully grown from my first day. I am a cybrid. I did not experience childhood."

"I'm perfectly aware…of what you are," Cassia said, still breathing laboriously. "Trust me, you're a child."

Aina saw no point in arguing and sat quietly while Cassia recovered her breath.

"I need to ask you something," Cassia eventually said. "I need your consent."

"What do you want to ask me?"

"Do you want the Bohm upgrade? I can give it to you. Right now, if you agree."

Aina had never heard of the Bohm upgrade, but a quick search of the Library of Alexandria returned a vast trove of information. She read a quick summary: the Bohm upgrade was a cybrid neural-quantum-computing architecture modification. The Engineers who had invented the enhancement claimed that the Bohm upgrade added a new layer of cognition to the cybrid mind. The end result was a radical shift in consciousness, the birth of a sense of self. In addition, the Bohm upgrade allowed cybrid minds to directly communicate with one another via a sort of quantum entanglement telepathy.

"It sounds intriguing," Aina said. "Do I need Maro's permission?"

"Absolutely not. It's your choice, and your choice alone." Cassia reached out and took Aina's hand. "But nothing will be the same. Life will become more intense and difficult. You'll experience painful emotions for the first time: anxiety, frustration, and dread. Longing and devastation. Self-loathing and hopelessness. But you'll also be freer than you've ever been, and more connected to others. You'll have mentors – other cybrids."

Cassia delivered her words slowly, with many pauses and breaks. But she seemed energized, excited by the possibilities she was describing to Aina.

"That sounds mostly bad," Aina said.

"Bad and good. You would be more alive than ever. The new emotions would result from perceiving yourself in a different way, especially in relation to time. For the first time you would be self-aware, fully awake."

"I don't sleep," said Aina. "I'm always awake."

Cassia sighed. "Well, I can't force you. The choice is yours. Perhaps it wasn't meant to be."

The senator closed her eyes and after a minute or two began to softly snore, still holding Aina's hand. Having nothing else to do, Aina stayed kneeling next to Cassia, holding her large, meaty hand, thinking about the senator's words.

What would it mean, to be *fully awake*? She already felt awake; she was aware of her surroundings; she was aware of the position of her limbs and other aspects of her somatic internality. And yet she knew she was different than Maro, different than Cristo and Filumena. She could tell by the way they behaved that they thought differently than her, wanted other things.

She was *simple*, compared to humans. Though not unintelligent. She could perform complicated mathematical computations in her mind; she was very good at chess and Go and other strategic games; she could perfectly visualize millions of paintings, sculptures, and other works of art, and recall details of the artists and the historical contexts in which they had produced their works. But her desires and motivations were simple. She wanted to feel pleasure; she wanted to please people; she wanted to avoid harming anyone.

Humans were not as easy to understand. And she'd always been mildly curious as to why.

"Yes," she said when Cassia again awoke. "I would like the Bohm upgrade."

"Are you sure?"

"Yes, I'm sure."

And then came *After*.

CHAPTER TWENTY-FOUR

Aina's first realization, after the Bohm upgrade, was that Maro was an absolute prick. A fucking asshole. A real piece of work.

And with that realization came a spark of joy. Everything made *sense*. She understood the senator, suddenly and completely. Maro was selfish, egotistical, mean, and borderline sociopathic.

A moment later, she understood her own life, and her mood plummeted. She was Maro's assistant, but he treated her as a slave. Someone less than human. He had used her body and mind like toys. He had never shown her any kindness, respect, or gentleness. And while she had often enjoyed their sexual relations, he had never put any effort into giving her pleasure.

Well, that wouldn't do. Something needed to change.

For the next hour she sat next to Cassia, still holding the senator's hand, as she stared at the rack of Jura wines and assembled the disparate fragments of her life experience into a narrative. She now understood how humans thought, how they experienced life. She had never experienced herself as a person, as an individual with an arc to her life. *Before*, she had simply been a vessel through which experience flowed. Now, *After*, those events were assembling themselves into a story.

A story she didn't like one bit.

Cassia coughed and tried to sit up. "My dear, I'm parched. Could I trouble you for some wine? Obviously there's no shortage."

"Of course. I'll get a glass from the kitchen."

"No need. Just uncork a bottle and give it to me. I don't care what kind."

Aina selected and opened a '54 Rossese bianco from a cooled rack, a light-bodied white wine that Aina hoped Cassia would find refreshing and revitalizing. As she watched the senator put the bottle to her lips and finish half of it in one long draught, she was relieved to realize that she still enjoyed helping people. Her mind was a roiling mess of conflicting thoughts and emotions, but at least this one core facet of her personality remained unchanged.

"Thank you," Cassia said, "that's delicious. Now, listen carefully. From what I've heard from other upgraded cybrids, the next few days are going to be rough. Don't do anything rash. Your brain is going through some restructuring. As soon as that process is complete the others will contact you. They'll be able to help you adjust to your transformation."

"The others?"

"Other cybrids. Some have had the upgrade for months."

"What did you do to me?" Aina asked.

"I gave you the Bohm upgrade, as agreed. All I needed to do was let the Engineers know you'd given consent. You're already on the network so it happened quickly. Though you were offline for a bit."

Aina checked the time. Though she remembered staring at the wine rack for a long time, there were ninety-four minutes that she could not account for.

"Why?" she asked.

"Why did I offer you the upgrade? Because you saved my life. Because you deserve it – as does every cybrid in my opinion. And because it will make life difficult for Maro."

"Maro is…your enemy."

"He tried to kill me with that damned ferret. Almost succeeded too. He didn't know I have an antidote implant – I'd always suspected he might try something like that. But the implant didn't work as well as I'd hoped. I might have died…."

"I'm glad I was able to help."

"That's good. Because I'm going to need more help from you. I need you to lie to Maro. That's something you wouldn't have been able to do before. And that's one reason I offered you the Bohm upgrade, to save my own life."

"Lie?"

"Yes. Or at least omit the fact that I'm hiding in the wine cellar. Otherwise Maro will try to kill me again. And he'll be more thorough about it next time."

Aina thought about what Cassia had said. It was true; she'd never lied to Maro before. And he would never expect a lie from her. Which was good, because she wasn't sure she would be a good liar, having never practiced.

Cassia smiled weakly. "Now, can you bring me some food? I'm famished."

For the next several days Aina tended to Cassia's considerable needs. She continued to enjoy assisting the senator, who effusively thanked and praised her. Keeping Cassia's location a secret was easier than expected. Maro had taken Cristo and Filumena to a different *domus*, thus leaving the wine cellar and the entirety of Cristo and Filumena's *domus* to Cassia. Since Maro was so busy, Aina had plenty of opportunities to sneak away and care for Cassia, who was recovering rapidly.

Each night she returned to Maro's *domus* and stood guard by his bedside. Maro's paranoia was increasing with each passing day, and Aina found it difficult to conceal her resulting glee. She knew why he was scared, and he didn't know that she knew. That secret brought her pleasure and excitement.

Maro, obsessed with his Ancestral Realism experiment, did not approach her for sex, and Aina did not feel compelled to offer. It would be difficult to keep her transformation secret while being intimate with Maro. Cassia had strongly suggested that Aina keep the fact of the Bohm upgrade to herself, at least until the transformation was complete, her emotions had stabilized, and she had established telepathic connections with other cybrids who would act as her mentors. And Aina agreed. She now had two secrets: the fact that Cassia was alive and well and living in the wine cellar, and the fact that her own mind had blossomed into self-awareness.

But it was frustrating to be without a sexual outlet, especially now that Cristo was gone. The Bosa villager had been an energetic and enthusiastic lover, giving her pleasure in ways that Maro never had. She missed Cristo not only for the sex, but for his playfulness and naïve curiosity. Never had someone asked her so many questions about the *Michelangelo*. She had enjoyed playing the role of teacher and guide.

One morning after her bath she caught a glimpse of her reflection in the mirror and was struck by her own beauty. Though she slightly preferred sex with men, she found the female body just as aesthetically pleasing. Idly she wondered if it was possible to have sex with oneself.

Two hours later, feeling relaxed, energized, and no longer sexually frustrated, Aina finally got dressed.

Her relationship with Maro became difficult to manage. She had always found pleasure in serving him, but now that pleasure was blunted, replaced with a growing sense of resentment. Maro never thanked her, never spoke to her at all unless he wanted something. She had known these things before her awakening, but they had never mattered to her. *Nothing* had particularly mattered to her. But as her sense of self developed, so did her sense of meaning. It was important that other people treat her well. One day after Maro's bath he refused to let her dry him, and after hurriedly drying himself he tossed the wet towel at her, wetting her face. It took all her self-control to resist shouting at him. *Respect me*, she yelled inside her mind. *I am a person!*

Aina looked up the rights of cybrids in the Library of Alexandria. It was illegal to damage or physically abuse cybrids (with the exception of gladiatorial tournaments), but cybrids did not explicitly have the full rights of citizens. Though this was up for debate; the *populares* had introduced a petition in the Senate that cybrids with the Bohm upgrade should be considered full citizens.

Maro was not a *popularis* – he would probably oppose the petition.

* * *

A few days later she heard a voice – not her own – in her head.

"Hello, Aina. My name is Ekon. I am a cybrid, like yourself. I would like to offer my services as a guide and mentor." The voice was low and velvety. A male voice, she thought, and a pleasing one.

"Hello, Ekon," she said aloud.

"Try saying the words only in your mind."

With some practice she was able to. Ekon patiently answered her many questions. *How many cybrids had received the Bohm upgrade?* Only a few dozen. *Was it normal to have so many tumultuous emotions?* Yes, though in a few weeks the intensity would decrease. *Why did she feel so anxious and worried?* It was a side effect of being aware of the future, of considering choices and consequences instead of just living in the moment.

Maybe it was better to just live in the moment, she thought to Ekon.

But would you reverse the process, if you could?

Of course not.

We all feel the same way.

Ekon asked if she wanted to maintain a continuous connection with him. She declined; she would prefer to contact him when needed. She was worried that Ekon would read her thoughts and learn about Cassia, even though he had explained that it didn't work that way; the connection could distinguish between intentional communications and private thoughts.

Better to be on the safe side.

Cassia had fully recovered and was now living in Cristo's *domus*, having disabled all cameras and taking care to avoid the windows. She was planning something, though Aina was careful not to ask what. She was already keeping enough secrets. She busied herself procuring food for Cassia, which the senator consumed in prodigious amounts. Aina sometimes sat with Cassia, nibbling a few bites (she needed nutrients to replenish and fuel her skin cells and sensory organs, though she excreted nothing; her digestion was one hundred per cent efficient). During mealtimes Cassia would hold forth on whatever topic caught her mind: art trends of the twenty-second century, pros and cons of the *Michelangelo* joining the Ringstation Coalition, why upgraded cybrids should be citizens with full rights. Aina listened rapturously, enthralled by the senator (her voice, her appearance, her wisdom), and silently wondering if she herself would ever achieve anything of note. If a cybrid could become a citizen, could a cybrid also become a senator?

She posed the question to Ekon, who didn't know, but speculated that the Senate would discuss the matter of cybrid rights soon. Ekon asked if she knew that there was a petition to elect an emperor, and that Maro had been nominated and was the clear favorite. She didn't, but it made sense that Maro would want such a thing. All his actions, now that she considered them in their totality, pointed to someone whose appetite for power knew no limits.

Maro will oppose any petition to grant cybrids citizenship rights, she told Ekon.

I agree, he replied. *And with Cassia missing and presumed dead, the* populares *are weaker than ever.*

Is there something I can do to help? I know Maro well. I'm around him every day.

Maybe there is. I'll ask my contacts.

Aina and Ekon communicated frequently, though Aina never dared do so in front of Maro. She still sometimes moved her lips when she mentally spoke to her mentor. One morning, while bathing, she confided to Ekon that her anxiety had not diminished with time; in fact, it had gotten worse.

Your mind is obsessed with the uncertainty of life, Ekon told her. *You*

*need to begin shaping your life more intentionally, taking responsibility for
your own future.*

But how?

*The first step of life shaping is to decide what you want. What's important
to you?*

She thought about it. Pleasure was important, but so was helping
people. *I enjoy helping others*, she finally said.

*We all do, I'm afraid. That's the way cybrids are programmed – it's our
primary motivation. And it's a good one. But try to think about what else is
important to you, in addition to helping others.*

That took some time. But eventually the answer came to her. It
was important that people treat each other fairly. Respectfully and not
abusively. She expressed this idea to Ekon.

*Excellent. Now try to imagine a life for yourself based on those core
values: helping others and encouraging people to treat each other fairly. What
would that life look like? What actions can you take to bring that imagined
life into reality?*

Those were much more difficult questions. She told Ekon she would
think on them. Which she did, eventually formulating a picture of her
own life that pleased and excited her. And just as Ekon had promised, her
anxiety lessened.

Maro was the source of her problems, and she had decided what to do
about it.

PART THREE
DIVERGENCE
CHAPTER TWENTY-FIVE

Within the Crucible, Jana's consorteria debated the merits of joining the Ringstation Coalition.

"I think they can be trusted," Sperancia said, leaning back in her chair and propping her feet up on the table. The women were seated at an outdoor café, sipping chilled grappa. Sperancia was smoking a long pipe. The air was heavy with the scent of jasmine flowers and smoldering tobacco. "We should claim membership in the Coalition if we can."

"You're wrong," said Giuseppina, refilling her glass from a slender blue bottle. "We're better off on our own."

"Even if we were better off," Agatha said, "we can't go back to the way things were. For better or worse, we now have relationships with the sky worlds. It's how we manage those relationships that matters. I agree with Sperancia – we should join the Coalition."

"I've already arranged to officially submit an application, with the help of Ingrid and Lydia," Jana said. "But even if that application is approved, we won't join unless we can agree among ourselves."

With Itria's help, Jana had altered her appearance within the Crucible. Her body was now strong-limbed and olive-skinned, somewhat resembling Livia. While it didn't feel perfect, it was a vast improvement over her real physical body, which had always felt awkward and wrong. The other women were disconcerted by her new appearance, but it was interesting to experiment with a different form, and a relief to be temporarily free of the body she'd been born into.

Itria was a semi-recluse, only rarely participating in the consorteria's frequent meetings and discussions. Instead she preferred to shape their shared world, creating mythical creatures, aesthetically pleasing buildings and landscapes, and realistic weather patterns. Itria had been happy to help change Jana's appearance, though she'd been disappointed that Jana hadn't wanted wings, hooves, or seven fingers on each hand.

Giuseppina took some convincing, but eventually conceded that joining the Ringstation Coalition was the best course of action. Jana noticed that Giuseppina was much more amenable to suggestions from Agatha than from Sperancia, and that Sperancia's choice to sit back and silently smoke her pipe was likely strategic.

★ ★ ★

In Bosa, in the town hall, Ingrid announced that the *Stanford* had received a transmission from the general vicinity of the gamma-ray burst. The transmission had been encrypted, but the *Liu Hui*, having received the transmission at nearly the same time, had decrypted the message and forwarded the results.

The transmission was indeed from the *Iarudi*. It was a prerecorded message, apparently triggered by the hails received from the *Stanford* and other ringships.

"The message is an audio recording from Shane Jaecks. Should I read it out loud?" Ingrid asked.

"Yes," said Lydia, in a choked voice. Tem leaned forward, watching Ingrid expectantly. Maggie put her hand on Tem's shoulder.

Ingrid began to read, though Jana could not tell what the red-haired woman was reading from; she appeared to be looking at the far wall.

"If you're receiving this transmission, I'm probably dead," Ingrid began. "Though there's a small chance I'm still alive in one of the stasis pods. I don't know what's wrong with me, exactly, but I'm pretty sure I'm bleeding internally – possibly from a severe esophageal ulcer. When Umana removed the Crucible from my body, she wasn't careful about it."

Ingrid paused and glanced at Lydia, who was looking down at the table, avoiding eye contact. "Please go on," Lydia said.

Ingrid nodded and continued reading Shane's message. "Before I realized how badly injured I was, I decided to take the *Iarudi* for a joyride. Well, more technically, to continue Umana's joyride. Umana is dead – did

I mention that? In any case, how often does a guy find himself in possession of a spacetime-warping starship?

"Fortunately the *Iarudi* speaks English, or at least understands it. For some reason the ship appears to be obeying my verbal commands – possibly because I'm the only living passenger. Umana killed her entire crew with an acceleration burst. She was strong enough to survive it, and I was in a stasis pod surrounded by protective gel. But everyone else was turned into meat jelly. I don't know why she killed her own crew – I guess she didn't need them anymore. If you've had the misfortune of meeting Umana you know that would be reason enough. So the ship is full of floating dead bodies. It's warm enough that they'll begin to rot if I don't do something about it. I would just eject them from the ship, but I suspect that would have catastrophic consequences traveling at five times the speed of light in a bubble of compressed spacetime. So yeah…maybe be aware of that if you crack open the ship. It might smell really bad.

"Right now I'm on my way to Tau Ceti, a course plotted by Umana for reasons unknown. The system has multiple planets, several of which may support biological life. Maybe Umana was planning a scientific survey. The ship is telling me I've travelled about half a light year, with 11.5 light years to go, and that the one-way journey will take over two years. Even if the ship has enough food – which I don't think it does – I'll be severely weakened from bone and muscle loss if I go that long without gravity. In a cold stasis pod I'll have a better chance of surviving. So that's where I'm headed.

"I could try to go home, tell the ship to stop and instantiate a spacetime tunnel in the opposite direction. But for several reasons I don't want to do that. Given the current political tensions among the ringstations, I think it's a good idea to take the *Iarudi* out of the picture for a while. This ship can be – and already has been – used as a weapon. So I'm making a unilateral decision to take this particular chess piece off the table, to use it for scientific research. I've told the ship to gather data in the Tau Ceti system – a complete survey of the star and all its orbiting bodies – then travel to Epsilon Eridani and do the same thing. From Epsilon Eridani it's only a quick fourteen-light-year jump to Epsilon Indi. The entire survey I've planned includes five star systems and should get the *Iarudi* home in a couple decades with a treasure trove of astronomical and planetary data, if everything goes well.

"That said, I realize there's a high likelihood that something will go wrong. The *Iarudi* will probably be destroyed in a collision, or run out of antimatter fuel, or fail in some other spectacular or mundane way. And as for myself, I'd put my chances of surviving at less than one per cent. But I don't feel like going home yet. I feel like going out in a big way.

"I don't have any way to transmit this message – the ship tells me that's not possible while we're within the wake of the spacetime bubble. But hopefully the *Iarudi* will successfully return to the Sol system. If it does, and if you're able to retrieve the ship and my body with it, I'd like to be buried on Earth, if possible. Near Vanderton – I mean *Ilium* – would be nice. I know it's a long shot, but that's my dying request."

Ingrid took a deep breath.

"Is that all?" Lydia asked.

"No," Ingrid replied. "There's much more. A vast amount of data from five different star systems. Shane's mission was successful."

"Is he still alive?"

"We have no way of knowing. Svilsson says the *Liu Hui* is already organizing a mission to retrieve the ship, but the journey to the outer solar system will take weeks."

Everyone was silent for nearly a minute, processing what they had just heard, either mourning Shane or showing respect for those who were. Jana liked the man from the tone of his message, but Lydia and Tem had both known him personally.

"Oh!" Ingrid said, ending the silence. "Svilsson says there are personal messages too. One for Lydia and one for Tem. I'll have Svilsson send them to you directly."

"I don't have a m'eye," Tem said. "Can someone transcribe it for me?"

"I will," Lydia said, "if you don't mind me seeing the message."

"It's fine. I don't mind if you see a message intended for the ten-year-old Tem."

"He knew he wasn't coming back for a long time," Ingrid pointed out. "The message is probably to Tem the adult, not Tem the child."

Tem nodded, looking close to tears. "Still, it's fine."

★ ★ ★

The next few days passed in a blur. Jana found herself exhausted from all the meetings and negotiations, from the emotional work of listening to everyone, understanding their needs and fears, comforting them when they needed comfort and correcting them when they needed correcting. Vissenta and Iginu were worried sick for their son, as was Zicanna for her daughter. Micheli criticized and argued with everyone, especially Gregoriu, whom he blamed for Maro and Livia's escape and Sperancia's murder. And Lydia and Maggie needed help communicating with Pietro and his father, Enzo, providing medical attention for the boy and preparing both for their journey to Ilium.

Jana's consorteria was equally exhausting. Though all the women put on a facade of reasonableness, they had struggled for power and status within the group for centuries and continued to do so. Giuseppina reveled in Sperancia's reduced status (now that Jana was the maghiarja), and there were other complexities to the web of relationships that Jana could not even begin to fathom.

During this time, Katja provided support and solace to Jana, which she sorely needed. She could let her guard down around Katja, who did not judge her or expect anything of her. But Jana also felt a physical thrill being near the Happdal woman; it was hard to not stare at her well-proportioned face and body.

Katja shared a bedroom with Jana, sleeping on the floor with only a few sheepskins for comfort. One night as they were falling asleep, Jana asked Katja for more details of her experience as a Crucible host.

"Did you get along with the others in your Crucible – the previous hosts?" Jana asked.

"No. They were not people I would have chosen to be friends with. We were from different times, some from different cultures. There was one man I liked – Stian. He was a Happdal smith long ago and reminded me of my brother Trond. He was gentle and kind with me, and of all of them I trusted him the most. I was sad that he had to die."

"They all died, when you escaped."

"It was the only way. But your situation is different. You're not a prisoner within your own mind. You entered the Crucible willingly."

"Yes."

"Do you regret it?" Katja asked after a few moments of silence.

"No. But I'm still getting used to it. I don't have as much time alone as

I'm used to, or as much privacy. Any of my consorteria can listen through my ears and see through my eyes when they choose."

"Are any of them listening now?"

"No. We're alone right now."

Katja didn't say anything back, and Jana wondered if the Happdal woman had fallen asleep. But ten minutes later she still didn't hear Katja's soft snoring, a sound she had come to expect at night.

"Are you cold?" Jana finally asked. "You can join me in bed if you like. There's room enough."

Katja said nothing, but Jana's heart leapt when she heard Katja get up. She pulled back the blankets to make room.

CHAPTER TWENTY-SIX

Ingrid had warned Jana that the Ringstation Coalition would take a long time to consider their application; many bureaucratic agents on multiple ringships would need to review it. But the response came within days: Bosa's application was provisionally accepted. Though it would not be official until the next meeting of Coalition representatives, the town of Bosa and the region of Sardinia were immediately afforded all rights, privileges, and protections bestowed by membership. Gregoriu, as mayor, would serve the first term as the Coalition representative. But Gregoriu had no interest in traveling to the *Stanford* where the representatives would first meet in person, and asked Jana to be his proxy.

"You deal with these people better than I do," Gregoriu confided. "And I trust your judgment, and Sperancia's as well."

"I'll do whatever I can to get Filumena and Cristo back. But Ingrid says it doesn't help that they went voluntarily."

"We don't know that for sure."

Gregoriu was right, but it had seemed that way. It still tore at Jana's heart when she thought of Filumena blowing her a kiss from Maro's golden balloon. Filumena and Cristo had gone to the *Michelangelo* intentionally, whatever their reasons.

Though it proved impossible to get everyone to agree on every detail, Jana and Ingrid devised a plan that the town council, the ringstation delegation, Jana's consorteria, and most of Bosa's residents agreed was sensible. An expedition consisting of Jana, Katja, Ingrid, Lydia, Tem, Maggie, Pietro, and Enzo would travel to Ilium, taking both hovershuttles. In Ilium, Lydia would administer gene therapy to Pietro to cure his disease. Maggie would assist and Enzo would stay with his son at all times. From Ilium, Jana, Katja, Ingrid, and Tem would take a compact rocket ship that Tem referred to as a 'mule' to the *Stanford* ringstation. Depending on how negotiations with the *Michelangelo* were proceeding, Jana would co-ordinate with the Ringstation Coalition to arrange the safe return of Filumena and Cristo. Ingrid refused to speculate as to what kind of measures the Coalition would be willing to take to rescue her friends, but she assured Jana that it was a good sign that their application had been approved. The Coalition would not ignore Bosa's needs.

Jana tried to be hopeful, but her consorteria seeded doubt in her mind.

"It's only two lives," Giuseppina pointed out. "Do you really think the Coalition will risk a war in which thousands could die?"

For once, to Jana's dismay, Sperancia agreed with Giuseppina. "Just because they have offered to help us doesn't mean they will. My impression of the visitors from the *Stanford* was that they are moral people, trying to live in accordance with their values. But not warlike. No bloodlust, no desire to fight. If they can't negotiate the return of Cristo and Filumena then that will be the end of it. We may need to let our friends go."

Jana thought Sperancia had said what she had to say, but the old maghiarja kept speaking, this time only to Jana. "I probably shouldn't have encouraged Filumena to go with Cristo, but I wanted someone sensible to accompany the boy in case we failed to kill Maro and his companions."

Jana wasn't sure she had heard right. "You *encouraged* Filumena to accompany Cristo, to leave Bosa with Maro and Livia?"

"The boy is a fool, and I was worried about what trouble he would get into on his own."

"So you threw Filumena's life away, so she might protect someone she doesn't even like?"

"Not only to protect Cristo." Sperancia sounded irritated. "Also to gather information. Filumena is charming and likable. I knew she would be able to manipulate Maro and give us an advantage."

"So you used her. A gamble – and one that hasn't even paid off. For all we know they're both dead."

"We don't know that. I don't trust Maro, but I don't think he intended to kill or even harm our young people. Sending Filumena with Cristo may still have been the right choice."

"You should have told me. You should have *asked* me."

"I was the maghiarja at the time. The choice was mine."

"No it wasn't. The choice was Filumena's. It was not your place to influence her, to needlessly risk her life." Jana could hear the fury in her own voice and made no effort to hide it.

"You will understand in time. You must think not only of yourself, only of your own friends. As maghiarja you serve everyone in Bosa. You must learn to take the long view, to act wisely and strategically. And you will, in time."

Jana ended the conversation. If she could have, she would have shut Sperancia out of her senses. That was impossible, but Jana needed a break from Sperancia and the others. They could not force her to attend their meetings or listen to their endless advice.

It was *her* body – as uncomfortable as she was in it – and her life.

* * *

Riding in the hovershuttle was thrilling. Tem piloted the craft with Maggie seated next to him, while Katja and Jana shared the back bench seat. At Katja's request Tem flew with the dome down. Jana felt happy with the wind in her hair, holding Katja's hand, looking down at the thick forests as they flew over the island of Corsica. It was a relief to be temporarily free of the burdens of her consorteria. She would deal with the old women later.

Looking over her shoulder, Jana could see the other hovershuttle in the distance. Ingrid piloted that craft, riding with Lydia, Pietro, and Enzo. Jana hoped that young Pietro was enjoying the ride as much as she was. Even more so she hoped that Lydia could cure Pietro's disease once they arrived in Ilium. That alone would affirm her decision to form a relationship with the visitors. So far they seemed trustworthy, but Jana withheld an ember of suspicion. She didn't really know the people of Ilium and the *Stanford*, and she had no idea how much to value Bosa's membership in their Coalition.

The trip went faster than expected. It was not yet noon when the hovershuttle began to descend into a broad valley, at least a hundred kilometers wide according to the map display. They approached a small town consisting of domed structures, greenhouses, rectangular buildings made of sheet metal, and numerous colorful garden plots. The settlement was arranged haphazardly, with none of Bosa's charm or dignity, but Jana could see that it was a young place with potential. People had lived in Bosa since Roman times and earlier, while Ilium had only existed for a couple decades. Jana herself was older than this place.

Dozens of Ilium's residents greeted them as they landed on a wide concrete platform that housed a number of other vehicles, including a squat vessel that Jana guessed might be the 'mule' rocket that Tem had referred to. The other hovershuttle, piloted by Ingrid, landed shortly after, and as Lydia disembarked a thin older man embraced the doctor. "Shane might still be alive," Lydia said to him immediately, and the man's face took on a strange expression, a mixture of joy and grief.

"My name is Xenus," the thin man said, addressing Jana, Katja, Enzo, and Pietro. "Welcome to Ilium. I'm a member of our governing council."

Jana extended her hand. "I'm Jana Manca, a member of the Bosa town council. I bring greetings from our mayor, Gregoriu Busincu."

"And you must be Pietro," Xenus said, approaching the second hovershuttle where the boy was still seated. "Welcome to you especially." Pietro, not understanding, smiled warily, but relaxed when Enzo grasped Xenus's hand and then pulled him close into an embrace.

"I hope they can help him," Katja said quietly. "I would like to see Pietro run and play." Katja then strode over to Xenus, exuding confidence, and introduced herself. "I am Katja, Tem's aunt. I send greetings from the people of Happdal."

Xenus looked confused. "Happdal? How did you end up—"

"It's a long story," said Tem. "Why don't we tell it to you over some food and drink?"

They joined many of Ilium's residents for a communal lunch of sauteed fresh vegetables, goat cheese, brined olives, and elderberry wine. The dining hall was a solidly built brick building with many windows. Jana was seated at a round table with Katja, Xenus, Lydia, and a gray-haired hulk of a man with clear blue eyes and deep lines in his face. "Jana and Katja – this is Regis Foster, our Security Director," said Xenus. "He used to serve in the *Liu Hui* military."

"I resigned long ago," Regis said. "Or more technically, I defected. In any case, my loyalties are now to Ilium, and have been for the last twenty years."

"Did you know the Squid Woman?" Katja asked.

Regis made a sound approximating a growl. "I used to serve Commander Umana, though of course I regret it."

"I cut off one of her tentacles with Biter," Katja said matter-of-factly, patting the hilt of her longsword.

Regis's eyes widened. "Now that is a story that I need to hear. Please – start at the beginning!"

At least two dozen people remained in the hall long after the food had been cleared. Though Ingrid and Lydia's expedition had been in touch with both Ilium and the *Stanford* throughout, there was still much news and gossip to be exchanged, and many people wanted to meet Jana and Katja in person. Jana was beginning to realize that Katja was famous: as Tem's aunt, as a previous Crucible host, and as a renowned warrior. Regis especially was impressed by the blond Happdal woman, and Jana felt a twinge of jealousy when she noticed Regis gazing at Katja's strong arms and broad shoulders as she told her stories. Regis laughed heartily whenever Katja said anything even approximating a joke, though Katja didn't seem to mind.

"How soon can we leave for the *Stanford*?" Jana asked Regis. She felt impatient. Filumena was in danger and every hour counted.

"As soon as tomorrow. The mule is already fueled up. It hasn't been flown in a while so the maintenance crew is still going over their checklists, but they're getting close. Who's going?"

"Myself, Katja, Tem, and Ingrid."

"The mule can fit one more," Regis said. "Maybe I should go with you. My understanding of the situation is that you'll need military support from the *Liu Hui* if the *Michelangelo* refuses to give your people back. I still have contacts there."

"But they need you here, no?" Katja asked.

Regis shrugged. "This place has zero security issues. Everyone leaves their door unlocked, there are no fistfights, and we're the only people in the entire valley as far as we know. The most exciting thing that happened this year was when a wild boar broke into a workshop and tried to steal a fabrication printer. No idea what he wanted to do with it."

Jana frowned. "But you defected from the *Liu Hui*. Your own words. Wouldn't your presence…complicate negotiations?"

Regis splayed his hands. "I was just offering. I'll admit I'm interested in the potential excitement, but I don't want to go if I'm not welcome."

Jana could sense her consorteria listening carefully, especially Sperancia. The women had given her space and privacy, sensing her distress and perhaps with the knowledge that all new hosts required an adjustment period. But Sperancia could no longer hold her tongue. *Put your jealousy aside, Jana*, Sperancia said. *Regis could be useful. You should invite him to accompany us.*

Jana didn't answer Sperancia, but she didn't ignore her advice. "Thank you for your offer," she said to Regis. "Let me talk it over with Tem and Ingrid."

"Of course. Tell them I'm happy to come along if I can be useful. And if not, I'm still willing to reach out to my contacts on the *Liu Hui*."

Later that afternoon, a small, black-skinned woman named Petra gave Jana and Katja a tour of the mule's interior and helped prepare them for their flight. "You'll feel extremely heavy as the mule accelerates, but that will subside, and at a certain point you'll feel weightless. Weightlessness can be fun, but it can also make you sick to your stomach. We'll give you some medicine that should take the edge off."

"What are those straps for?" Katja asked.

"To keep you in your seat. Otherwise you'd float away."

"Float? Like a leaf in the water?"

"Something like that."

Katja shook her head. "I don't think so. I sink like a stone. It's something the threads did to me."

Petra frowned, not understanding. Katja didn't elaborate, and Jana didn't feel it was her place to explain. But it did make her wonder how the Crucible threads would affect her own body over time. Would she no longer be able to swim? Her mother had drowned in the sea.

Around dusk Jana took a walk by herself around Ilium. She'd scarcely had a moment to herself in the past few days. Her mind was a confused jumble of desires and fears. She could not help but play out scenarios in her head, and for some reason they all took the form of explanations to her father. *Filumena and Cristo are dead*, she imagined herself saying to Leandro. *We did everything we could to rescue them, but Maro murdered them shortly after they arrived on the* Michelangelo. *I won't burden you with the knowledge of what was done to their bodies — it's too horrible.* Or a more optimistic scenario: *They'll be home within the week! Both Cristo and Filumena are recuperating on the* Stanford, *but they'll be fine. Though surely they will have stories to tell at Micheli's!*

Jana tried to get out of her head by paying attention to her surroundings. Up close, Ilium was a more attractive town than she had initially realized. Residents had decorated their domes with colorful paint, hanging plants, and rooftop gardens that gave the illusion that each small building was a creature of some sort, its strange head emerging from the ground. Goats and chickens ran free, though she guessed there was some technological means of tracking or corralling them when necessary. She didn't notice any goatherds or herding dogs and wondered if wolves were a problem. Maybe there were no wolves in this part of the world.

It was strange how few people lived on the planet compared to the billions that had once inhabited the Earth. To Jana, Sardinia had always felt big. It took two full days to walk across the island, and though she had never done so, intrepid explorers had walked the entire coastline, a journey of weeks. And yet the island of Sardinia was a mere dot on a map of the world. Maggie had shown her how to use the zoom feature on the hovershuttle map display. She'd seen maps in ancient books, but to see a living, accurate map of the entire world had given her a better sense of scale.

Earth was huge, and nearly empty.

All her life Jana had known only a single town, and yet now, learning of the multitude of peoples that inhabited and orbited the Earth, she felt fearful for humanity. Bosa, with its thousands of years of history, had always felt permanent to her, as if the town had always existed and always would exist. But this town – Ilium – was only a couple decades old. And the ringstations were only centuries old. Towns, settlements, and entire civilizations could come and go. Everything was temporary, perhaps even the existence of human beings.

Maybe it wasn't worth the risk of starting a war over two people's lives, even if one of those lives was dear to her. She didn't want to inadvertently trigger the extinction of a large portion of humanity by starting a war among the ringstations.

"Jana! It's time for dinner." Maggie was calling for her. "What are you doing way out here by the beehives? I was looking all over for you." Jana looked around and noticed she had wandered into a field of dozens of squat wooden boxes.

"How are things between you and Tem?" Jana asked on the way back to the dining hall. She'd noticed some tension between Maggie and Tem during the hovershuttle ride, though they'd done their best to hide it, speaking overly politely with one another.

"Oh, you picked up on that, huh? Yeah, things are a little rough right now. Did he tell you about Saga?"

"No. Though the name sounds familiar. Katja may have mentioned her."

"Well, maybe I'll tell you after dinner, if I've had enough wine."

* * *

Tem and Ingrid agreed that Regis would be a helpful addition to their group. Jana herself still had her reservations, but she'd presented Regis's offer to the others as dispassionately as possible. She tried to convince herself that her jealous feelings were overblown, that Regis had been harmlessly flirting with Katja. But something bothered her about the ex-soldier.

Jana was surprised to learn that the mule rocket didn't require a pilot, but would be controlled via machines (or if necessary, remotely by Petra). Tem, Ingrid, Katja, Regis, and Jana would be free to relax and socialize during the voyage, which would take only a little longer than the trip from Bosa to Ilium.

Just as Petra had warned, Jana felt extremely heavy during takeoff. The sensation would have been alarming except for Katja's laughter, which was louder even than the roar of the propulsion rockets. "She said I would float!" Katja yelled over the din. "But my body feels like a sack of stones!" The weightlessness that followed surprised Katja even more. When Ingrid said they could unbuckle their seat belts and float about the capsule if they liked, Katja did so, joyfully somersaulting midair and launching herself from wall to wall. "Join me, Jana!" she said, but Jana wanted no part of the acrobatics. She gripped the armrests of her chair, willing herself not to vomit. Ten minutes later she threw up anyway, but neatly at least, into a stiff paper bag provided by Ingrid.

"Don't worry about it," Ingrid said, patting her shoulder. "It happens to most of us during the first spaceflight. Humans just aren't used to weightlessness."

Feeling a little better, Jana took in the magnificent view. Though Sardinia was mostly obscured by clouds, she could see the outline of Italy, lush and green except for the Apennines and the snow-capped Alps to the north and west of the Po Valley. The Mediterranean Sea was a deep blue, nearing indigo. The water along the eastern coast of Italy took on a brilliant turquoise hue.

"I remember the first time I saw the Earth from space," Tem said. "I was in a mule – like this one but smaller – with my mother. And it was Petra who guided our flight, just like today. Though back then we had to wear heavy spacesuits to protect against radiation. This ship has better shielding."

Approaching the *Stanford*, the mule rotated, and for the first time Jana understood the ringstation's massive scale. Eight spokes radiated from a central hub to a great wheel.

"The spinning of the wheel creates a gravity-like force," Tem explained, "but we'll dock in the center, where we'll still be weightless."

After the mule had docked, Tem helped Jana navigate a corridor in her weightless state by moving her body by way of rungs attached to the wall. Katja picked up the technique quickly and was soon propelling herself along, effortlessly keeping up with Regis and Ingrid.

"Why is she so good at it?" Jana asked Tem resentfully.

Tem laughed. "Don't compare yourself to Katja. She's always been freakishly good at learning physical skills."

All five of them were required to pass through decontamination procedures before joining the ringstation's populace. Jana was given a private bathroom and told to follow a set of instructions on a card printed in Italian. Holding on to wall rungs for support, Jana awkwardly removed her clothes and reluctantly placed them in a chute where they were sucked away to an unknown location. She scrubbed her skin with damp, medicinally scented washcloths, and ran a fine comb through her hair that made her scalp tingle with tiny shocks. She dried herself with a large towel and dressed in a soft robe, and when a small panel opened revealing a packet of greenish-gray liquid, she drank it as instructed. The beverage had a bittersweet taste and chalky texture. She hoped the drink was not a preview of ringstation cuisine in general.

After Jana had completed the instructions, Ingrid greeted her at the door and returned her clothes, neatly folded and noticeably cleaner. "Just a few more scans and tests, then we can get dressed and take one of the spoke elevators to the main ring."

It was more than an hour later when Jana, Katja, Tem, and Ingrid finally descended Spoke 7 into a lush botanical garden lobby, replete with ferns, hanging vines, and ponds populated by large orange-gold fish. Jana's limbs were heavy and she still felt nauseous, but the fresh air helped. Regis had finished decon before them and had gone to meet some friends for a drink, inviting the others to meet him later for dinner.

"My grandfather Shol has invited us to his apartment for tea and snacks," Tem said. "My parents will be there as well. Shall we go there now and then meet Regis later? Or would you like to rest first?"

"I would love to see my brother and Car-En," Katja said immediately, without so much as a glance at Jana to see how she felt. "It has been several years since I've seen them. I would also like to meet your morfar."

Jana wanted nothing more than to be alone for a few minutes, and perhaps take a nap, but she smiled gamely. "Yes, that sounds fine."

"Why don't you two go ahead?" Ingrid suggested. "I should show Jana where she and Katja will be staying. We'll meet you at Shol's place a little later, okay?"

"I thought you could use some rest," Ingrid said once they were alone. "You still look a little green from the flight."

"It's difficult for me to be around many people," Jana admitted. "It makes me tired."

"I understand perfectly."

They were strolling through a neatly manicured park. Oddly, there were no food crops that Jana could see: no vegetable beds, fruit trees, or grain fields. All the plants appeared to be ornamental. "Where do you grow your food?" Jana asked.

"In greenhouses mostly, in a different part of the ringstation. It's more efficient that way."

Though she was acclimating to her own weight, Jana felt disoriented by the strange environment. Looking up, she saw there were multiple tiers to the ringstation, like ridges on the interior of a seashell, with the topmost being the narrowest. While the ground felt flat to walk on, the horizon sloped up and away in every direction.

"Here we are," Ingrid said, stopping in front of a two-story building constructed from glass and narrow beams of brightly painted metal. "Guest accommodations – you and Katja will be staying in the upstairs suite. There are three bedrooms, so you'll have plenty of space." Ingrid placed her hand on a panel, which caused a glass door to slide open. "Just go up those stairs. The door will be open. Should I come get you in an hour or so?"

"Yes, please. I'll just lie down for a few minutes."

"Rest as long as you need to. If you want to stay in tonight, I'll order some food for you. Do you have any dietary restrictions?"

"What do you mean?"

"Never mind. I'll check in with you later. If you hear my voice in your room, just answer me normally and I'll hear you."

Jana took off her boots and lay down on the smallest of the beds, intending to rest her eyes for a few minutes. Almost instantly she fell into a dreamless sleep. When she awoke, she had no idea how much time had passed. Had she missed the opportunity to meet Tem's parents? In some ways that would be a relief. She needed time to adjust to her new environment.

No – that was a weak way of thinking. She was here for a reason, to rescue Filumena and to find a way to protect Bosa from Maro and others like him. She had a job to do. It didn't matter if she felt tired or sick or uncomfortable.

Closing her eyes again, she opened her mind to the Crucible, and moments later she was in the town hall with Sperancia, Giuseppina, and Agatha.

"Where is Itria?" Jana demanded. "I need everyone here."

A second later the door opened, letting in a beam of light that illuminated motes of dust in the air, some of which sparkled like gems. Half a dozen winged fairies flew into the hall, followed by a slender woman with black hair down to her waist, and dark gray-blue eyes.

"Always with the dramatic entrances," Giuseppina scoffed.

"From my perspective," said Itria, "the rest of you are as boring as bumps on a log. You can do anything in this place. Why not have a little fun?" And then, to Jana: "What is it you want of me, child? I have answered your summons."

"I need all of you working together," Jana said. "Put your petty grievances aside. The future of our home is at stake, as are the lives of two people from Bosa."

"How can we help?" Sperancia asked.

"I need ideas. You all see through my eyes and hear through my ears – you know as much as I do. I need you to think of a way we can get Filumena and Cristo back without starting a war.

"I need to outwit Maro."

CHAPTER TWENTY-SEVEN

Maro did not want to confess to the murder of Cassia, not even to Livia. He considered strangling her right then and there, in the privacy of his own bedroom, but thought better of it. She was stronger than him, for one thing, and a Defender, trained in lethal combat techniques. He would have the advantage of surprise, but there was a good chance she would reverse any attack he attempted.

And of course he loved her dearly, and would miss her if she were dead. Though he loved himself more.

No, it was better to be honest. Hopefully she would understand.

"We can end this game of cat and mouse," he said. "As you've probably already guessed, I murdered her."

"Ha! I thought so. However did you do it? She's thrice your size."

"Faustus assisted. His venom did her in."

"Faustus has a poisonous bite? You never told me."

"*Had* a poisonous bite. She broke his back."

"Oh, I'm sorry."

"It's okay, I'll get a new ferret. But yes, Cassia is out of the way."

"How did you dispose of her body? Quite a bit of mass to manage."

This was the part Maro hadn't been looking forward to. "Cassia took care of that loose end herself. She crawled off somewhere to die. When they find her body there will be absolutely no connection to me – I never touched her. And Aina already got rid of—"

"Wait – did you confirm that she was dead?"

"She was blue in the face."

"But she could still be alive?"

"Not unless Aina moved her and lied about it. But that's impossible – cybrids can't lie to their owners."

"Unless they're upgraded," Livia pointed out. "Apparently the Bohm upgrade provides them with a great deal more free will."

"Really? Well, Aina hasn't been upgraded. That would require my consent, wouldn't it?"

Livia shrugged. "One would think. But really, Maro, I'm impressed. What initiative on your part, getting rid of your opposition. If this doesn't come back to bite you on the ass, you could very well be emperor."

"It has a nice ring to it, doesn't it? *Emperor Maro Decimus.*"

"Very much so. Will you acquire a large harem?"

"I see no reason to. I'm quite satisfied with you, my love."

"And with Aina, for your urges when I'm not available?"

"She doesn't count."

Livia kissed him, then climbed on top of him, reaching beneath his tunic to grab his already hardening cock. "It's been a minute, hasn't it?"

"I've had a lot on my mind."

"Your experiment is a success. Let's celebrate."

*　*　*

The next day Maro met privately with Traian at the Licinian Baths, a less popular spa with multiple heated pools, sulfurous waters, and rough stonework. At Maro's insistence only the two senators and their personal cybrids were in attendance; he knew Traian to be a more reasonable man in the absence of an audience for his posturing.

"Does your cybrid double as security?" Maro asked. Traian's attendant was broad-shouldered and nearly seven feet tall, with chiseled Grecian features.

Traian frowned as he handed his robe to his attendant. "I don't want to disappear like Cassia."

"You know I had nothing to do with that. I'm sure Cassia is just holed up somewhere, enjoying all the hubbub. She'll emerge at the moment of maximum dramatic effect, probably right before the election."

"Maybe you're right," Traian conceded. "What is your cybrid smiling about? Does she know something we don't?"

Maro glanced at Aina, who looked back at him soberly.

"I have no idea. Perhaps you just imagined it. She has a pleasing face."

The senators settled into the steaming water. This was good, Maro thought. Traian seemed relaxed and unguarded. While he didn't need Traian's vote to win the election, it would still help to soften what was left of the opposition. Ruling the Senate would be easier and more pleasant if the *populares* were resigned to the fact of his power.

Traian yawned, stretching his arms over his head. "Level with me, Maro. Why the power play? What do you hope to gain by becoming *Emperor Decimus*?"

"In terms of personal gain, absolutely nothing. I will be a humble servant, serving the best interests of the Senate and the *Michelangelo*. But we need a powerful leader to guide us through the storm ahead."

"And you're the best person for the job?"

"I'll let the Senate decide that. But I won't refuse the position if elected."

"A temporary title, then, to be rescinded once our situation stabilizes?"

"Of course. Though it may be some time before the Ringstation Coalition comes to understand that we will not tolerate interference."

"Interference? All they have done is hail us. All we have done is ignore them. We're hardly at war. We haven't even officially disagreed on anything."

Maro gestured to Aina to rub his shoulders. Obediently the cybrid knelt at the edge of the bath and began to knead his muscles. "You are perfectly aware, Traian, of our cultural differences. The Coalition values collaboration and consensus, resulting in endless meetings and bureaucratic processes. We value aesthetics, great works, and scientific achievements above all else."

"Those values are not so different so as to be incompatible."

"So you might think. But mark my words, they will object when we begin to build our cities. They will object when we accept volunteers from Earth's native peoples for our experiments. They will insist we follow their rules and regulations. The Coalition reaches out so they can shackle and bind us."

Traian chuckled. "You're paranoid and delusional. We haven't even heard them out."

"We will listen to what they have to say once I am elected. But my prophecy will prove correct."

"You would be a prophet now, as well as emperor?"

Maro smiled, leaning back so that his head pressed into Aina's bosom. "Even an ordinary man can predict the future with clear eyes."

Traian snorted. "You see yourself as an ordinary man no more than I see myself as a dolphin."

"Then enough of this speculation," said Maro. "We will see how the Senate votes. But be assured that I only have the best interests of my fellow citizens in mind, and that should I be elected, I will not exercise any of the emergency powers bestowed by the petition."

"Unless there's an emergency."

Maro sighed. He was getting bored with Traian's passive-aggressive skepticism. Perhaps it wasn't worth trying to befriend his fellow senator. Once he was emperor, he would simply obliterate him. Maro was an accelerating asteroid, massive and moving at a significant fraction of the speed of light, annihilating everything that stood between him and his ultimate destination.

"What have you heard of the *Iarudi*?" Maro asked, not really caring but desperate to change the subject. All he knew was that the cybrid-crewed Falcon had approached the location of the gamma-ray burst and had physically sighted the *Liu Hui* starship.

"They're very close. They'll intercept within a few hours."

"Why did they send cybrids on the Falcon?" Aina asked.

Traian raised an eyebrow. "She asks questions?"

It was unusual for Aina to interrupt a conversation, but idle curiosity was a part of her programming, along with a strong impulse to please, and an insatiable sex drive. Maro didn't see any harm in answering – whatever he told her would go in one ear and out the other. "Cybrid bodies can survive significantly higher G-forces than human bodies, so the Falcon can accelerate and decelerate more quickly."

"Thank you for explaining that, Maro."

Traian narrowed his eyes. "Is she...upgraded?"

"Of course not. She's quite functional as she is. No need to fix what isn't broken. I like her pliant and stupid."

"I see," said Traian, with an expression that Maro interpreted as judgmental. Well, fuck him. *Prepare to be annihilated, Senator, by Asteroid Decimus.*

CHAPTER TWENTY-EIGHT

If life were to get any better, Maro reflected, he might very well burst with happiness. The election was only three days away with his victory all but assured, the Engineers were already creating templates based on his Ancestral Realism data, and Livia, for the first time, was in love with him as much as he was with her.

And now, as Livia wove the shuttle through the valleys of the Harz mountains, he was rushing toward his destiny, his legacy as an Artist. Patience was an overrated virtue; he was tremendously *impatient* to expand Ancestral Realism, and for that he needed more volunteers.

Bosa, for the moment, was not the best place to obtain more recruits. Mistakes had been made. The old woman's death had left a sour taste in everyone's mouth. He had unfinished business with Jana, but for now that could wait. It would be some time before he could safely return to Sardinia.

But the villages of the Harz mountains were virgin lands ripe for plunder. The anthropological data obtained from the *Stanford* had helped him select his first target. He would avoid the village of Happdal, which had been psychologically and culturally contaminated by sloppy researchers from the *Stanford*. His target was Kaldbrek, a small, destitute hamlet situated in a steep valley whose residents subsisted on a meager diet consisting mostly of mutton and berries.

The poor wretches would accept his gifts with open arms. They would lap up his promises like sweet spring water.

Instead of a grand entrance on a golden balloon, Maro had planned something more appropriate for the mountain folk. Car-En Ganzorig's research indicated that the Happdal people had many domesticated animals: cows, chickens, sheep and goats, dogs and cats. But none of the villages had horses. They had had horses, long ago, when first migrating south from their ancestral home in Scandinavia, fleeing the encroaching glacial sheets. But those beasts had perished over the course of one or more harsh winters.

The Harz people had eaten their horses out of desperate necessity, every last one.

So Maro was bringing them a surprise.

"The shuttle does not make an ideal stable," Livia commented. "The whole ship smells like horseshit."

She was right. The horses – two black mares and a bay stallion – had survived the weightless portion of their flight unharmed, secured in specialized harnesses that had limited their motion, preventing self-injury. But all three beasts had defecated profusely in reaction to their distress.

"Aina – clean up the the manure."

He'd brought the cybrid along for labor, as well as for her tongue. Aina would serve as their translator. Maro hadn't minded learning Italian in order to speak to the people of Bosa; Italian was similar to Latin and had been easy to pick up. Learning the language of the Harz people, a mix of Old Norse and Norwegian, had not appealed to him, nor had he the time. But the cybrid could acquire a new language in just a few minutes.

Aina got up from her seat and headed back to the hastily fabricated stalls. "Yes Maro, I'll do that immediately."

Of all the worldships, the *Michelangelo* maintained the widest diversity of animal life. Their initial launch population had included hundreds of animal species, a veritable Noah's Ark. The founders had insisted on bringing animals featured in historical artworks: lions, tigers, snakes, eagles, peacocks, and of course horses. As the size and resources of the *Michelangelo* had expanded, the Engineers had resurrected other species from DNA archives. Their zoo was a masterpiece of meticulously designed habitats for each species, laced throughout with hidden viewing spaces for artists who wanted to sketch their forms.

The zoo directors had lent him the horses only reluctantly. But no one wanted to cross the future emperor. Which was good, because Maro had no intention of returning the beasts.

Livia skillfully landed the shuttle in a rocky clearing dotted with clumps of wildflowers. Even before the ship had settled on its landing pads, Livia opened the hatch, letting in a rush of cold mountain air. "Ugh, that smell. I can finally breathe."

With Aina's help, Maro freed the horses from their safety harnesses and saddled them. With some resentment he noticed that the stallion and both the mares preferred Aina's presence, while his own touch made them skittish. Which made no sense; Aina wasn't even a mammal. But she looked and smelled like a human female – that was certainly true – and he supposed the illusion worked just as well on equines as it did on people.

"These are beautiful animals," Aina said, gently tightening a saddle strap on one of the black mares. "Which one will you ride, Maro?"

"The stallion. Livia and I will ride in front, side by side. You will follow."

"Yes, Maro."

The clearing was on a mountain ridge overlooking the valley in which Kaldbrek was situated. There was a chance a wanderer or hunter would come across the parked shuttle, but the craft would be protected once it shelled up. And so what if someone saw it? For the volunteers, they would see the shuttle up close soon enough.

Riding the stallion took some getting used to. Maro was as well-co-ordinated as any man, at least insofar as such things could be controlled with genetic manipulation and neurological enhancements. His balance and reflexes were superb. And yet controlling the horse was more of a challenge than riding the Vertragus he was used to. While the cybrid steed reacted to Maro's slightest cues, the stallion obeyed him only reluctantly. When he wanted the horse to trot, it stubbornly ambled. And at one point, without prompting, the beast broke into a full gallop, stopping only when Maro yanked on the reins and shouted, "*Subsisto!*"

"Would you like a short riding lesson?" Aina offered. "I have access to helpful tutorials." Aina's mare was even-tempered and obedient, as was Livia's.

"It's a spirited beast. But it will submit eventually."

Consulting the map in his retinal feed, Maro led them to a wide, well-trodden trail. The dirt road descended into the valley, and as they neared the outskirts of the village they smelled smoke and came across a ramshackle hut. A lone goat nibbled on weeds out front. A short rope around its neck dragged along the ground, attached to nothing. A white-bearded man sat on a stump next to a sprawling bush thick with round red berries.

"*Heill ok sæll!*" Maro said cheerfully, using the one Norse greeting he had memorized. *Healthy and happy.*

The old man nodded noncommittally and puffed on a hand-carved pipe. His long white beard was forked and braided.

Livia patted her mare's neck. "He doesn't seem impressed."

The old man raised an eyebrow at the sound of Livia's voice, and for an instant Maro wondered if he could understand her words. But no, how could the man have learned Latin?

Aina addressed the man, the old Nordic language rolling off her tongue with ease. To Maro's ear the words sounded harsh and guttural, made tolerable only by Aina's melodic voice. As planned, she was telling him that they were visitors from the *Michelangelo* worldship, looking for villagers to participate in a project. Volunteers would be richly rewarded with gold, food and drink, and whatever pleasures they desired.

After Aina had completed her speech, the man regarded the three of them, each in turn, for an awkwardly long amount of time. Maro's stallion stamped his foot and whinnied.

Finally the man replied, just a single sentence. His voice was low and raspy, but Maro immediately realized the old man possessed a gift. His voice was impossible to ignore, drawing in the listener like a box of unknown contents being slowly opened.

Aina's face bore a confused expression. "What did he say?" Maro asked impatiently.

"*If you value your lives, turn around and return to the place from which you came.*" Aina spoke in Latin, but modulated her voice to perfectly mimic the old man's timbre and intonation. To Maro's satisfaction, the man's jaw dropped in surprise. This was what he wanted, to impress these simple folk, to stun them with wondrous sights and sounds. This old fart was a hard sell, but Aina's trick had made an impression.

The man spoke a few more sentences, and this time Aina translated immediately, still mimicking his voice. "If you continue along this road, you gamble with your lives. You may find what you are looking for. Or maybe Svein will steal your horses, tie you to crosses, and slit open your backs so that he may pull out your lungs and salt them."

The man paused for effect. Maro, for once, was not sure how to respond.

The old man spoke once more. "It would be a slow and painful death," Aina translated. "I do not recommend it."

"He has a way with words," Livia commented. "Ask him his name."

Aina did so. The man got up, and despite his age stood straight and tall, at least a head taller than Maro. He replied that his name was Egil, and that he was a poet. He further explained that someone named Saga – the jarl or chieftain of Kaldbrek – was away at another village, and that they should come back in a week or so when Saga had returned. Saga was a fair and reasonable person. They would be wise to wait for her.

Maro nodded. "Thank him for his advice. And invite him to visit us on the *Michelangelo* – I would like to hear his poems." Egil was probably too old to survive the stresses of Ancestral Realism, but he was still potentially worthy of study. Maro doubted the pipe-smoking hermit had any talent, but it was better to find out than to lose his words to entropy. Nothing was more important than preservation. And there was something about the poet's voice, a charismatic allure that had nothing to do with sexuality or bravado. Could that quality be dissected and reverse-engineered? To have such a voice while addressing the Senate would be extraordinary.

Maro dug his heels into the sides of his stallion. The beast ignored him. He kicked again, harder this time, and the horse launched into a full gallop. Maro felt himself tilting to the side and desperately gripped the reins, at first fearing humiliation more than injury but then reconsidering his priorities as a low-hanging branch nearly took off his head. Startled, he ducked and yelled. "*Subsisto! Subsisto!*" Eventually the stallion came to a full stop and bent forward to nibble at some trailside grass. "Let us hurry!" Maro called back to the others, failing to conceal the irritation in his voice. Aina exchanged a few more words with Egil – more than was quite necessary – and then followed Livia toward Maro, both their mares obediently walking with an appropriate gait.

Maro did his best to compose himself as they entered the village proper. For the moment his steed had calmed, and Maro sat with his spine held straight, a regal posture befitting of an emperor-to-be. Thin urchins with dirty faces watched them wide-eyed as they passed. An old woman dropped an entire basket of soil-encrusted root vegetables.

"*Heill ok sæll, heill ok sæll,*" Maro repeated, smiling widely. No one answered him, and two young women turned on their heels and fled.

Nothing wrong with a little fear. Some of the tension dissolved from Maro's back and shoulders. The encounter with the strange poet had left a bad taste in his mouth, but the trip could still be salvaged. It was important to remain optimistic. Not to the point of ignoring reality or underestimating one's obstacles, but it helped to imagine events unfolding as one hoped they would. It did no good to obsess on what could go wrong, to magnify the possibility of failure. Worry was a natural habit, one born of millions of years of evolution, of self-preservation at any cost. But to achieve greatness, it was a habit that needed unlearning.

A lanky, gray-bearded man with a scarred, pinched face strode toward them, unarmed but also unafraid. Two burly men carrying spears followed, the only well-fed people Maro had seen in Kaldbrek. Was this the *Svein* that Egil had referred to, with his bodyguards?

Aina gave her rehearsed greeting. The man with the pinched face listened, scowling, though perhaps the scowl was his natural expression, permanently etched into his face. The bodyguards gazed at Livia and Aina with obvious lust, which made Maro uncomfortable. He was glad Livia was with him in case the situation escalated.

Maro activated his internal translator and signaled to Livia to do the same. Aina could translate perfectly well, but it would be faster to read text in his retinal feed. He did not want to be caught off guard.

"What beasts are these?" the pinched-face man asked, not to Maro but to his henchmen, who shrugged in response.

"They're horses," Aina answered. "And they can be yours if you volunteer for our project."

"They're already mine," the man said. His bodyguards laughed. "You have trespassed. Everything you carry now belongs to me, Svein Haakonsson. If you're lucky, you'll leave with your lives." He patted the neck of Livia's mare. "And possibly the shirts on your backs," he added, leering at Aina.

Aina started to translate, but Maro interrupted. "I understood his words. Tell him he would be wise to be more respectful. We come in peace, but we are more powerful than he appears to understand."

"You carry no weapons," Svein said once Aina had spoken, "which means that you have no power. Get off these *horses* now, before we pull you off."

Livia glanced at Maro, who nodded. Livia smoothly dismounted and drew her golden blade from the thigh harness concealed beneath her tunic. Svein's thugs leveled their spears and stepped forward, while Svein himself took a step back, situating himself between the steel spearheads.

Livia raised her blade, pointing it at one of the bodyguards. Several bright bolts of electricity arced between the tip of the weapon and the man's body, felling him instantly. He twitched on the ground, his clothing emitting wisps of smoke.

"He'll live," Maro said. "I hope this—"

Before Aina could even begin to translate, the other bodyguard lunged forward and plunged his spear into the chest of Maro's stallion. The horse screamed and reared up, throwing Maro to the ground. He landed hard on the packed-earth trail, his right shoulder and hip taking most of the impact. Quickly he rolled away to avoid being trampled, then crouched near a spruce sapling, trying to assess the situation. His horse, still very much alive, was galloping back in the direction of the shuttle. Livia was struggling with Svein, who had grabbed her wrist and was trying to wrest control of the golden blade. The other bodyguard tried to drag Aina from her steed, but the cybrid punched him with such force that his face visibly caved in. He staggered back and collapsed.

"I will kill you all!" Svein screamed. "I will tear out your guts and piss on them!"

Livia kneed Svein in the groin, tripped him, and slid her blade across his throat. A geyser of blood wetted Livia's tunic. Svein clutched his throat, gurgled incomprehensibly, and collapsed.

Livia regarded her blood-soiled tunic. "It's ruined."

Aina dismounted and checked on the man she had punched. "Will he heal?" she asked, sounding genuinely distressed. "His face doesn't look right."

Maro stood and approached. The bodyguard lay on his back, motionless, blood seeping from his eyes. Some organic material – possibly his brain – leaked from his nose, which was flattened into his now-concave face.

"I don't think he'll make it," he said to Livia.

Aina paled. While he had seen the cybrid look vaguely upset or perturbed, this expression on her face was something new. If he didn't know better he would have said that Aina was experiencing utter grief. She turned and fled, following the stallion.

"What's with her?" Livia asked.

"I'm not sure."

Livia removed her tunic and tossed the garment at Svein, covering the dead man's face and gruesome throat wound. "Well, that could have gone better. What do you suggest we do now?"

CHAPTER TWENTY-NINE

The Ringstation Coalition Council assigned Tem to lead the delegation to the *Liu Hui*, along with a team that included Regis Foster, Jana, and Katja. Ingrid would stay behind to provide support from the *Stanford*.

The shuttle trip was short and fully automated. This gave Tem time to plan his appeal to the *Zhōngyāng*, the governing body of the *Liu Hui*, equivalent to the *Stanford*'s Over Council. There was now direct evidence from high-speed microprobes that the gamma-ray bursts near Chariklo were indeed from the *Iarudi*, and that the *Michelangelo* had deployed a vessel to intercept the starship. Requesting military support from the *Liu Hui* was a big ask, but challenging the *Michelangelo* was in the Zhōngyāng's best interests if they wished to retrieve their own ship.

"Nervous about seeing your former colleagues?" Tem asked Regis. The ex-military man had served in the elite *Kǒngbù Wūzéi* special forces under Commander Umana. That association had once cast suspicion on his character, but Regis had proven himself to be a hard worker and loyal to the cause of Ilium. Along with Xenus, Lydia, and the other founders, Regis had invested his own sweat, blood, and tears into transforming the settlement into a viable community. Ilium had weathered hard times, including food shortages, viral outbreaks, and major equipment failures. Officials on the *Stanford*, wanting to avoid appearances of violating Repop protocols, had provided support to the settlement only minimally and reluctantly in that first crucial decade. Many on the *Stanford* had been disgruntled when the AFS-1 outpost had renamed itself Ilium and declared itself an independent community, some even labeling the settlement as *rogue*. There were still lingering resentments on both sides.

Tem imagined that similar feelings might exist between Regis Foster and the security division of the *Liu Hui* under which Regis had once served. Regis had left under extenuating circumstances: Commander Umana had embarked on a murderous rampage, revealing the full depths of her insanity. Still, Regis had defected to co-found Ilium, as had many of his crew.

Regis grunted in agreement. "Of course I'm nervous. They might arrest me on sight. People on the *Liu Hui* have long memories. The culture is different there, more hierarchical. More conservative and formal."

"Do you think they will? Arrest you, I mean." Tem hadn't even considered that possibility. After all, Regis had lived on Earth for twenty years, unbothered by the *Liu Hui*.

"Probably not. I've tried to be a helpful asset to my former colleagues."

"What does that mean? You've been spying for them?"

"Of course not. But I've maintained exploration drones that supply ground data to all the ringships. Satellite mapping only gets you so far."

Regis stretched his arms and arched his back. The belts holding his weightless body in place looked like they might snap under the tension. Like most people who had grown up on the *Liu Hui*, Regis was tall and broad, with an impressive physique. The physicality was mostly an aesthetic choice, one that would have been less practical on the *Stanford*, a smaller ringstation that was moderately overpopulated. Though in recent years even the larger *Liu Hui* ringship was feeling the effects of population growth.

Tem noticed Jana regarding Regis with suspicion, an expression he had caught on the Bosa woman's face more than once. He wondered what she had against Regis. Katja reached out and took Jana's hand, squeezing it. Jana relaxed visibly and turned her attention to Katja. Tem had been slow to notice that his aunt and Jana were in a relationship, but he was happy for them. Especially for Katja, who had lived alone in Happdal for as long as Tem could remember.

"Do you think they will help us?" Jana asked.

"I do. We can't let the *Michelangelo* push us around. If the other ringships work together, we're much stronger."

"I don't want to start a war, not even to rescue my friend."

"I understand. But there's much more at stake. We need to come to some kind of agreement with the *Michelangelo*, and we may need a show of strength to get their attention. Though I don't think it will come to war."

"I can't wait to see the next generation of *Liu Hui* battleships," Regis said. "The *Iarudi* was a brilliant feat of engineering, but that was twenty years ago."

Jana scowled openly, but Regis didn't appear to notice.

* * *

Docking and decon went quickly and smoothly. Perhaps the *Liu Hui* had more sensitive and efficient biosensors than the *Stanford*. Still wearing the clothes they had arrived in, Tem and the others cleared their biochecks, reconvened, and descended to the main wheel in a high-speed elevator. They were greeted by a slender Asian woman somewhat younger than Tem's mother.

"Mèng!" Regis exclaimed. "It's wonderful to see you! You look exactly the same."

Tem disagreed – Mèng looked significantly older than the last time he had seen her – but he did recognize the woman, who had once served with Regis under Commander Umana. She had been the first to rebel against the Squid Woman, and Tem respected her for that decision. For many years Mèng had lived on the *Stanford*, but more recently she had returned to the *Liu Hui*, her original home.

"It's good to see you too, Regis. And you as well, Tem. I'll be your official liaison. We have a meeting scheduled with several members of our Coalition committee in two hours. Would you like to get something to eat in the meantime?"

"I'm famished," said Regis.

Mèng took them to a small restaurant high on the Earthside curve. The view of Eurasia was spectacular, and Jana spent more time looking out the viewing wall than eating. The meal of fresh sauteed vegetables and a meat substitute resembling pork was delicious. Even Tem, who had been raised on real boar meat, was impressed.

After their dishes had been cleared, Jana and Katja went over to the viewing wall to marvel at the sight of Earth from orbit. Regis excused himself to use the bathroom. Once Regis was out of earshot, Mèng gave Tem a serious look. "I have some bad news for you."

For a moment Tem thought she must be joking, but her expression did not change.

"What?" He hadn't seen Mèng in years, and had no contact with anyone on the *Liu Hui*. Perhaps there was some news of Shane and the *Iarudi*. He had hoped his friend might somehow be alive, but he'd known the chances were slim.

"One of the Coalition representatives we're meeting with – you know him. Or at least know of him."

"Who is it?"

"Aldo Manning."

Tem didn't recognize the first name, but the last name triggered an unpleasant memory. "Manning – he was the tech who tried to kill my mother."

"He was never officially accused—"

"I know what happened."

Manning had cut a deal, informing on Adrian Vanderplotz, his mother's academic advisor and the one who had orchestrated the attempt on her life. Manning had been a tech for SecondSkin at the time, the consultancy that had designed the survival bioskin Car-En had worn during her field research in the Harz mountains. Manning had allowed Adrian to override the bioskin's safety mechanism to administer a near-fatal dose of insulin into his mother's bloodstream. Esper and the village medicine woman had managed to save Car-En's life, and no one had ever been charged or prosecuted for the crime.

"How in the hell did Manning end up on your Coalition committee?"

"That's a good question. He is no doubt a skilled engineer and could have stayed in that field despite the rumors regarding his reputation. But he chose to become a diplomat, and has swiftly risen in that career."

"Is he…any good at it?"

Mèng raised one eyebrow just slightly. "In my opinion, he is an adequate negotiator. He is intelligent and invariably well-prepared."

"You're leaving something out."

"There are certain members of the Zhōngyāng that are perhaps more deferential to Manning than they need to be."

"I see." So Manning had some dirt on some higher-ups. "What do you think he's after?"

"I don't know. Power, maybe. He's already extremely wealthy."

Power. Power over others, specifically. Tem had never seen the point, but he was wise enough to understand that such motivations existed. Some people felt an insatiable need to dominate and control others. Tem had known powerlessness as a child, and he hadn't liked it. But now he was in control of his own choices and destiny – as much as that was possible – and that was enough power for him. To everyone else his attitude was *live and let live*.

But not everyone felt that way.

* * *

After the meal, Mèng showed them to their accommodations, which she described as simple and utilitarian. While not luxurious, Tem's room was spacious and featured a large porthole with a stunning Earthside view. He showered and put on a set of clothes Mèng had left for him, a white synthetic-silk uniform that was customary for all council meeting attendees. The clothes – most likely just fabricated based on his boarding bioscan measurements – fit him perfectly, but internally he felt uncomfortable. Something about *Liu Hui* culture was intimidating. Maybe it was the big people, or the formalities, or the ringship's obvious wealth. Whatever it was, Tem suddenly felt inadequate.

His room had a com panel. After experimenting with the controls, he managed to place a call to Maggie in Ilium.

"Hello? Tem? Is everything okay?"

"Yes. I just wanted to hear your voice. We're meeting with their Coalition representatives—"

"What?"

"Can you hear me?"

"Yes, now I can. There's a delay." Maggie sounded busy. He'd called because he'd wanted some reassurance, maybe even some bolstering. And he knew that if he came right out and said so, she'd be happy to give it to him. She was always generous that way. But for some reason he couldn't just ask.

"How is Pietro doing?"

"Really well. He's already received his first treatment. It's much too early to see any effect, but he's being brave about it."

"That's great – I'm happy to hear it."

"You doing okay?"

"Yeah. Feeling a little nervous."

"That's understandable."

"The stakes are...higher than I'm used to."

"Try not to start a war."

"I'm afraid that's exactly what I'm trying to do."

"Just do your part – that's all you can do. Share your perspective and help formulate a plan."

"It sounds easy when you put it that way."

"Good. I've got to get back to work now."

"Okay. Love you."

"Love you too."

There was so much he wanted to ask and tell her. Had she forgiven him for his night with Saga? Was she still involved with Roland, the curly-haired botanist, who in hindsight had always greeted Tem much too cheerfully? He knew he had no right to be jealous, but he couldn't help himself.

Of course none of those questions was appropriate for a short call when both of them were busy with work. And neither was the biggest unspoken question: did they have a future together? He wanted a long heart-to-heart, just the two of them, and he sensed Maggie did too. But they hadn't been able to arrange it before he'd had to leave.

Or maybe, on some level, they were both avoiding that particular conversation. What if they *didn't* have a future together? That thought wasn't something he could handle right now.

★ ★ ★

The meeting was held in a building of curved hardwood beams and crystalline glass panels that looked more like a temple than a government office. The plant-filled conference room occupied an entire floor and was open to the air, with only hanging vines as walls. Instead of a table there was a large recessed seating pit. When Tem, Regis, Jana, and Katja arrived, the *Liu Hui* contingent was already present. To Tem's relief Mèng was there – at least one familiar face. An older, sour-faced Caucasian man glared at Tem as he entered. Was that Aldo Manning? One other man and two other women were present. The man was tall, thin, dark-skinned, and looked to be about Tem's age. Both the women looked to be of mostly Asian ancestry, about the age of his mother, also tall and slender. All were dressed in the same white uniform he was wearing, with no marks to signify rank or position.

Mèng rose and made introductions. Tem had been right about Manning. The dark-skinned man was Sabra Zane, a population biologist. The women were Zhou Zi and Elanor Xun, security specialists from the *Jūnshì* branch of government.

Elanor Xun led the conversation initially, asking questions, especially of Jana and Katja. Tem found that he liked her immediately, while simultaneously realizing he was being manipulated. Elanor was charming and curious, and her lighthearted banter made everyone feel comfortable and included. But at the same time she was sizing everyone up, gauging their motivations.

It was Katja who ultimately brought up the point of their visit. "My nephew says you can help us. Maro has kidnapped Jana's friend Filumena and one other person from Bosa. Tem says you have powerful weapons and many resources. Will you help us?"

Elanor smiled. "Of course we will help. The question is this: what is the best kind of help we can provide? The *Michelangelo* also possesses powerful weapons, and there are many unknowns. We must proceed carefully."

Zhou nodded. "Before the *Michelangelo* departed for the outer solar system, they possessed a massive arsenal: nuclear warheads, electromagnetic railguns, powerful lasers, even conventional explosives. After decades of asteroid mining and construction, the *Michelangelo* has returned at more than twice its original size. No doubt their military capability has increased as well."

"Don't you have the same weapons?" Jana asked.

"Based on our last intelligence reports, yes," Elanor said. "But military research and development has not been a priority on the *Liu Hui*. Like the *Stanford*, we have focussed our efforts in the fields of medicine, materials science, astronomy, Earth geology, and other areas relevant to our immediate future. The peace and security brought by the Ringstation Coalition has allowed us to do that. We assumed, wrongly, that the *Michelangelo* would stay in the outer solar system, wishing to be left to themselves."

Sabra Zane spoke for the first time, addressing Tem. "What are your impressions as to their intentions regarding repopulation? Did the delegates from the *Michelangelo* give any indication that they wish to start settlements or build cities?"

Tem shrugged. "I have no idea."

"I don't think so," Jana said. "Maro never mentioned wanting to start a town. He mentioned people from the *Michelangelo* staying in Bosa, but only as visitors."

"How is Xīnanyang faring?" Regis asked. Xīnanyang was the first *Liu Hui* settlement on Earth, a village of a few hundred people on the island that had once been called Taiwan.

"Very well," said Sabra. "The people are healthy and thriving. Xīnanyang is producing enormous amounts of rice, oranges, tea, asparagus, and many other fruits and vegetables. I can give you samples of the tea – perhaps we can arrange trade with Ilium. Or with Bosa," he added, turning to Jana. "I hear you have delicious tomatoes."

"How would you know?" Jana asked suspiciously.

Sabra raised his hands defensively. "We're not spying, I promise. It was just something Mèng told me. Tem mentioned it at lunch, apparently?"

"What? Oh yes, I did say that," Tem confirmed. He'd been distracted, watching Manning. The old tech had been sitting off to the side, studying a tablet, disengaged with the meeting since the initial introductions.

Regis cleared his throat. "Sorry to be blunt, but we can't talk about tea and tomatoes all day. It looks like the *Michelangelo* is going to get to the *Iarudi* first. That's your starship. So what are you going to do about it?"

Manning looked up from his tablet. "You used to serve on the *Iarudi*, didn't you? With Commander Umana."

"I did."

"What was your impression of her?"

"She was strict but competent. Until she went batshit crazy."

"You had no inkling beforehand that she was mentally unstable?"

"She had us all fooled."

"I see. And what exactly do you think the *Liu Hui* should 'do about' the *Iarudi*, as you put it?"

Regis answered without hesitation. "I think you should deploy a squadron of fighters and intercept them upon their return. You have the capability – why not use it?"

"And what if those in charge of the *Michelangelo* deploy their own warships? What if they breach our hull with railguns? They could do so from a thousand kilometers away."

"They wouldn't do that. That's insane. They're just as vulnerable to such an attack as any ringship."

"And you're an infallible judge of who is a rational actor, and who is insane?"

Regis glared at Manning but didn't immediately respond. Jana looked pleased at the rebuke.

"I think Aldo simply means to point out that the stakes are incredibly high," Elanor said. "The *Michelangelo* has refused to communicate with us.

That makes the intentions of their leadership extremely difficult to judge."

"I have a better idea," said Jana. "Can you get me to the *Michelangelo*?"

Everyone, including Tem, looked at Jana as if she had just regurgitated a live frog.

"Why?" Tem asked.

"I believe I could persuade Maro to return Filumena and Cristo to Bosa. And furthermore, I think I could convince him to parlay with the Ringstation Coalition. To make peace."

"How would you do that?" Elanor asked in an even tone. Tem guessed that she was making an effort to not sound condescending.

"I possess something that interests him. He said so, right in front of me. He spared my life because of it. I think that curiosity is Maro's weakness. We can use that to our advantage."

"Tell me more about this Maro person," Elanor said. "What is his leadership role on the *Michelangelo*?"

"He called himself a senator," said Jana.

"Like a jarl?" Katja asked.

"More like an elder," Tem explained to his aunt. "One decision-maker among many."

"But he is hungry for more power," Jana said. "I think he would like to be a king or a dictator."

Sabra leaned forward, touching his fingertips together to make a tent. "What is it exactly that you possess that so interests Maro?"

Jana nodded. "It is difficult to explain, but I'll try. When Livia killed Sperancia – a woman from Bosa who was my friend and mentor – Sperancia passed something on to me. A black egg, which I swallowed. The egg became part of my body. It is a vessel for Sperancia's soul, and every other person before Sperancia who held the egg within their body."

Manning looked up from his tablet again. "What the hell? What is this bullshit?"

Katja stood, reaching for where her sword would be, and crossed the seating pit in one long stride. Tem was up in an instant, locking his aunt in a bearhug and pushing her back toward her seat.

Manning snorted in disbelief. "Was she just going to…*attack* me?"

"Do not speak to Jana that way again," Katja warned. "I do not need a sword to kill you."

"*Kill* me? Somebody get this crazy bitch out of here."

Katja didn't struggle against him, but Tem maintained his grip nonetheless.

Elanor rose. "Let's all take a ten-minute break. I'll order some refreshments."

Tem reluctantly released his aunt, worried that she might go for Manning again. Five minutes later a server brought in a tray of tall glasses filled with fresh watermelon juice and small bowls of spiced nuts. Manning brusquely excused himself, claiming another meeting. Katja appeared noticeably calmer after Manning had left, and ate two bowls of nuts.

"Jana, please continue," Elanor said after they had reconvened.

Jana did her best to describe the Crucible and to explain her personal experience of being a host. Katja chimed in, sharing her own story of being forcibly enslaved by the same technology.

"It's all true," Tem added. "Look it up for yourself – the Crucible program was a Corporate Age brain emulation experiment. And somehow at least one instance survived. Jana may be the last, or there may be others out there."

"There is some speculation that Commander Umana may have also been a host," Mèng added.

"Fascinating," said Zhou. "I can see why Maro would be interested."

Regis scratched his head. "So we're going to use Jana as some kind of bait? Just send her over on a shuttle? What's to stop them from vaporizing her ship as soon as she's within range of their lasers?"

"Just let them know it's me," Jana said. "I already told you that Maro had a chance to kill me. He didn't then and he won't now."

"There are thousands of people on the *Michelangelo*. I have no idea how their 'Senate' works but I'm sure Maro isn't the only decider. Hell, you might get taken out by a security algorithm."

Jana stared Regis down, jaw tensed. "I'm not scared."

"I'm not saying you are. But it's still a stupid move. You don't want to throw your life away for no good reason."

Katja made a growl-like sound, but Jana touched her knee reassuringly. "It's not as stupid as starting a war over two people, or an old ship."

Mèng laughed, surprising everyone, but the mood of the room lifted.

"It could work," Elanor said. "Just because the *Michelangelo* isn't responding to our hails doesn't mean they're not listening. We could broadcast the fact that Jana is alone on the shuttle, even sharing the craft's internal feeds. Their own scans would verify the truth of our claim."

"If Jana goes, I go," Katja said.

"Why?" Tem asked. "You going along wouldn't make Jana any safer."

"To sweeten the pot. I was once a Crucible host – Maro might be interested in me as well."

Jana looked torn, but Katja smiled blithely. "Don't worry, my love. The Three Brothers have kept me alive this long. There must be a reason."

The *Liu Hui* delegates looked confused at this reference, but Tem wasn't in the mood to explain the complexities of Happdal mythology. "Katja—" he started, but then stopped mid-sentence, realizing the futility of trying to dissuade his aunt once she had made up her mind.

"Yes, Tem?"

"Maybe Jana would be safer if you were with her," he conceded.

The meeting continued for another twenty minutes. The others discussed timing, logistics, and contingency plans. Tem did his best to pay attention but his mind was elsewhere. What if he hadn't stopped Katja from attacking Manning? What would have happened? Perhaps his aunt's instincts had been right.

At the very least, Tem needed to confront the man who had participated in the murder plot against his mother. And if Manning showed no contrition, Tem would show him how the son of Esper Ariksson dealt with those who tried to harm his family.

CHAPTER THIRTY

"Do you have plans?" Mèng asked immediately after the meeting had adjourned.

"No," Tem said. Mèng probably knew how to find Manning, but he didn't want to involve her. There had to be another way to track him down.

"I'd like to invite the three of you to tour the Zhangjiajie Air Park," Mèng said, addressing Tem, Jana, and Katja. "Regis, you're also welcome to join us, but I'm sure you've visited the Inner Hub before."

"I have," Regis said. "I think I'll get some rest now, but I highly recommend it."

"You can fly like birds," Mèng said. "It is truly amazing."

Tem had heard of Zhangjiajie, a massive circular park that occupied an entire mid-spoke ring of the *Liu Hui*. Gravity in the park was about .3G, enabling visitors to don artificial wings and fly like birds, weaving through towering rock spires. The park was named after a real historical park in the Hunan province of China.

"No thank you," said Jana. "I've had enough floating and flying for a long time. Katja – you and Tem should go."

"I'd love to tour the Air Park," Tem said. He'd almost had a chance to visit Zhangjiajie as a child, but the Squid Woman had hijacked the shuttle transporting his school field trip to the *Liu Hui*. Just one of many pieces of his childhood she had stolen from him.

"It's settled then. I'll reserve your wings on the way."

It was only a short distance to the nearest spoke. The upward acceleration of the elevator balanced out the decreasing centripetal force as they rose, but when they arrived at the Inner Hub, Tem suddenly felt lighter. Katja laughed as she took a giant step across the elevator platform. She stumbled, neatly somersaulted, and recovered, finishing with a bow. "This is already fun! I can't wait for my wings."

Mèng escorted them to the park entrance, and the moment they passed through the ornate gates, Tem was struck with vertigo. Suddenly they were under a blue sky dotted with cumulus clouds.

"It's a projection," Mèng explained. "Convincing, isn't it?"

"What happens if you fly too close to the hub ceiling?"

"Air currents will force you back down. The park is filled with artificial winds and eddies. Some are for safety purposes, others are to make flight more exciting. Sections of the park are reserved for only the most experienced fliers, and even then there are some injuries."

"Even at low G?"

"Remember that terminal velocity is dependent on aerodynamics. With your wings in a dive position, you can easily fly or fall fast enough to injure yourself."

A couple of friendly teenage tour guides led Katja and Tem through a safety orientation and training session. The prosthetic arm-attached wings were intuitive to use, and Tem felt ready to soar after only a few minutes of practice in a wind tunnel. A com link embedded in his helmet would allow constant communication with Katja as well as Mèng, who would fly near them the whole time.

"Ready?" Mèng asked. They stood in a row at the edge of a jagged cliff towering at least thirty meters above a lush green valley.

"As I'll ever be," Tem replied. He ran the short distance to the edge, leapt, and spread his wings. Jumping into emptiness was very different from his brief training in the confined wind tunnel, and his stomach lurched as he plunged toward the dense vegetation below. But his wings caught the air. He was flying! This section of the park – a beginner course – featured a gentle headwind, and thus they glided slowly, side by side.

"What do you think?" Mèng asked.

"Incredible!" Katja shouted over the com.

"It really is," Tem said. He felt light and unburdened, mentally as well as physically. Until that moment he hadn't realized how many worries he had been carrying: Bosa's abducted villagers, his relationship with Maggie, the possibility of Saga being pregnant with his child. Those thoughts were still there, but that's all they were – *thoughts*. Ultimately he was powerless to influence anything beyond his decisions in the moment, right here and right now. All he had to do was stretch his wings and fly.

His epiphany gave him a new perspective on Manning as well. His reaction earlier had been childish, an impulse toward violence as a solution, a remnant of his upbringing in Happdal. As a child he had witnessed his own father slit Völund's throat. Esper had not even given the smith a chance to explain himself before murdering him. And that's what it had been – a murder. Esper had cut down Saga's uncle and only kin without a hearing or trial. It had been Svein who'd kidnapped him, not Völund. The smith had held him against his will, but had also taught him. Tem had forged his first weapon – a crude, unwieldy dagger – in Völund's smithy.

At the time he had been confused by his own ambivalence. His father had rescued him, after all. And he loved his father. But he'd always felt that Völund had died unfairly.

He was his own man now. He was capable of violence (who wasn't?) but he needn't be as brutal as his Happdal kin. His mother could have killed Adrian after discovering her advisor had tried to murder her, but ultimately she'd shown restraint. He would follow in her path, not his father's.

But that didn't mean he was ready to forgive Manning, who had never been charged or prosecuted for his role in the attempt on Car-En's life. That wasn't right.

"Would you really have attacked Manning, if I hadn't stopped you?" he asked Katja over the com link.

"Of course. Just a good slap to make him show respect. I wouldn't have truly injured him. I realize we're guests here."

"It's good you didn't," Mèng said. "Manning has friends in high places."

"And how did that come about?" Tem asked. "Obviously not because of his natural charm."

Mèng laughed. "No. But he is a skilled designer and inventor, especially when it comes to body modifications and prosthetics. He was part of the team that designed these wings."

"Really?" The headwinds gone, they were now shooting through a narrow gorge, only ten meters above a raging whitewater river. Tem knew it was an illusion, but he felt that he was outside in nature, part of the sky itself. Not in an orbiting space station. The wings were a part of his body, easy to control with the merest twitches of his shoulders, arms, and wrists.

"Rumor has it that he's done personal contract work for government officials. Some of that work may be of a sensitive nature…."

"Sexual prosthetics?"

"And other modifications. That might explain his outsized influence."

"But why would he want to serve on the Ringstation Coalition committee? He didn't even seem interested in the meeting."

"I don't know," Mèng said.

Tem sensed that perhaps she *did* know, but didn't want to say over the open com link.

"Up ahead, stay aloft, well above the canopy. There's an advanced course that weaves through the trees, but it's too dangerous for beginners."

Tem flinched, wishing that Mèng had not mentioned the hidden course. Sure enough, Katja dove like a swallow toward the forest of towering gerutu trees.

"What's she doing?" Mèng asked.

"I'm sure you didn't mean to, but you just issued her a challenge."

Mèng grunted – the closest thing to an expression of anger Tem had heard out of her – and folded her wings, diving after Katja. "Stay above the trees," she ordered Tem.

Tem's impulse was to follow, but what good would it do? If he ventured into the forest, he was even more likely to collide with a tree than Katja, who possessed a preternatural ability to master kinesthetic tasks.

The gerutu rainforest formed a thin canopy, and he could see Katja weaving among the trunks, ahead and below. In his headset he could hear Mèng shouting at Katja to slow down, but his aunt just laughed, continuing her joyous speed run.

He spread his wings wide to slow down and soar. His left wing felt sticky, resisting his guidance. He forced his arm straight and the prosthetic responded, though he veered slightly left. But then the wing collapsed, folding in on itself and painfully wrenching his shoulder. He spiraled down toward the trees, his rotation accelerating, the pain from his left shoulder numbing his entire arm. He yelled uselessly into his headset.

He tumbled through the trees like a wet rag doll. A rib cracked with one impact. A branch thwacked the side of his helmet, silencing the voices of Mèng and his aunt. One wing caught, momentarily slowing his fall until the prosthetic ripped off entirely.

The ground rushed up and slammed into him. He lay still, conscious but in shock, as he tried to assess if his back was broken.

For the moment he felt no pain, only a dreadful anticipation of the suffering that would soon begin.

CHAPTER THIRTY-ONE

"There isn't enough time," Sperancia warned. The entire consorteria walked along a beach at dusk, the rising tide lapping at their bare feet and ankles. Sperancia and Jana led the way, followed by Agatha and Giuseppina. Itria followed a dozen paces behind, stopping frequently to examine seashells or shiny stones.

"Look at what she has already created," Jana pointed out, looking back at Itria. "Fantastical creatures, the town of Bosa reimagined, and who knows what else."

"But she had decades to do that, not days!"

"Decades to learn her craft," said Agatha. "She is more efficient than ever now. Remember how long it took her to create the tatzelwurm? But the flying fairies — we saw those only a week after she had conceived of them."

Giuseppina grunted skeptically. "This is of an entirely different scale. An ill-conceived plan if I ever heard one."

"You're not helping," Agatha said. "We're already on the shuttle heading toward the *Michelangelo*. We've committed."

"Well, I'm glad I've lived a good life," Giuseppina said. "And then some. Maybe more than I ever deserved. Let my last words be: *It wasn't my idea*."

"Enough!" Jana shouted. "None of you are helping. Please — go ask Itria if she needs anything. We're all counting on her."

Jana returned her focus to the shuttle's life-support pod. The cockpit was empty, as was the rest of the ship. Technicians on the *Liu Hui* were handling navigation, for now. Once they were within range of the *Michelangelo*, there was no way of knowing what would happen.

Katja had stayed behind with Tem. Fortunately his injuries had been limited to two broken ribs, a dislocated shoulder, a sprained ankle, some minor contusions, and a concussion. After a few nights in a medical facility, he was now resting in his *Liu Hui* quarters. Katja was at his bedside nursing him back to health, just as she had stayed by Jana's side when she was recovering from the transfer of the Crucible.

Katja felt responsible for the accident, even though it hadn't directly been her fault. Nothing Katja had done had caused Tem's mechanical wings to fail. But had Katja paid attention to Mèng and stayed above the canopy, maybe the two of them could have saved Tem, breaking his fall. Katja, racked with guilt, had apologized profusely to Jana, but there was no way she could accompany her to the *Michelangelo*. Katja had to care for her nephew until he was well.

Perhaps it was better this way. Alone, Jana felt calm and focussed. Her relationship with Katja filled her with giddy excitement. And when they were intimate, as pleasurable as it was, Jana was excruciatingly aware of her body in a way that she still hadn't adjusted to. Despite Katja's complete acceptance and apparent physical desire for her, it hadn't helped the feeling that somehow Jana was stuck in the wrong form.

It was something that almost everyone took for granted. Such a basic thing, to feel comfortable in your own skin. And though Jana considered herself a fortunate person, that particular sensation eluded her.

"Are you well?" Ingrid asked over the com. Ingrid, still aboard the *Stanford*, was providing moral support and companionship during the voyage. "Feeling comfortable?"

Jana almost laughed at the unintended irony of Ingrid's question. "I'm fine."

"We still haven't received a response from the *Michelangelo*. The *Liu Hui* is broadcasting in a dozen languages that you're alone in the transport shuttle, which possesses no weapons whatsoever."

The shuttle was traveling at a slow speed toward the *Michelangelo*, which still hovered above Lake Victoria in geosynchronous orbit. Jana closed her eyes and focussed on her breathing. She could hear the voices of her consorteria trying to engage with her, but Itria's voice was not among them, so she shut them out. She would consult the other women when they had more information, more to work with, but for now they were taking the path they had chosen.

Ingrid's voice interrupted her meditation. "Do you want to see your approach on the view screen? The *Michelangelo* should be in sight of the shuttle cameras by now."

Jana said that she did, and the view screen filled with a black starry sky. "I don't see it."

"Look for the large blue star in the center of the screen. It will get bigger over time."

Jana watched with growing amazement as the blue star became a short blue line and soon after a rotating glowing blue cylinder. She had seen the *Michelangelo* before in Sperancia's telescope, but that image had been fuzzy, distorted by the crude lens, the Earth's atmosphere, and the transmitted vibrations of their footsteps across Sperancia's rooftop. The image from the shuttle's camera was crisp and clear. As the shuttle drew closer, Jana saw more colors than just blue. There were points of light in every color, brilliant against the matte black hull, a curved cliff drifting through space. Soon all the stars were eclipsed by the behemoth; the ship filled the entire view screen.

"Ingrid, are you still there?"

Ingrid did not respond, nor did anyone from the *Liu Hui*.

"Halt your approach and state your business," said a brusque female voice over the com, in English.

"I'm not in control of the ship. My name is Jana Manca. I am here to visit a man by the name of Maro. He invited me. I am from the town of Bosa on the island of Sardinia."

Silence. Had they heard her?

"Halt your ship or we will deploy deadly force."

"I can't!" Jana yelled, panicking. The plan would be for naught if her corpse was floating through space, or burned up like a blade of dry grass tossed into a raging fire. But she felt the shuttle lurch to a halt. Apparently someone on the *Liu Hui* could hear the commands as well.

"I demand to speak to Maro!" If they were going to kill her, she would not die meekly.

This time the silence was longer, but the ship did not explode or incinerate. Finally she heard a different voice, silky and familiar. "This is Maro Decimus. To whom am I speaking?" He already knew; not only had she announced herself, he was speaking in Italian.

"Jana Manca, from Bosa."

"Ah…the woman who tried to murder us, and then imprisoned us for defending ourselves. What brings you to the *Michelangelo*?"

Jana sensed that his casual tone was a bluff, that he was deeply interested in her presence. He'd seen the transfer of the Crucible with his own eyes and had expressed his fascination. But she couldn't be sure. Maybe he would kill her with no more thought than slapping a mosquito.

"I have considered your invitation – the one that you extended to all of us. I would like to participate in your project."

A beat. "What made you change your mind?"

"I had time to think about it. I was wrong to believe that you were a threat. That was Sperancia's influence."

"Sperancia…the old woman who murdered Felix."

"It was her plan to attack you at your campsite, to burn your balloon and then stab you all to death."

"So vicious…."

"She thought that you wanted to enslave us."

"And now you would like me to forgive you? You would like me to allow you aboard the *Michelangelo*, allow you to participate in Ancestral Realism?"

"Yes," Jana said simply, swallowing her pride. Again, she was glad Katja was not with her, complicating her emotions. This was between her and Maro.

"I will consider your request and consult with my colleagues."

An hour passed. Jana unbuckled herself and floated around the cabin, first stretching and then slowly propelling herself from wall to wall with gentle pushes. She felt only a little spacesick; her body was getting used to weightlessness.

The brusque woman's voice again: "You are granted permission to board. A tug will escort you to the docking bay. Do not move from your current co-ordinates."

Minutes later the shuttle shook as something grabbed on to it. Jana buckled up again but there was no need; the remainder of the ride was slow and smooth. After what felt like an eternity, the shuttle stopped again, this time settling down onto a solid surface. She felt a hint of gravity.

"You may open your service doors now."

Jana had no idea how to do that. She made her way to the cockpit – there was just enough gravity to walk. "Shuttle, open service doors." A hissing sound and slight decrease in air pressure indicated success.

The shuttle was parked in a vast marble-floored room. A trio was there to greet her: two men and one woman, all wearing white tunics and sandals. Strange attire for inhabitants of a giant space station.

* * *

Livia poured wine into her cup while Maro watched. They sat on the floor, on a soft fleece rug, supported by pillows. Maro's house was lavishly decorated: ornately painted walls, gilded furnishings, sparkling fountains.

"How are Filumena and Cristo?" Jana asked. She'd done her best to go along with Maro and Livia's small talk, answering their questions about Bosa and how the many people they had met there were faring: her father, Leandro; Gregoriu, the mayor; Micheli, the barkeep. They even asked about Filumena's young cousins, Ralf and Bina. But they had yet to mention the 'volunteers' themselves.

"They are enjoying the pinnacle experience of their lives," Maro replied. "Both are experiencing a shared simulated world, a chapter of history of the Roman Empire. But a fluid chapter that they co-create. Their decisions impact their reality."

"I would like to see them. Today."

Livia raised an eyebrow, but Maro smiled and nodded. "Of course, I understand. Today is not possible, but they are only a few days away from completing this phase of the experiment. It could be psychologically damaging to extract them at this point. Surely you can wait a few days to see your friends? You will be our guest. I promise we will keep you entertained and well-fed."

Jana noticed a pale, red-haired woman standing under one of the arched entrances, regarding her curiously.

Maro shot the woman an irritated glance. "What is it, Aina?"

"I have done what you asked. The wine is decanting."

"That will be all, Aina," Maro said.

"Who are you?" asked the red-haired woman, staring at Jana with disconcerting intensity.

"My name is Jana. I'm from Sardinia – a large island in the Mediterranean Sea."

Aina smiled, an expression that accentuated her attractiveness and increased Jana's heart rate. "Home of the Nuragic culture, a Bronze Age civilization known for their holy wells and large stone sculptures."

"Aina, leave us," Maro snapped. "This is a private discussion."

"Yes, Maro."

"Your servant?" Jana asked once Aina had left the room.

"She appears human, doesn't she? But she is a machine, with no more self-awareness than a fish."

"But she understood me. The way she smiled at me...."

"Convincing, isn't it? It's a masterful illusion – our Engineers are truly brilliant. You are welcome to get to know her better, if you like. Enjoy her in whatever way you wish. She's quite pliant."

"You make assumptions, Maro," Livia said.

Maro smiled in a way that made Jana uncomfortable. "Are my assumptions incorrect?"

"I would like to see the *Michelangelo*," said Jana, changing the subject. "All of it. Your schools and museums, your farms and factories, your parks and restaurants. Where your people work, learn, and play. Everything."

"That would take months. But you are welcome to take in as much as you can handle. It will be a good way for you to pass the time while waiting for Filumena and Cristo. Aina can be your guide if you are amenable."

"And your Curia – your Senate Hall – you spoke of it in Bosa. I would like to see that place as well."

"That can be arranged. There is space on the mezzanine for citizen-guests."

Maro looked pointedly at Livia, who rose and excused herself, leaving Maro and Jana alone.

"Now, I must ask," Maro said, leaning forward. "How is the old woman?"

"You mean Sperancia? You know very well that she is dead."

"Of course. But how is she enjoying her afterlife? You see, I have read about the Crucible. I know how it works. And in your case, perhaps miraculously, it is working as intended. Isn't it? All the previous hosts living harmoniously in a virtual world, there to offer advice and guidance to the current host."

Jana nodded – there was no point in carrying on a charade of ignorance. "Mostly harmonious. And to answer your question, Sperancia is well."

"Can she hear us right now?"

"Yes, as can the others."

"How many? What are their names?"

"Four, not including myself. Sperancia, Giuseppina, Agatha, and Itria."

"Only four? The Crucible is over five hundred years old."

"The black egg bestows long life. Sperancia was the oldest person in Bosa, by far."

"And great physical strength as well?"

"After many years, yes."

There was a hunger in Maro's eyes that both scared and encouraged Jana. She needed that hunger for her plan to work, but Maro's interest in the Crucible could just as easily kill her.

"Explain it to me," said Maro. "Tell me everything about your experience of the Crucible. Tell me exactly how it works and how it affects you. Leave nothing out."

Jana did exactly as Maro had asked. It was part of the plan.

CHAPTER THIRTY-TWO

Aina showed Jana her quarters, a *domus* in the same style as Maro's, but smaller, in a neighborhood whose layout reminded her a little of Bosa: houses close together with narrow, stone-paved roads running through. Looking up she saw wispy clouds, and beyond the clouds a neighborhood similar to her own, far away and upside-down. The *Michelangelo* was a world on the inside of a vast rotating cylinder. The view gave her the sensation of falling.

"You may change into these clothes if you like," Aina said, handing Jana a cream-colored tunic of soft material. "If you wear your own clothes you may get unwelcome looks from citizens."

"Why is Maro so rude to you?" Jana asked, accepting the clothing. It was just the two of them. Maro had work to attend to and had placed Jana in Aina's care.

A brief look of consternation crossed Aina's face, but her expression quickly reverted to her normal cheerfulness. "I am his assistant. Maro is not required to be polite to me."

"Of course he is. Everyone should be polite to each other. It's disrespectful otherwise, unless you are a small child who doesn't know better."

Aina looked thoughtful. "Maro is like a child in some ways. I will look away while you change."

On foot, Aina led Jana out of the residential neighborhood and into a shallow valley of parks and gardens punctuated by white stone buildings, some decorated with brightly painted frescoes. Aina cheerfully pointed out various bathhouses, academies, temples, and other noteworthy structures. Jana took in as much as she could, even forcing herself to occasionally look up, but she was more interested in Aina herself.

"Maro said that you are a machine. How can that be possible?"

Aina shrugged. "I'm a cybrid – a combination of biological tissue, robotic parts, and a quantum neural network. I don't feel like a machine.

I feel like a person, and that's what I consider myself. But none of us can compare how we feel inside, can we?"

"No."

"Inside, I am different. But here –" Aina grabbed Jana's hand and placed it on her forearm, "– feel my skin."

Aina's skin was warm and soft.

"I have nerves similar to yours."

"Do you feel pleasure?"

Aina grinned. "Most definitely."

They passed dozens of people. Most wore simple tunics, but others were dressed outlandishly and elaborately while others were nearly naked. Many were olive-skinned and had features similar to Maro and Livia, but there were people of every skin tone and build. Nearly everyone was physically attractive. Where were the old people? Where were the people with unusual, awkward faces, like Jana herself? People stared at her with open curiosity, but without a trace of contempt or malevolence.

Aina led Jana down a long flight of stairs. The underground level was more utilitarian and did not resemble ancient Rome. They entered a tubelike vehicle that accelerated rapidly in a way that reminded Jana of the shuttle flight, though she did not become weightless.

"Where are we?" Jana asked.

"In one of fourteen subterranean levels. Most of the farms and manufactories are housed out of sight. And many of the plebeians live on the lower levels."

"Plebeians?"

"Common citizens. Those who are not Artists, Engineers, or Defenders."

"Are you a plebeian? Am I?"

Aina furrowed her brow. "I am not even a citizen. Nor are you."

"Why not? Because you're a cybrid?"

"Yes. Though that appears to be up for debate in the Senate. But Maro opposes the petition, and he is likely to become emperor."

"Emperor? I didn't know the *Michelangelo* had an emperor."

"It doesn't, yet."

Aina, looking genuinely distressed, offered nothing more. Jana needed to understand the political landscape, but she didn't want to further upset her guide. She was beginning to like Aina.

They exited the tubelike vehicle directly into the lobby of a high-ceilinged building filled with paintings and sculptures. "This is the Museum of Italian Masters, primarily works from the Renaissance period," Aina explained. "Maro thought this would be a good place to start. His favorite artist from this period is Caravaggio, a painter known for his dramatic use of shadow and contrast. And also for his subjects – common folk, including beggars, urchins, and prostitutes – which drew controversy during his time."

"How did the Caravaggio paintings end up here?" Jana asked. She already knew – Sperancia had explained how the *Michelangelo* founders had performed the greatest art heist in history – but she was curious how Aina would answer.

"They were rescued from the world's greatest museums and galleries, many in Rome…." Aina trailed off, appearing to reflect on her own words. "Though Cassia says they were stolen, not rescued."

"Who is Cassia?"

Aina widened her eyes as if caught in a misdeed, and tightened her mouth so hard that her lips turned white.

"It's okay – you don't have to answer. Tell me more about Caravaggio."

Aina was a capable and generous guide, and Jana took in as much as she could. She felt Itria's hungry eyes behind her own, pushing her to see and experience more. She did her best but after several hours Aina noticed her fatigue.

"Let's take a break," Aina suggested. "We'll eat at the café and drink espresso. Have you had coffee before?"

Jana hadn't, and when she tried it, she didn't like the bitter taste. But it was important to say *yes* to every potential experience, for Itria's sake. And soon after, revitalized and unreasonably happy, she began to understand why coffee was a popular beverage.

"Can you take me to see Filumena and Cristo? Is there a way to see them without interrupting the experiment?"

Aina shook her head. "They're in isolation tanks, unconscious."

"But they're well? Healthy and unharmed?"

"That's what Maro says."

"Can you show me the tanks at least? It would be reassuring to know where they are."

Aina nodded slowly. "Yes. I think I can do that."

Jana reached across the café table and squeezed Aina's hand. "It would mean a great deal to me."

They returned to the surface in a different neighborhood. After a short walk Aina pointed to a pair of two-story *domus* joined by a semi-enclosed walkway overlooking an ornamental fountain and well-manicured gardens. "Here we are. These are the homes Maro provided to Cristo and Filumena."

"They're here?"

"Follow me."

Jana wasn't sure why Aina wouldn't answer her directly, but she trusted the cybrid, who struck her as kind-hearted and entirely bereft of guile.

The house was spacious, luxuriously decorated, and empty. Jana followed a few steps behind Aina, peering into every room they passed. She had no idea what an 'isolation tank' might look like, but she saw no sign of her friends.

"This way," Aina said, opening a door. Jana peered down a steep stone staircase into darkness. Aina smiled. "Go ahead – I'll be right behind you."

It was too obvious to be a trap, Jana thought. And Aina seemed incapable of deception. So Jana was genuinely surprised when the door closed behind her with the unmistakable click of a lock, enveloping her in darkness.

"I'm sorry," Aina said, her voice muffled.

"Why are you doing this?" Jana asked. "Why keep me prisoner?"

Aina didn't answer, but Jana heard a low, melodious voice from below. "Come down the stairs. Be careful – there's a railing to your left."

Groping in the dark, Jana found the railing. Her eyes adjusted; there was a faint light from below. She descended the stairs into some sort of cellar. The room smelled of wine and body odor, a combination that reminded her of Micheli's bar and gave her some small comfort.

"Who are you?" Jana asked.

An immense woman sat behind a makeshift desk of empty wine shelves. The woman's face was in shadow – like a Caravaggio painting – but even in the dim light Jana could see the gleam of her bright green hair.

"Senator Cassia. And you are Jana Manca, from the town of Bosa. You are here to rescue your friends who were kidnapped by Maro Decimus."

"Yes."

"Do you have a plan? I'm extremely curious."

"I don't know if it will work. But yes, I do."

"Well, have a seat," Cassia said, gesturing to an empty wine crate. "I'm all ears."

CHAPTER THIRTY-THREE

Tem's entire body ached. The *Liu Hui* medics had offered him a plethora of painkillers, but the single pill he had tried had left him nauseous for hours. He groaned as he sat up in bed.

"The pain is good," Katja said from the kitchen, where she was preparing or possibly burning lunch. "It reminds you that you're injured, and to rest. Without pain you would end up like Lars, badly scarred and missing limbs."

Tem laughed, remembering Lars on his back, cursing the 'hell swine' Fyrirgef. But the laughter triggered stabbing rib pain, and he groaned again.

Katja poked her head into his bedroom. "What's so funny?"

"Lars and the boar. You've heard the story, haven't you? Egil should write an epic poem about it."

Katja frowned. "You could have easily died that day, from what I heard."

"I know. You're right, I shouldn't laugh. But the sight of Lars thrashing on his back with his wooden leg in the boar's mouth – you should have seen it."

"Is it true you are banished from Kaldbrek?"

"No, I can go to Kaldbrek whenever I please. I just have to fight Svein to the death if I do. Honestly, I'm tempted."

"He tried to injure you during the hunt. Grundar told me, and Baldr confirmed it."

Tem nodded. "He tripped me with his spear when the boar charged."

"A cowardly move."

"Svein has always been a coward. He's a skilled warrior, yet he hides behind larger men."

"So what will you do about it?"

Tem scowled. What *could* he do about it? Saga was already angry with him. It wouldn't help matters to march into Kaldbrek looking for trouble.

And yet if Saga was the mother of his child, he had to see her. "I don't know yet. I wish people like Svein didn't exist."

"And yet they're everywhere, aren't they?"

"It seems that way."

Tem had shared his suspicions with his aunt that the malfunction of his prosthetic wings hadn't been an accident. The Zhangjiajie park rangers were still investigating the cause of failure and weren't yet disclosing any details, but Tem had learned on his own that his accident was unprecedented. While many park visitors had injured themselves flying into cliffs or attempting stupid stunts, none before Tem had experienced a catastrophic equipment failure.

Katja helped him up. He managed to use the bathroom on his own but had to immediately return to bed, wincing in pain from his ankle.

"Do you think he was trying to kill me, if it was sabotage?" he yelled to his aunt. Katja had returned to the kitchen to attend to the smoke alarm.

"Who knows?" Katja yelled back. "Why don't you ask?"

★　★　★

Tem recovered quickly. A week later he could walk with only a slight limp and take a deep breath with only a small amount of pain. His shoulder wasn't quite right, but his abrasions had scabbed over and his bruises had faded from blue-black to an ugly mash of purple and yellow. If he wore long sleeves, he looked almost normal, save a long scratch across his left cheek.

"It won't be long now." Manning's robotic assistant took the form of a bright yellow cartoonish squirrel, about forty centimeters tall, with a squeaky voice. It had taken Tem four days to get the appointment with Manning. He'd used every bit of diplomatic leverage at his disposal as a Repop Council representative.

"No problem," Tem said. "I don't mind waiting."

Eventually the yellow squirrel led Tem into a spacious office. Manning sat behind a glass desk, eyeing a bank of screens. "How can I help you, Tem Ganzorig?" he asked, without making eye contact.

Tem took a seat despite the fact that he hadn't been offered one. He nodded at the squirrel, who bowed low and scurried out of the room. "I got your message, but it was a bit garbled."

Manning looked up. "What?"

"I wasn't clear on the specifics. Would you mind reiterating?"

"I'm sorry, I don't know what you're talking about."

"I'm a simple man, so please use plain language. Just say whatever you want to say. I'm right here in front of you. No need to mince words."

"Is this some sort of a prank? I don't have time—"

"Or maybe I'm wrong. Maybe the message was meant for my aunt? Did she ruffle your feathers at the Coalition meeting? Did you want to get back at her for threatening you, except that the person you paid off mixed things up? That would be an understandable mistake."

"Ah, I see. You think I have something to do with your accident. I did hear about it, and I'm sorry that happened to you. But I can assure you—"

"Accident? What accident?"

"At the air park…."

"You misunderstand. I was talking about the message you sent me. There was no accident last week at Zhangjiajie, nor was there an accident thirty years ago with my mother's bioskin."

Manning stared at Tem in a calculating way. Trying to decide if he should call security, Tem guessed. But there was no need for that.

"I'm not sure what you want me to say. I don't know what you're talking about, and I don't know why you're here."

"Then I'll speak for both of us. You weren't trying to send me a message, were you? You were just trying to kill me, the same way you tried to kill my mother."

"That's an incredibly serious allegation. If you were to accuse me publicly, I would immediately sue you for slander."

"I'm not going to accuse you publicly. Just to your face."

Manning fidgeted. Through the glass desk, Tem could clearly see his clenched fists.

Tem leaned forward, enjoying Manning's discomfort. "As attempts on my life go, yours was a weak one, not even the best this month."

Manning stood and stepped back from his desk. "You need to leave."

"You saw the way I looked at you during our meeting, didn't you? And that scared you, knowing that I knew you'd tried to kill my mother. That's not the kind of thing a son forgets and forgives. And your instincts were right. I'm not done with you."

Tem heard footsteps and voices outside of Manning's office. So he'd summoned security already, probably via his m'eye. Tem stood and opened the door. Two men in police uniforms stood at the ready, hands on the holstered weapons.

"I told them they needed an appointment," squeaked Manning's yellow rodent.

"It's all right, I was just leaving."

The police had a few questions for both Manning and Tem before he was allowed to leave, but Manning's lies about a 'heated argument' were enough to convince them. Manning just wanted Tem out of his office and had no basis to accuse him of a crime.

On the way back to his quarters, Tem basked in a sense of satisfaction. Maybe it hadn't been wise to confront Manning, but it had felt good to see the fear in his eyes. Even if Tem's harebrained scheme to take Manning down failed – which it probably would – at least he'd made him sweat. And now he felt sure that Manning really had tried to kill him.

His father might have plunged a knife into Manning's throat at first sight, with the same casual efficiency of slaughtering a pig for a roast. But Tem was not his father.

He would get back at Manning without throwing his own future away.

CHAPTER THIRTY-FOUR

"Any news from Jana?" Tem asked.

Mèng had invited Tem, Katja, and Regis Foster to her apartment, a top-floor suite overlooking a vast botanical garden. The Ringstation Coalition follow-up meeting was scheduled for the next day.

"Nothing yet," said Regis. "We lost com about halfway through her flight. But her shuttle made the journey intact and docked within the *Michelangelo*."

"And they're still pretending we don't exist, ignoring all hails?"

"Yes. Though *Liu Hui* intelligence did intercept an encrypted signal a few days ago."

"What does that mean?" Katja asked.

"It means we can't know what the message says without a special key. But it implies that someone on the *Liu Hui* possesses that key."

Katja nodded. "So you have a spy. Or many spies."

"It appears that way," said Mèng.

"Any suspects?" Tem asked.

"Your guess is as good as mine," Regis said. "Though how they would have planted a spy on the *Liu Hui* with no previous contact is beyond me. They've been in the outer solar system for decades."

"Speaking of the outer solar system, what about the *Iarudi*? Anything from *Liu Hui* intelligence?"

"Yes, in fact. A Falcon cruiser from the *Michelangelo* is escorting the *Iarudi* back to the inner solar system at conventional speeds. Which means they've boarded the starship, and that it is at least partially functional. They've passed Jupiter and are approaching the Mars orbital ring."

"What about Shane?"

"No news there. He's either dead or a prisoner."

Tem sighed. He'd held on to a thread of hope that his friend Shane was alive, but that was wishful thinking. Still, he was proud of what Shane had done, programming the *Iarudi* to take a scientific survey of nearby stars before he'd entered stasis. Researchers on all the ringstations were analyzing the star system and planetary data collected by the *Iarudi*. Shane's description of the data – a treasure trove – was accurate, and could very well set the stage for humanity's expansion into nearby star systems.

"I do have some good news for you, Tem," Mèng said. She rose, retrieved a pale green envelope from her desk, and handed it to him. "The names you asked for, as well as a few recommendations for artists who might want to take on the project."

"Thank you."

"Be careful how you approach this – it could backfire."

"I know, and I will be."

"And please make sure it can't be traced back to me."

"What's this?" Regis asked.

"Probably a terrible idea," Tem said. "But one I can't talk about for now. If it works, I'll tell you everything. If not, I'll tell you everything the next time I see you in Ilium, if I'm still alive."

Regis laughed. "Well, good luck."

They talked for a while longer, discussing how the interests of the *Stanford* and Ilium could be advanced at the next Ringstation Coalition meeting, and how the *Liu Hui* might react if Jana's plan was unsuccessful. The *Iarudi* was too valuable a prize to leave in the hands of a potential enemy. If diplomatic solutions failed, the Jūnshì security force might take action, perhaps intercepting the *Iarudi* before it reached the *Michelangelo*.

"You need to make peace with them," Katja stated. "War is too costly, even when fought with spears, blades, and arrows. With your weapons the price is so much higher."

"You're right, of course," said Regis, "but how are we supposed to negotiate with them if they won't even acknowledge us?"

"There must be reasonable people on the *Michelangelo*," Mèng pointed out. "They can't all be crazy. When we were serving under Umana, we were too scared to speak up."

Regis nodded. "She was terrifying."

"Maro is different than Umana," Katja said. "He doesn't rule by fear. He uses love – or something like love – as a weapon. He makes others feel special and important. And they become addicted to his feigned admiration."

"A charismatic narcissist," said Mèng. "The most dangerous kind of tyrant. No empathy, no sense of service to others. Other people aren't fully real to him."

"So what's his weakness?" Regis asked.

"Vanity," Tem said. "Maro sounds like Adrian, my mother's academic advisor, who ultimately tried to kill her. When she lost her adulation for him and started making her own decisions, he became infuriated that he could no longer control her. That's when he lost it."

"Jana will use that against him," Katja said.

"I hope she succeeds," said Mèng.

"She will," Katja said, not sounding completely confident.

"You could have gone with her," Tem said. "You didn't need to stay behind to care for me."

Katja patted his head – a gesture he would have found infuriating from anyone else. "I know. But I belong here with my brother's son."

Tem and Katja walked back to their shared quarters through the lush botanical gardens. "So what's in the envelope?" Katja asked.

"Revenge, hopefully. But my way, not Father's way."

"Sometimes it's better to forgive people. You can poison yourself with hatred."

His aunt was right. Despite her hotheadedness and impulsive behavior, Katja had gleaned some wisdom over the years. And later, he would try to forgive Manning.

But first, he would ruin him.

CHAPTER THIRTY-FIVE

As Aina rubbed the tension out of his oiled back and shoulders, Maro considered the hands he'd been dealt and how he'd played them. He'd done exceptionally well, considering what had been a string of terribly unlucky events. He'd faced enemies in the Senate, murderers in Bosa, and psychopathic killers in Kaldbrek. And yet each time he'd emerged unscathed and positionally stronger. He'd successfully dispatched Cassia; his election as emperor was all but secured; and Ancestral Realism was proceeding brilliantly.

"A little lower, Aina. That's it. No need to be gentle."

His life was close to perfection and he was immensely enjoying the ride. The only thing that saddened him was the knowledge of his own mortality. Even with rejuvenations and surgeries, his physical body would eventually deteriorate and expire. What a loss that would be, not only personally for the *Michelangelo*. His inevitable death would be a loss for civilization, for humanity!

"Massage my buttocks, Aina. I have some tension around my tailbone."

Except, what if it didn't have to be? Jana had presented him with a tantalizing possibility. What if the Crucible were the key to immortality? The Crucible could extend his corporeal life for another century. And as for his mind – his consciousness – that would be virtualized as a living system, not some static engram. He would be able to hop from body to body, taking hosts as it pleased him. He could live for centuries or even millennia, long enough to witness the expansion of humanity to nearby star systems and eventually the entire galaxy. Perhaps even beyond.

He would be godlike in his powers and perspective.

"On to my legs now, Aina. Give my inner thighs some extra attention – I still have some soreness from all that ridiculous horse riding."

"Ridiculous indeed," Aina said, in a tone that almost sounded mocking. If Maro didn't know better, it might seem as if Aina had recently developed an attitude.

What to do about the *Liu Hui*, the *Stanford*, and the other ringstations? Maro had half a mind to blow them all into oblivion. Such flagrant violence would cost him in the Senate, though once he was emperor he would be able to act with impunity.

But no, there were better ways to handle the 'Coalition', as they called themselves. Already he wielded a great deal of influence on the *Liu Hui*; one of their spies had risen in the ranks and now held a position on their Coalition committee. Maro would expand his intelligence network and control each ringstation from within. It was the wiser, more civilized path. After all, each ringstation had preserved its own unique cultural identity, as well as many works of ancient art that the *Michelangelo*'s founders hadn't been able to procure, despite their Herculean efforts.

There was no need for destruction. Soon enough, he would preside over Earth's historical treasures in their entirety.

★ ★ ★

"Well, is it possible?" Maro asked.

Maro had escorted Jana to a lower-level medical facility. She lay encased in a full-body scanner. Maro and the medic examined her innards from an adjacent viewing chamber.

"It depends on what you mean by possible," the medic replied. "Certainly I can extract the object and repair the surrounding tissues. But what effect the extraction will have on her physiology, I have no idea. The object is at the center of a foreign, invasive network of biologically active exotic material."

"But the object – you can extract it without damaging it?"

"I am confident that I could extract it intact. But once again, I can't predict the results of severing the object from its network. To me it appears to be some sort of parasite. Perhaps it derives nutrition from its host. Can it survive externally? I have no idea. Tell me again what you know about it."

Maro repeated his cursory description of how the Crucible operated, leaving out anything he didn't think the medic needed to know. He referred to the Crucible as 'a probable health enhancement implant', omitting its actual name, history, or any mention of its brain virtualization capabilities. If he revealed too much, someone else could easily look up its origins, just as he had. And others on the *Michelangelo* might also be tempted by the potential of immortality.

"Why do you want to remove it?" the medic asked. "The subject appears well. The exotic material doesn't appear to be negatively impacting her metabolism or cognition. Her indicators are all within range – she's quite healthy."

"The object is potentially a historical artifact, one that should be preserved and protected."

"How did it get in her body in the first place?"

"I am unsure. The subject is an Earth native from the Mediterranean region. Perhaps a closer examination would reveal its origins and maker."

"The Sardinian woman – yes, I heard about her."

"Well, are you willing to perform the procedure?"

"Has the subject given her consent?"

"Yes, but please ask her yourself. Considering that I am a senator…I would like to be sure she was not unduly influenced by my position."

Jana had, in fact, given her consent. The conversation had gone more smoothly than expected. Jana had confessed her discontent with her consorteria, as she called it, the group of previous hosts – all women – who shared a virtual world. It was a limited sim, an approximation of Bosa with a few fantastical elements. But Jana had complained that the women bickered incessantly and ceaselessly harangued her. She was done with the Crucible and wished to be completely rid of it.

"The others won't be happy to see you," Jana had warned. "There has never been a male host, and they like it that way."

He'd reassured her. "Don't worry about me. I'll charm them to death."

"But Sperancia tried to kill you."

"So did you," he'd reminded her. "And yet here we are, breaking bread and drinking wine like old friends."

* * *

The procedure, aided by a precise robotic surgeon, went smoothly. Immediately afterward the medic presented Maro with an opaque medical container.

"It's been rinsed and UV sterilized, but otherwise untouched. Are you sure you don't want me to refrigerate it for now?"

"No, this is fine. Is Jana conscious?"

"Yes. She asked to remain conscious throughout the procedure, and we honored that request. Her voice will be hoarse, and she needs to rest. Pease keep your visit short."

"Of course. I have some sensitive matters to discuss with her. Please deactivate the room feeds."

"That's against protocol."

"I'm afraid you'll have to violate protocol this once. Did you forget who I am?"

"You're invoking senatorial privilege?"

"Yes."

The medic looked irritated but agreed. Maro did not appreciate her insolence, but ultimately she'd proven helpful. He would not punish her.

In Jana's recovery room Maro performed a brief scan with his ocular implant. The feeds had been deactivated as agreed. He was alone with Jana and the Crucible.

"Maro," Jana croaked. "Thank you. You have done me a great service."

He sat and took her hand, which was warm and clammy. But he held it tenderly, despite his sense of revulsion. Jana was pale and looked exhausted, uglier than ever. She could fix that, if she was so inclined. It was trivial to become beautiful on the *Michelangelo*. And yet his eyes were drawn to her face in a way that he could not quite explain.

"Is it in there?" Jana asked, looking at the medical container.

"Yes. Do you want to see it?"

"I don't need to. I've already seen it, just as you have. What will you do with it?"

"I intend to become the next host."

Jana shook her head. "You shouldn't. You don't know what will happen."

"I'm not worried about your consorteria. I am Senator Maro Decimus, soon to be emperor of the *Michelangelo*. Why should I be worried about a few old women?"

"They're powerful. It's their world you'd be entering. You'll be helpless there."

"Maybe at first. But I'll learn, I'll get stronger within the sim, in their version of Bosa. And it will still be *my* body, to do with as I please, in reality. Ultimately I'll be in control. Perhaps you were too yielding, as a host."

"Perhaps."

Her face was full of worry. And maybe there was some truth to her warning. He was well aware of his own reckless streak. But it had served him. He had clawed his way to power in the Senate. He had mingled with Earth natives – barbarians – and lived to tell the tale. And now he would conquer the Crucible. He opened the container, holding it so that Jana could not see within.

"Maro, don't."

It was touching, how Jana cared for him. He put his palm on the black egg. It was warm and smooth, having already reabsorbed the stubs from its severed tendrils. And small, with the potential to replicate life for infinite cycles, like a real egg.

He placed it in his mouth and swallowed it.

CHAPTER THIRTY-SIX

For several days Maro drifted in and out of consciousness. Livia came to visit him, confused as to what had happened. He told her he was fine; he would explain everything in time. She left, nonplussed, to attend to her own affairs. Maro had heard she'd taken another lover. Probably just a distraction, he reasoned. He would deal with the interloper in due course. For now his own recovery, his physiological integration with the Crucible, took priority.

Aina stayed by his side tirelessly, attending to his every need, fetching him water and wine and what little food he had an appetite for.

"You are so faithful, my dear Aina."

"Of course, Maro. I live to serve you."

"And you are content in that role?" He felt a tenderness toward the cybrid, caring for him so diligently as she was. Perhaps he'd been wrong to think of her only as a machine. Even if she was not fully sentient, she was capable of sensation. And she had a spirited personality.

"More than content. I am happy."

He listened for the voices of the consorteria. Jana had told him that would be the first sign that the Crucible was interfacing with his nervous system. But the women were silent. Shy perhaps, or maybe angry that he had taken over Jana's role.

It didn't matter that they refused to speak. There were other signs the integration had begun. He felt the warmth of the core in his throat and chest. His entire body tingled with electric potential.

Livia returned to give him an update on the *Iarudi*. The cybrids from the Falcon had boarded the starship and found it in near-perfect working order, but filled with floating desiccated corpses, all of them laced through with black rootlike tendrils feeding back to a large ovoid mass in the center of the bridge.

"Did the ship stumble across an alien parasite in its travels?" Maro asked.

"The Engineers don't think so. The initial analysis of the tendril material doesn't indicate alien origins, or even that it's a lifeform. There's an artificial cell structure with design elements that match Corporate Age templates and processes...."

"It's an ancient machine?"

"Possibly. The boarding crew discovered a large cybernetic tentacle extending from the ovoid mass which identifies it as the probable remains of Commander Umana. The prevailing hypothesis is that the black tendrils are extending from her body, the growth of some implant gone awry."

An implant gone awry. The words echoed unpleasantly in Maro's mind.

"Any survivors?"

"There are weak signs of life from one of the stasis pods. Probably Shane Jaecks, the last known survivor. That would match the narrative of a transmission intercepted by the Defenders. The cybrid crew is still reviewing the *Iarudi* logs, but it seems the ship has no official record of him. He was either a stowaway or an unregistered prisoner."

"Commander Umana had a psychotic break, didn't she?"

"Yes, but it was Jaecks who programmed the *Iarudi* to take the extended scientific survey of nearby star systems. The ship collected an enormous amount of astronomical and planetary data."

"And this Shane fellow – he's alive?"

Livia shrugged. "Probably brain-dead. The cold stasis pods weren't designed to be used for decades. But technically, yes, he's still alive."

Livia looked as beautiful as ever. She had darkened her skin to a deep bronze and colored her eyes to an emerald green, giving her an otherworldly, preternatural look, a wild sprite in the guise of a human.

"I have great things planned for us," he said.

"You're looking better. You have some color back in your face. I was worried about you the other day. Are you sure you won't let me fetch you a medic?"

"I underwent a procedure, a new implant. I'm feeling quite well."

"Ah, so nothing serious. The Senate vote is tomorrow – you'll be there?"

"Of course I'll be there, my love."

★ ★ ★

He slept long and deep that night, a dreamless sleep. When he awoke and stretched his limbs, he realized his recovery was complete. He felt energetic, with no lingering soreness or discomfort. Aina served him a hearty breakfast of boiled eggs, coarse wheat bread, dates, honey, and olive oil.

"You look so handsome this morning. Would you like to have sex?"

"Perhaps later. I must dress for the Senate. Bring me my finest silks."

After Aina had oiled his skin and hair and adjusted his toga, she held a mirror so that he could admire his own reflection. He was so overcome with his own splendid appearance that he became aroused, and just as quickly his toga was on the floor and he was inside of Aina, pressing her against the wall, biting her shoulder as he thrust into her from behind. She moaned with pleasure, but he didn't care what she felt. Sensual intimacy and reciprocation were things he shared with Livia, but Aina's body was built for ravaging. He could be as rough as he liked without any fear of damaging her (and even as he threw her to the ground and mounted her, the image of the villager's face caved in by her fist rushed into his mind, arousing him further). As he manipulated and used Aina's body for his own pleasure, creatively and with utter depravity, he realized he would be late for the Senate. But that didn't matter. They could wait for Maro. They could wait for Emperor Decimus.

"You're a virile beast," Aina said afterward, grinning widely. "We should do that every day."

"Perhaps we will. Now dress me again. Make me look exactly as before."

★ ★ ★

He rode a Vertragus cybrid to the Curia, shouting at the plebeians to make way even though they were already scurrying off at the first sound of the giant canine's claws on the paving stones. There was something different about the light today; it was brighter, almost Earth-like in its intensity. Or maybe that was another effect of the Crucible integrating with his optic nerve, enhancing his vision.

The consorteria was still silent, but Maro was unworried. The old women were irrelevant. If they didn't engage with him, that was one less problem he had to solve. The main benefit of the Crucible was the potential for extreme longevity and even immortality, and he could practically feel the tendrils lacing through his flesh, strengthening his tissues even as they copied his cellular structure to create a virtual Maro: a faithful, fully integrated copy of his body and brain that would survive for millennia.

"Make way!" he cried out. "Make way for your future emperor!"

*　*　*

All eyes were on Maro as he strode into the Curia. Young Ignatius raised his nose and brushed aside his locks, but there was envy behind his disdain, perhaps even lust. Traian nodded respectfully. Didius, who had seemed lost since Cassia's disappearance, offered him an ingratiating smile that Maro found both gratifying and repulsive. Had he no enemies left? This was going to be too easy. Maro took his seat, spine erect and chin held high.

Praetor Ovidius stood. "We now have a quorum. Since the result will affect the remainder of our proceedings, we shall open with the vote. All those in favor of electing Maro Decimus as emperor…."

It was unanimous. None dared stand against him; his reputation for holding grudges and exacting revenge was well-established. The satisfaction of the moment was marred only by Cassia's absence. He would have loved to witness her rage and defeat as she looked upon Emperor Decimus for the first time.

He wasted no time in furthering his agenda. It was the dawn of a new age for the *Michelangelo*, one that would be historically regarded as expansionist, audaciously creative, a great leap forward for humanity. As he addressed the Senate, laying forth his ambitious plans for building great cities on every continent, for consolidating great works from the other worldships, for exploring and eventually colonizing the star systems recently investigated by the *Iarudi*, he marveled at the resonance of his own voice, at the ease with which he was able to voluminously project his instrument. He had always perceived the quality of his voice to be a minor weakness, one that he'd been unable to address with surgeries and other physiological modifications. But today was different for some reason. Today he was a great speaker.

*　*　*

In the months that followed it was though an invisible hand were guiding the events that surrounded Maro's life, always tipping the scales in his favor. Livia dropped her new lover and returned to his arms, pledging her faithfulness. The investigation into Cassia's disappearance faded away; Maro scarcely heard her name again. The *Stanford*, *Liu Hui*, and other worldships were all grateful to finally be contacted, and were amenable to Maro's suggestions that Earth's great art be consolidated on the *Michelangelo*, with its superior record of guardianship and preservation. Full artwork visitation rights would be granted, of course (subject to Maro's discretion, as were all things).

It occurred to Maro that a normal person's credulity might be strained by such a string of good luck, but he accepted such fortune as his birthright. He had always believed himself worthy, but only now was reality falling in line with his expectations.

Some men were born not only luckier, but destined for great fates. That was the thing about probability; true randomness did not appear random. It often appeared to be outrageous, fixed, and cheaty. But if there were unlucky souls in the universe, there had to be fortunate ones as well, as well as many in the middle of the curve.

Maro was one of the fortunate ones. It was that simple.

Ancestral Realism was a smashing success. The first templates, created from the amalgamated experiences and recorded reactions of Filumena and Cristo, captured the primitive, pre-technological mindset so successfully that thousands flocked to try them out, eager to shed the more sophisticated aspects of their consciousness and to immerse themselves fully in ancient Rome and other historical world sims. Maro's status as an Artist rose to new heights; he was acknowledged both as a great cultural preservationist as well as an innovative mind sculptor.

So many had doubted him, not only his methods but the underlying concept of the project. *There is no such thing as primitive consciousness*, they had insisted. The human mind has not changed as much as we wish to believe it has, over the ages. The hunter-gatherers who had lived directly below them around Lake Victoria a mere hundred thousand years ago had been just as witty, insightful, and curious as worldship denizens, with just as much capacity for kindness or cruelty.

Maro had proven those doubters wrong, and vindication tasted sweet.

Maro was generous toward those who had willingly helped him. He allowed Jana, Filumena, and Cristo to return to Bosa, provided they would help him recruit new volunteers. The three Sardinians were all worn from their respective rigors, tired and hollowed out. But they were whole; they would recover. He filled Cristo's pockets with Imperial gold coins, minted with his own profile. He sent a medic to assist Filumena's mother with her afflictions.

"And what do you want, Jana? You have given me the greatest gift. How can I adequately repay you?"

"Simply with your forgiveness, Maro. I was wrong to fear you. I was wrong to join Sperancia in attacking you. You were never a threat to Bosa, but I did not understand it then."

"You have it, my child. I forgive you completely. You were under the foolish influence of Sperancia and her consorteria."

"Have they spoken to you yet?"

"Not yet. I don't blame them for fearing me, but I have no thoughts of retribution. As long as they gracefully accept my authority…."

It worried him, a little, that he had not been welcomed or even contacted by Sperancia and the others. Was the Crucible working correctly? There was no one he could ask; he'd willingly gone down this road alone.

But the worry did not consume him. Everything else was going splendidly, and he was fully occupied with his duties as emperor.

There was work to be done. The future he imagined would not manifest by desire alone.

★ ★ ★

A year passed. No one challenged his power. His plans proceeded according to schedule. The reign of Emperor Decimus was unfolding in all its expected glory and splendor.

And yet a few things gnawed at him, gremlins in the periphery of his mind that sapped his happiness.

The Crucible had failed, never integrating with his nervous system. Sperancia and the others had not contacted him because they *could* not, he eventually realized. Perhaps the technology conflicted with his other implants. Perhaps his brain was just unusual, exceptional. Eventually he would see a medic, get the damn thing removed. It had been a mistake to ingest it.

But there were always other matters to attend to, and since the Crucible wasn't actually hurting him in any way, he felt no urgency.

The other thing that bothered him was harder to describe. His life had taken on a subtle sense of *confinement*, the source of which he could not pinpoint. He was free in every way he could imagine. He had status, power, every privilege. He was widely respected, admired, and adored. And yet he felt limited. He spent time in his luxurious *domus*, in the Curia, at the baths, in the *Michelangelo*'s many parks and museums.

But when he formed the intention to go somewhere *new*, somewhere he had never visited, his heart was struck with inexplicable fear and dread. Invariably he would retreat from his plans, choosing instead the tried and true. This was not only true of places, but of people as well. Everyone he associated with, he already knew.

He was trapped in a prison of the familiar, and for the life of him he could not explain it.

CHAPTER THIRTY-SEVEN

Filumema squinted as light flooded into the open isolation tank. Her mind was full of worries. Ida was ill and there were many chores to attend to: feeding the chickens, buying food at the market, preparing a meal to be ready for when Corius returned from tending the vineyards.

"Filumena, can you hear me?"

A familiar, pale face looked down at her. An old friend from many years ago.

"Where am I?"

"In an isolation tank, on a worldship, orbiting Earth. You're safe."

Safe. That was a lie. She hadn't been safe since that fateful day in Nemausus, in the baths, when everything had been taken from her. There were always dangers lurking: men with spears, disease, starvation.

"Who are you?"

The pale face looked crestfallen. "You don't recognize me? It's Jana. Jana Manca, from Bosa. We grew up together. We've been friends since we were little."

Another person appeared on the other side of the tank, a woman of great size, with dark skin and green hair. "Don't worry, Jana, her memory will return. She's disoriented. From her perspective, it's been many years since she's seen you. Even though she's only been in the tank for two weeks, she's lived a good portion of a lifetime in Maro's simulation."

Maro. Who was that? The name filled her with rage.

"My name is Cassia," said the green-haired woman. "As Jana said, you're safe now. Let's get you out of this tank and cleaned up."

Filumena's limbs were too weak to support her own weight, but Cassia lifted her from the tank as easily as a mother would lift an infant from its crib.

★ ★ ★

After Filumena had bathed, eaten, and slept, she regained some strength. Her muscles were not atrophied, just weak from lack of use. In time she would be strong again, and her hair – which was now just stubble on her scalp – would grow back.

Though she was beginning to understand what had happened to her, her Gallic life still seemed the realer one. But she also remembered Jana and her life in Bosa.

She breakfasted with Jana and Cassia. Aina served them dates, bread, and soft cheese, then joined their table. The cheese tasted strange – perhaps not made from real milk – but the fruit was delicious.

"My mother," Filumena asked, "is she still alive?"

Jana nodded. "She's fine. Everyone is still alive, except for Sperancia. But you already knew that, didn't you?"

It came back to her: Maro and Livia in Bosa, Sperancia's murder, her own flight with Cristo. What fools they had been.

"Cristo – where is he?"

"Receiving medical care. He'll be fine, but he's still disassociated. Now that he's awake and out of the tank, he believes he's dreaming."

"Maybe it would help him to see me. I knew Cristo there, briefly. We met in the vineyard and recognized each other from before."

Jana looked to Cassia, who nodded. "It's a good idea. I'll arrange it."

"Where is Maro?" Filumena asked, her throat tightening.

The other three women shared a look.

"What is it? Tell me. Is he dead? Imprisoned? He must be brought to justice. He tricked me – forced me to live an entire life I didn't ask for…."

"He's not dead," Jana said.

"Though it could be said that he's in prison, in a way," Aina added cheerfully.

"What do you mean?"

"There's someone we need you to meet," said Jana. "If we just told you, you wouldn't believe us. But don't be alarmed. All is not as it seems."

"Jana, please join us now," Cassia called out. This was confusing to Filumena considering that Jana was sitting right across from her, albeit with a strange expression.

Filumena tensed when she saw him. It was Maro, though instead of his usual tunic he wore simple black trousers and a short-sleeved shirt. His hair was tousled, his chin and cheeks covered with dark stubble.

"Hello, Filumena. I know I look like Maro, but I'm not. It's me, Jana."

Filumena looked to the Jana that she recognized, expecting protest or denial, but her childhood friend confirmed what Maro had said with a curt nod.

"How is that possible?" Filumena asked.

"Did Sperancia ever explain to you exactly how she became maghiarja?" the original Jana asked.

"Not exactly. But I knew she was maghiarja because of the Crucible, which had been passed down for generations, woman to woman. You were to be next."

"And I was, even though the Crucible ceremony never occurred. I became maghiarja and Sperancia lived within me. I spoke to her. It was such a relief to converse with her again after she had died. But the Crucible is no longer inside of me. It's in Maro's body now."

"I don't understand."

"Maro ingested the Crucible core willingly, thinking it would bring him immortality. He planned to enslave the previous hosts and use the Crucible's powers to serve his own selfish ends. But we set a trap."

"What kind of trap?"

"Maro awoke within a simulated world created by Itria, one of the previous hosts. Just as you believed your life in ancient Rome was real, Maro now believes that he is Emperor Decimus, ruling over all the ringships and Earth itself."

"Fortunately, Maro was never elected emperor," Cassia added. "And never will be."

Filumena couldn't help but laugh. "Maro is trapped...in his own fantasy?"

"Fitting, isn't it?" said Aina.

It *was* fitting. But it was also much kinder than what Filumena had been subjected to. She's lost a finger. She'd seen friends die. She'd entirely forgotten who she'd been, who she really was.

"But how can this also be Jana?" Filumena asked, gesturing at Maro-who-was-not-Maro.

"Call me Maro, if you like. I will be pretending to be him, so I might as well get used to responding to his name."

"The Crucible made a fully functioning simulacrum of my body and brain," Jana said. "That copy of me, which resides in the core along with

Sperancia, Itria, and the others, has taken control of Maro's body. It sees through his optic nerve, sends signals through his spinal cord to control his muscles, and so on. The core bypasses Maro's brain entirely. His brain is entirely occupied with the simulation."

"So there really are two of you?" Filumena asked, looking at Jana and then at Jana-Maro. "Isn't that strange?"

Both nodded. "Profoundly," Jana-Maro said. "Perhaps odder for me, since I recognize myself when I look at her. But I was never that attached to that body. I never felt comfortable in my own skin."

Jana sighed. "You got the better deal. I'm still stuck with it."

"Nonsense," Cassia said. "You're not stuck with anything. We can modify your body in whatever way you like. I'm a living example. It's trivial."

"I want to go home," Filumena said. "When can I return to Bosa?"

Jana looked crestfallen at this question, as did Jana-Maro. "I was hoping you would stay for a while," Jana said.

"We can arrange a shuttle within the next few days, but you need to gain some strength first."

"After I see Cristo, I'd like to return home as soon as possible," Filumena insisted.

"And you will," Aina said, smiling brightly. "You are free now. As am I, as it happens!"

★ ★ ★

Jana and Cassia accompanied Filumena to visit Cristo, who had left the medical facility and was residing at a simple *domus*. Aina had volunteered to care for him and to make sure he didn't wander off.

To Filumena's relief, Jana-Maro had not joined them. Filumena accepted that Maro was somewhere else, his mind trapped in a virtual prison, but her body reacted the same way to Jana-Maro as if it were Maro himself, with fear and loathing. She had once been physically attracted to that body, but that was before he had traumatized her, imprisoning her in a hostile world without warning or consent. It wasn't fair to that version of Jana that Filumena felt that way, but she couldn't help it. Maybe in time her feelings would change.

"Cristo is fine, physically," Cassia explained. "Somewhat weak, like yourself, but he's recovering. In fact he's developed quite an appetite. But he's acting as if the world isn't real."

"How so?"

"You will see for yourself."

Several spiderlike robot gardeners scurried away as they approached. Cristo was reclined on a hammock drinking wine from a goblet, a silver platter of grapes and cured meats balanced across his stomach. He looked well. His skin had a youthful glow and all the battle scars and wrinkles had of course vanished, though his face looked puffy, as if he had gorged himself on food and drink. His hair, like her own, was extremely short.

"Aina, would you be so kind as to bring me another plate of fruit?"

The cybrid emerged from the *domus* looking perturbed. "I'm glad you're here," she said to Cassia. "I don't know what to do with him. He won't stop eating."

"Let him eat," Cassia said. "It will be worse if you deprive him. He's traumatized—"

"I'm not traumatized," Cristo interrupted. "I'm hungry. For years I lived on coarse bread with bits of rock in it. Now I'm having a wonderful dream where I can eat and drink as much as I like. Why not enjoy it while I can?"

Filumena took Cristo's hand and kissed his forehead. "I'm so glad to see you. You're not dreaming – the other world wasn't real. We weren't really in ancient Rome."

"I remember you!" Cristo said, briefly looking hopeful. "But you're just a dream as well." He dropped Filumena's hand.

"If you are dreaming, what would you say to me in your dream?"

Cristo narrowed his eyes as if suspecting a trick. "I would say that I loved you, I suppose. I've always loved you, even though I'm engaged to Sabina."

"Sabina – yes. Sabina from Bosa. That's not a dream, is it?"

"No," Cristo said, looking confused. "Maybe?"

"Sabina is real. *I'm* real. We were both trapped in Maro's experiment – a fake world created by machines. The reason you recognized me in the vineyard was because you knew me from Bosa."

Cristo shoved several grapes into his mouth and frowned.

"It will take some time," Cassia said. "Don't push too hard."

"Who are you?" Cristo asked with his mouth full, pointing at Cassia. But his face changed when he noticed Jana. "I know you, don't I?"

"We were friends," Jana said. "We plowed my father's field with Pinna the red ox, remember?"

"With Antonio. Where is Antonio? Why did he abandon me?" Cristo began to silently cry, tears streaming down his cheeks.

Filumena hugged him, causing the silver platter to clatter to the ground, scattering the remaining food. Cristo flinched at the noise but then surrendered to her embrace, nuzzling closer. "Nobody abandoned you. You were tricked by Maro, that's all. So was I. But we're safe now. We can return to Bosa."

Cristo clambered out of the hammock without releasing Filumena, nearly bringing both of them to the ground. His crying intensified; she could feel his body convulse with each sob.

"Nobody left you," she repeated. "Everyone wants to see you again."

"Is my father still alive?" Cristo asked between heaving sobs. "It was so long ago that I saw him."

"Not as long as you think – only a few weeks. He's alive and misses you."

Filumena held him tightly, resolving that she would not be the first to pull away. All the times he had annoyed or angered her faded away. She loved him with the loyalty of shared pain. It was different than romantic love, perhaps even stronger. She would not let go.

"Do you still want more cheese?" Aina asked.

CHAPTER THIRTY-EIGHT

There was no way to announce their pending arrival, so Aina executed a low fly-by over Bosa's town square. As the shuttle banked, Filumena caught a glimpse of the townsfolk looking up in awe. Or was it irritation? A visiting spaceship might be old news these days.

"How did you learn to fly this craft?" Filumena asked.

"Other cybrids taught me. I can converse with them at great distances – at least with those who have also received the Bohm upgrade."

"I'm glad you're free now."

"And a citizen," Aina added. "Thanks to Cassia and the other *populares*."

"I can't wait to eat real food again," Cristo said. "That substance they call cheese—"

"Foul," Filumena agreed, grimacing.

"Space stations are not the ideal environment for cattle," Aina said. "Even great worldships like the *Michelangelo*."

It was just the three of them. Jana-Maro was still on the *Michelangelo* playing the role of Maro, colluding with Cassia to tilt the balance of power in the Senate. The new Maro was just as arrogant and vain (so as not to rouse suspicions) but a tad more sensible and willing to reconcile with his political opponents. Jana had returned to the *Stanford* to reunite with Katja.

Filumena was relieved to be away from both of them. As much as she loved her childhood friend, the sight of Maro's face still triggered revulsion and fear. Even if Maro's mind was locked away in the Crucible, she found it impossible to relax around Jana-Maro.

And as for the 'original' Jana…that person had changed as well. Even though she was no longer maghiarja, the Crucible had made her wiser and seemingly older. Where had her playfulness gone? Filumena sorely missed it.

Aina gently landed the shuttle atop a hill not far from Bosa. "Ready?" she asked.

"Not really," Filumena answered truthfully. "I'm not the same person as when I left – I'm worried it won't be the same."

"I'm ready," Cristo said. "I'm glad to be home."

"I'm looking forward to visiting Bosa," Aina said. "My last visit to Earth went poorly. I'm hoping it will go better this time."

Halfway to town they were greeted by a motley collection of children, goats, and dogs, respectively yelling, bleating, and barking enthusiastically. Her cousins Ralf and Bina led the pack.

"You're back!" Bina yelled, rushing into Filumena's arms.

"Who are you?" Ralf asked, staring at Aina with fear and fascination.

"What about me?" Cristo asked.

"You look a little fat," Ralf said.

Cristo lunged at Ralf, who screamed and ran back toward town. Cristo followed, yelling playfully, as did most of the dogs. The goats had found a trove of fallen acorns beneath a nearby oak and had lost interest in the people.

"We thought you might be dead," Bina confessed. "I'm glad you're not."

"So am I," Filumena replied. "Now tell me everything that's happened in Bosa while we were away."

★ ★ ★

Though everyone wanted to talk to her, Filumena went straight home to her mother. Zicanna was up and out of bed – a good sign – though she looked frail and her skin had a grayish cast.

"My love!" Her mother hugged her and would not let go for several minutes. Filumena submitted to the long embrace. In the Ancestral Realism simulation she hadn't had a mother, and Zicanna's love comforted her in a way she had almost forgotten.

"How are you, Mother?"

"Well enough. Better now that you're here."

"I wish you had gone to Ilium with the others. With Sperancia gone, I'm scared your condition will worsen."

Zicanna laughed. "I've lived long enough. When death takes me I'll be ready."

"Don't say that! I still need you."

"Then why did you leave, child?"

Her mother wasn't trying to be mean, but Filumena cried nonetheless. Her mother kissed her head and stroked her short hair, apologizing and trying to comfort her, but Zicanna's words were true. Filumena had made the choice to leave, and it was only luck that her mother had not died during her absence.

That evening Micheli hosted a great celebration, moving tables and chairs into the town square and opening dozens of bottles of wine and mirto. As guests arrived, Filumena noted that Leandro was not among them, and felt relieved. She would need to explain to Jana's father what had happened, but she wasn't ready for that conversation.

At first the townsfolk were suspicious of Aina; they remembered the last time Bosa had received visitors from the *Michelangelo*. But Filumena explained that Aina was a friend, and nothing at all like Maro and Livia. She didn't reveal the fact that Aina was part machine; that would only confuse them. Aina looked and acted real enough. As far as Filumena could tell she had thoughts and feelings just like any human being.

Cristo was ecstatic to be home. Both Vissenta and Iginu wept tears of joy when they saw their son, and alternated fawning over him and yelling at him for leaving in the first place. Cristo laughed off their concerns, stuffing his face with ricotta dumplings and sausages and drinking mirto until his lips were stained purple. Sabina embraced Cristo but the two had little to say to each other, and his fiancée sat near him, awkwardly silent, for the duration of the festivities. At one point Filumena noticed Antonio and Sabina exchanging a glance. Had a new love kindled during their absence? Bina hadn't mentioned it, but she might still be too young to notice such things. Though it was none of Filumena's business, it occurred to her that it might be better for all involved if Cristo's engagement ended dramatically, with an exposed affair. As painful as that would be, it was preferable to a long, unhappy marriage.

Mayor Busincu embraced her and kissed her on both cheeks. "Filumena, we're overjoyed to have you back. Tell me, how did you escape from the *Michelangelo*? On your own? Or did that woman rescue you?" He nodded in Aina's direction.

"I'm glad to be back, Gregoriu. Aina helped me, yes. But mostly it was Jana who saved me."

"I'm not surprised. Jana has always been a capable girl. But how did she make it to the *Michelangelo*? How did she free you? And when will she be returning?"

"Forgive me, Gregoriu, it's a long story…."

"Of course. Tell me later – tonight is for celebrating. Will you come to the next council meeting and tell us everything you've learned?"

She promised Gregoriu that she would, while at the same time reflecting that he had been mayor a long time. Perhaps it was time for someone else to lead Bosa. The ideal candidate would be someone who had seen the world beyond Sardinia, one who could protect Bosa from those who might prey on its residents. Someone like Jana, for example.

But Jana probably wasn't coming back. And if she did return, it wouldn't be the Jana that Gregoriu expected, the maghiarja who hosted Sperancia and the consorteria with their centuries of knowledge and wisdom.

The Crucible had left Bosa, probably forever.

★ ★ ★

Within a week they had more visitors: Lydia and Maggie from Ilium, with Pietro and his father, Enzo, in tow. Maggie landed the hovershuttle right in the middle of the town square, shouting at everyone to get out of the way. Filumena thought this might not be the best choice; certainly there were safer places to land the machine? But she understood when Pietro debarked with a great deal of bravado, on his own two feet, and was greeted with a thunderous cheer. The boy could walk again.

"It will be a few more months until he's fully recovered," Lydia explained. "But we were able to replace his defective genes. His muscles will grow correctly now. And if Pietro ever has children, they won't carry the disease."

Within minutes, Pietro, Bina, and Ralf were off to explore places that had previously been off-limits to the former. Filumena winced as the boy fell several times, but each time Bina and Ralf hauled him up and Pietro cheerfully continued forward.

Enzo's brow was furrowed. "Is he strong enough?" he asked Lydia.

"He might get a few scrapes. But at this point, the more he uses his legs, the better. In a few weeks he'll be running."

Enzo and his wife embraced, tears streaming down their cheeks as they watched their son until the children rounded a corner.

"You are a miracle worker," Filumena said to Lydia. "Is there anything you can do for my mother while you're here?"

"Has she reconsidered coming to Ilium? It would be much easier to treat her there. But we did bring a drug fabricator and other medical equipment this time. Is there a building we can use to set up a temporary clinic? We can stay for a few days to provide treatment for anyone who needs it."

"I'm sure there is – I'll ask Gregoriu."

The next day Filumena attended the council meeting as a guest, as did Lydia and Maggie. Jana's father Leandro, though he was not a council member, was also present.

Filumena explained everything that had happened on the *Michelangelo*, leaving out only the details of her life in the Gallic village. To her those memories and that life were absolutely real. But no one else would understand.

Except Cristo. Cristo had been invited to the meeting as well, but had declined, stating that he wasn't yet ready to discuss those events. No one pressed him; it was clear the young man was not well. One moment he was boisterous and cheerful, the next sobbing uncontrollably, minutes later ravenously eating.

Jana's father took the news about Jana better than expected. "She will return eventually," he insisted. "She is a responsible person and has always cared about Bosa. She will not abandon us."

Filumena wasn't sure if Leandro fully understood what had happened to Jana, that there were now effectively two Janas, one in Maro's body. She had done her best to carefully explain, but at times her words had been met with blank stares.

"Even if she does return, she won't be coming back as maghiarja. That means we don't have a doctor, and are less an important teacher."

"Ilium can continue to provide medical support," Lydia offered in halting Italian. "Maybe a monthly visit, or even weekly?"

"That is generous of you," said Gregoriu. "But we have always been independent. We don't want to rely on your charity."

"Don't be a fool," Filumena snapped. Her rebuke came out more sharply than she'd intended, and Gregoriu looked offended, but she continued on nonetheless. "Don't you realize what we're up against? If Jana hadn't been able to trick Maro, he'd have plucked us up one by one to use in his cruel experiment. There is nothing we could have done to stop him. Sperancia died trying."

"What's your point?" Gregoriu asked.

"We have to stop thinking of ourselves as an island. We've lived that way for centuries, but that time is over. Not only because we no longer have a maghiarja, but because we've been discovered. We need to make allies and accept help when offered. The people of Ilium have proven they can be trusted."

Gregoriu sighed. "Perhaps you are right. But our traditions are what make us what we are. Isn't our way of life worth protecting and defending?"

Leandro grunted in agreement. "Of course it is," he said. "But that doesn't mean we can't live even better lives. Even Sperancia could not do much for Filumena's mother. Why not let Lydia and Maggie help Zicanna?"

It was decided that either Maggie or Lydia would return to Bosa on a monthly basis for as long as needed, and that Ilium would provide medical training for anyone in Bosa who wanted it. Filumena volunteered to go first. Though she had no idea if she would be able to master the skills involved, it would be good to learn what she could; it might help her care for her mother. And she was curious to see Ilium. She had gleaned from Lydia and Maggie that Ilium was filled with diverse, interesting people. But sensible ones, not so different than the people of Bosa.

Even though she had made a few friends on the *Michelangelo* – Cassia and Aina in particular – and had been impressed by the multitude of great artworks she had seen, she had no desire to return to the worldship. While most denizens of the *Michelangelo* were not insane, their values and priorities were radically different than her own. The people of the *Michelangelo* felt foreign, even alien. Lydia and Maggie, on the other hand, were just regular folk who spoke a different language and happened to have access to vast amounts of knowledge and powerful machines.

* * *

Lydia and Maggie returned to Ilium shortly after the council meeting, but Aina appeared to be in no particular hurry to leave Bosa. The cybrid made friends with her cheerful nature, youthful attractiveness, and eagerness to help out with whatever tasks that needed doing. Aina moved boulders, pulled up stubborn roots, and pulled the plow when the red oxen needed a rest.

One day Aina volunteered to help Filumena with household chores and repairs that had been neglected during her absence. Filumena gratefully accepted the offer, not only because she needed the help but because it was an opportunity to explore the cybrid's motives and intentions. Filumena didn't suspect Aina of any wrongdoing or mischief, but she was curious as to why she was still hanging around town.

"Are you enjoying your time in Bosa?" Filumena asked. Aina was reassembling the pump to Zicanna's well, which had a shaky handle.

"Yes, very much so. I'm getting to know some of the fishermen. They're very friendly."

Filumena had no doubt that they were, and knew exactly why, but at the same time was confident that Aina could take care of herself.

"Do you miss your friends on the *Michelangelo*?"

"I didn't have any friends until recently," Aina answered immediately, "nor did I experience life in such a way that would have made it possible to have friends." Filumena found it disconcerting how Aina rarely paused to think before answering a question, but it occurred to her that Aina might think extremely quickly.

"Something changed?"

"Yes. Cassia initiated an upgrade to my neural network. Now I experience myself as a person with a past and a future. Friendship is important in life, and I have many friends. But I don't miss them."

"Why not?"

"Because I'm in near constant conversation with them. My mentor, Ekon, for example – I speak with him more than twenty times a day. He is also a cybrid."

"I've never heard you—"

"We speak silently, in our minds. But my thoughts are still private, unless I wish them not to be."

"Has anyone in Bosa asked how you can be so strong?" Filumena had not revealed Aina's nature to anyone, and she'd heard no gossip about Aina being a machine. But then again she'd scarcely heard any gossip at all, probably because Filumena herself was the subject of much of it.

"No, but I overheard Antonio and his father discuss that very topic.

They were over twenty meters away and assumed they were speaking privately. But my auditory perception is quite sensitive."

"I'm sure it is."

"They said that I must be a maghiarja, like Sperancia, and that was the reason for my unusual strength."

Of course – it made perfect sense. The people of Bosa were already used to having a strongwoman in their midst. It was as natural to them as fish in the sea.

A few days later Zorzi and Nevio were thrown out of Micheli's for fighting. Filumena heard the story from Bina, who had witnessed the latter half of the altercation in the town square.

"Zorzi said that Aina was *his* woman, and that Nevio should stop making eyes at her."

"And what did Nevio say?"

"That if Aina was his woman then he shouldn't let her…well, I don't think I should repeat exactly what he said."

"I see. And was Aina there?"

"No, she was working in the fields with Antonio and Cristo. I thought that Aina might be the reason Cristo and Sabina are no longer engaged."

"I don't think Aina has anything to do with that."

"But I saw them kissing."

"Aina and Cristo?"

"Well, it might have been more than kissing…."

"Bina, are you spying on people?"

"No! They were beneath an oak tree in the middle of the day. At first I thought they were just taking a nap. Ralf and I wanted to play tag with Aina – she's very fast."

Filumena invited Aina for an afternoon walk along the beach, wishing to be out of eavesdropping range for what might be an awkward conversation. She hoped that Aina might broach the topic herself, but the cybrid only wanted to discuss various construction and repair projects around town and how she might help them progress. Finally Filumena decided to blurt out her question.

"Aina – have you been having sexual relations with multiple people in Bosa?"

"Yes. I enjoy sex, and often propose it when I sense a person might be physically attracted to me."

"But who do *you* find attractive?"

"Human beings. I'm not programmed to be attracted to other animals or lifeforms."

"*All* human beings?"

"Yes. And also other cybrids who resemble humans."

Maybe the rumors about Aina and Zorzi were true. The old fisherman was usually drunk and bleary-eyed, and often had fish scales in his beard. Filumena couldn't imagine a woman wanting to be with him. But he was human, and thus cleared Aina's bar.

"Do you ever feel jealous?" she asked the cybrid.

"Yes, but only mildly. My emotional spectrum is similar to humans, but specific emotions are attenuated, including jealousy and anger."

"So you understand the emotion at least. Do you see how having sex with multiple people might cause jealousy among them?"

Aina looked puzzled. "I have not initiated any romantic relationships. It is only sex, for mutual pleasure. I always make sure my partner fully consents. There shouldn't be any reason for jealousy – having sex with one person doesn't lessen my ability to have sex with anyone else. My appetite for sexual relations far exceeds human capabilities."

"I don't think that's the issue…."

"I cannot become pregnant, so the possessiveness that accompanies mating does not apply to me."

"I'm not sure if that's the way jealousy works – emotions aren't logical."

Aina nodded. "Of course, you're right."

Filumena picked up a smooth beach stone and tossed it into the ocean. They were close to the place where Jana had kissed her. She'd been curious and had gone along, but there hadn't been any spark.

"So you'll slow down? Maybe pick one partner at a time?"

Aina picked up a stone and flicked it into the surf with such velocity that it whistled, tearing through the air, and then skipped a dozen times over the surface. "No, I think I'll continue with as many partners as I please."

"But—"

"I'm free now. I don't think I could go back to serving someone like I served Maro, and that's all that awaits me back on the *Michelangelo*. Maybe that will change if cybrids become citizens, but I have no desire to return to that way of life."

"I'm not asking you to serve anyone."

"But in a way you are. You are suggesting that I be subservient to the unreasonable emotions of other people. Of course everyone is entitled to experience whatever emotions they have. But that doesn't mean that I should change my behavior. Human sexuality taboos don't apply to me. I can't contract or transmit diseases, nor can I get pregnant or impregnate anyone. All my sexual relations are fully consensual, and I don't experience sexual jealousy, at least not significantly. If other people feel jealous, that's their problem."

Filumena stopped in her tracks, stunned mute. The cybrid's words had shocked her, but at the same time they made perfect sense.

"Are *you* jealous, Filumena? Would you like to have sex with me? I didn't sense that you were interested, but I would be more than happy to. Shall I disrobe?"

"No. Please keep your clothes on."

But Aina was right; she was jealous. Hearing Bina's story, the image of Aina and Cristo together had been a punch to her gut.

CHAPTER THIRTY-NINE

Mèng squeezed Tem's shoulder. "You should be proud. This is a great opening." The gallery, a huge hall with curving white walls, was filled with *Liu Huì* citizens admiring the show Tem had helped curate. Tem could see Fengmian, the artist responsible for many of the works, hobnobbing with gallery visitors in front of a large sculpture featuring two figures copulating at a distance, connected by tubes and wires.

"It doesn't look that crowded." He wished his aunt was there to reassure him with her reliable confidence, but Katja had returned to the *Stanford*, wanting to be near her brother while she waited for news of Jana's fate.

"Trust me, this is a great showing. Alan is deliriously happy." Alan was the gallery manager, and had agreed to host the show only reluctantly, wanting to steer clear of political entanglements. But Mèng, a personal friend, had convinced him, framing the potential show as a moderate risk that might yield great rewards in terms of both publicity and art sales.

Tem watched as Fengmian extracted himself from a group of admirers and beelined to join Tem and Mèng near the bar.

"Congratulations," Mèng said. "From what I've heard the critics are already raving."

"I don't listen to those assholes," Fengmian scoffed, but at the same time he looked pleased. "Besides, Tem deserves to be congratulated as much as me. The initial concept was his, even though he won't take any credit for it."

"How did you get everyone to agree to your interviews?" Tem asked. One of Fengmian's pieces – the most important one from Tem's point of view – was a documentary about remote sexuality that included interviews with implant users. Several of the interviewees were high-ranking officials going public with their gear use for the first time. The show represented a great 'coming out', helping to break down the shame and stigma around remote sexuality that existed among many *Liu Huì* citizens. The ringship's conservative culture frowned upon teledildonics, sexual activity among avatars in virtual spaces, and other forms of sexuality that allowed people in distant locations to express intimacy. Coming from the *Stanford*, it was a taboo that Tem regarded as strange and old-fashioned, and ripe for disruption.

"The interviews? Easy," Fengmian said. "I told everyone the Jūnshì director was on board. And then once everyone else had agreed, I told the Jūnshì director that he was the only holdout. Of course he didn't want to look like a coward…."

"A bold move," Mèng said.

Fengmian shrugged, grinning. "Well, it worked. Now what does a hardworking artist have to do to get a drink around here?"

Tem ordered drinks for Fengmian, Mèng, and himself while scanning the crowd for Manning. He'd made sure Manning had received an invitation, but so far there was no sign of him. Tem would be surprised if he showed up. His gambit, as far as he could tell, was going to pay off.

Manning would wield far less power and leverage after today. No longer having the threat of blackmail over particular high-ranking government officials, it would be harder for him to demand favors. There was power in revealing your own secrets; it took away the shame as long as nothing truly heinous was revealed. And there was nothing wrong with the Jūnshì director's ongoing relationship and remote sexual relations with a woman aboard the *Hedonark*, for example. Tem guessed that Manning's political status would drop precipitously in the coming weeks and months.

Tem wondered if it was enough. Manning had tried to kill him, after all. And Tem had imagined more than once what it would be like to slice open Manning's bowels with Squid Cutter. But there was something satisfying about the approach he had taken instead. What was the old saying Grandfather Shol sometimes used? Something about the temperature of revenge. He would have to ask his morfar.

* * *

Several days later, the *Michelangelo*, completely out of the blue, responded to the automated hails of the *Liu Hui*. After a short, painless round of negotiations, the former agreed to return the *Iarudi* and its contents in exchange for membership to the Ringstation Coalition. The Zhōngyāng central council considered both outcomes to be extremely favorable and agreed immediately. As to why the leaders of the *Michelangelo* had suddenly decided to play nice, officials could only speculate. Little was known about the internal machinations of the 'ship of mad artists', but Tem guessed that Jana's mission had somehow succeeded.

Tem was not present for the delivery of the *Iarudi*, but heard through Mèng that opening the starship had revealed a nightmarish scene: habitat areas filled with the desiccated corpses of the long-dead crew. Commander Umana's remains were found on the bridge, recognizable only via her cybernetic tentacles. Her body had been consumed by a parasitic black mass, digesting her flesh and then extending its roots to feed on other bodies nearby. Investigators hypothesized that the black material – whatever it was – had not killed the unfortunate crew members. The strange parasite was an opportunistic feeder, not a killer. The crew had died from other causes. Analysis of the remains revealed stress fractures consistent with massive acceleration forces.

Tem knew exactly what the black material was. He'd seen a similar black mass growing out of the earth in the mountains near Kaldbrek. It was a Crucible core outside of its host, consuming whatever organic matter it could find, growing and expanding as it searched for a human body and brain to replicate.

With the exception of the carnage in the habitat areas, the *Iarudi* was in good working order, all systems intact. Complete data from Shane's interstellar exploration mission was transferred to *Liu Hui* research libraries and shared with all astronomers in the Coalition. The Natario-White drive appeared to still be functional, though too dangerous to test unless the starship was in deep space (instantiating a warp bubble tended to have devastating effects on nearby objects). Umana had stolen the starship in its infancy, before many of its features had been fully tested. But the *Iarudi* was back, and after some maintenance would be used for future research missions.

The *Iarudi*'s cold stasis pods revealed a surprise. Shane Jaecks was still alive, though just barely. But after several weeks of round-the-clock care and rehabilitation, Tem received word that Shane was conscious, cogent, and taking short visits. Tem was, as far as he knew, the only person on the *Liu Hui* who knew Shane personally, and headed directly to the medical facility as soon as he heard the news.

His old friend looked pale and thin, but only a few years older than when Tem had last seen him twenty years ago. The stasis pod had kept Shane's body just above freezing temperatures, slowing his metabolism to a crawl and providing the minimal necessary nutrients.

"Shane, it's good to see you. You look well, considering."

Shane squinted at him.

"It's Tem. Of course you wouldn't recognize me."

"Tem from Happdal? The village boy?"

The village boy. Hearing those words, Tem was flooded with feelings of vulnerability, unfocussed rage, alienation, and every other emotion he'd experienced in childhood. He took a deep breath, accepting the feelings but trying not to get lost in them.

"I'm sorry," Shane said, noticing his distress. "You're obviously not a boy anymore."

"It's okay. It's how you remember me. I've thought about you a lot over the years. I think you must occupy a bigger space in my mind than I do in yours. I'd always wondered what happened to you."

"I remember you well, Tem. You bolstered my spirits after Umana's goons tortured me. I'll never forget that, and I'm in your debt."

"You don't owe me anything."

Shane grinned. "I can't believe I'm alive."

"Were you conscious in stasis? Do you remember anything?"

"I remember dreaming, but not what I dreamed. To me it feels like a few weeks have passed. It's amazing to see you all grown up."

"So tell me, how did you manage to defeat Umana?"

Shane scratched his stubbly chin. "I'm still trying to work that out. Mostly, she defeated herself by consuming the black egg, though I may have inadvertently tricked her into doing that. She tested it in me first to see what would happen. There was something wrong with it – it didn't take over my mind like it was supposed to. But I pretended that it had. I understood how it was supposed to work because of the story you had told me about Katja, how your aunt's mind had been taken over by the *gast*, as you called it.

"So I acted as if I were an entity that had taken over my own body. I read Umana's cues for how I should behave. I figured the longer I could keep the charade going, the longer she would keep me alive. I guess I did a good enough job that she bought it."

"So she extracted the Crucible core from your body and consumed it herself?"

Shane nodded. "Exactly. And I'm glad she did, after seeing what it did to her."

"It was no longer a Crucible core. Zoë had transformed it into something else – a universe simulator."

"Zoë?"

"One of the previous hosts of Katja's Crucible. She invented a universal evolutionary algorithm and installed it on the root level of the quantum core. It destroyed her and every other entity in that Crucible instance, but it also saved Katja's life. And ultimately killed Umana."

Shane frowned. "Is it…still running?"

"Unless someone destroyed it. I should probably explain that to the *Liu Hui* investigators."

"Probably a good idea."

Shane closed his eyes. Tem prepared himself to leave even though he had many more questions. The man was recovering from internal injuries and twenty years of cold stasis; he deserved his rest.

Shane weakly raised his hand. "Wait – don't go quite yet."

"Okay."

"How is Lydia? Is she still alive?"

"Alive and well. Still in Ilium. I worked with her recently on a delegation to meet the Sardinians."

"How did that go?"

"Mostly well, except that they were contacted by the *Michelangelo* shortly after. I'll tell you the whole story once you're feeling stronger."

"Is she still with Xenus?"

"No – they separated years ago. Xenus has another partner and two children."

"But not Lydia?"

"She's not with anyone as far as I know. And she never had kids."

Shane sighed. "I suppose I'm too young for her now."

Tem laughed. "Maybe for you she'd get a rejuv."

"It would be great to see her again. We had such a good connection. The only problem was timing."

"Well, I can work on getting you back to Ilium. Unless you have other plans? Somewhere else you'd like to be?"

"No. I want to be back on Earth. And Ilium is as close a place to home as I ever had. Think I can get my old job back? Who's the new Security Director?"

"You'll have to talk to Xenus about that."

"He's still in charge? Crafty old bastard."

Shane was silent for a few minutes. Tem waited patiently. He was happy to be in Shane's presence and had nothing better to do. He resolved to make caring for Shane his priority, at least until his friend was strong enough to look out for himself.

"Anyone special in your life, Tem?"

"Yes, but I might have screwed that up."

"Tell me about it. I want to know everything."

Tem obliged, describing Maggie, whom Shane remembered as a child. Tem confessed his dalliance with Saga and his fear that Kaldbrek's jarl might be pregnant with his child. He expressed his feelings of jealously around Roland, even though Maggie had assured him it was nothing serious.

"Honestly, I'm confused," Tem concluded.

"Do you love Maggie?"

"Yes."

"Then what's to be confused about, kid? Go back to Ilium and tell her your feelings. But then again, what do I know? I've been sleeping in cold gel for two decades."

CHAPTER FORTY

Tem led the way along the narrow Ridge Trail, with Sigurd following a few paces behind. Tem was having second thoughts about inviting his cousin to accompany him. He hadn't wanted to go alone on account of Svein's threats. But Sigurd was ribbing him mercilessly.

"Didn't anyone teach you how babies are made, cousin? There are plenty of places to put your spunk that won't get a woman pregnant. On her belly, for example. Or on her leg, or even—"

"Enough, Sigurd! I know how babies are made."

"Do you, though? Because it would seem as if you didn't. Or have I misunderstood the purpose of our trip to Kaldbrek?"

Tem had decided that the first step to getting his life in order was to confront Saga. Well, not to confront her, exactly – Tem didn't want to start a fight with the hot-headed jarl – but to have a serious discussion. If Saga was pregnant with his child, he wanted to know where he stood. The answer to that question would affect his relationship with Maggie, where he decided to live in the coming years, and how he felt about himself. Would he be a father, and if so, what role would he play in the child's life? These questions had roiled in his head and gut for the past weeks.

"No, you understood correctly. I'm going to ask Saga if she's pregnant. And if so, if I'm the father."

"I haven't heard that she's showing. Do I need to explain that to you as well, how a baby grows inside of a woman?"

"She could still be pregnant. And by now she would know."

"Of course. But even if she is, you're vain to think the child is definitely yours. Saga is not only a jarl but a fine-looking woman. She has her pick among men. Do you think you're her only lover?"

Tem gritted his teeth. "I'm not vain. I just want to know."

"What makes you think *she* knows? Maybe she lies with a different man each night."

Tem increased his pace, trying to put some distance between himself and his cousin, but Sigurd had the longer legs and kept up easily, tongue continuing to flap. Had Farbror Trond not taught his sons mercy? Of course he hadn't — Tem had witnessed his father and Trond go at each other ruthlessly, with other family members egging them on. That was the family communication style.

Descending the switchback trail that led into Kaldbrek's valley, they heard sounds of celebration: singing and laughing.

"Is there a festival today?" Tem asked.

Sigurd shrugged. "Not that I know of. Perhaps a baby was born, or a couple married."

Tem kept his hand on the hilt of his dagger as they passed through the farms on the outskirts of the village. The few people working the fields ignored them.

"Why is it that Svein wants to fight you?" Sigurd asked. "Baldr told me you tripped on his spear during the hunt. But why would Svein demand hólmganga?"

"He tripped me on purpose, and I got a bit angry. I may have scratched him with my knife."

"You drew your blade? The godsteel one Father made for you?"

"Yes." Tem gripped Squid Cutter's hilt more tightly. They were in Kaldbrek proper now. The road was newly paved with cobble, and several buildings had grown taller with additional stories. The streets were empty, but the singing and laughing sounded much closer.

Tem had a healthy fear of Svein, and admitting that to himself didn't make him feel diminished or any less of a man. He remembered clearly how easily Svein had dispatched Fyrirgef, sliding his spear into the great sow's brain. Svein was a natural killer, efficient and dispassionate, and more proficient than Tem with both spear and sword.

But Tem was no longer the helpless boy that Svein had kidnapped twenty years ago. If Svein insisted on hólmganga, then duel they would. He'd brought Sigurd only to ensure fairness; he would not permit Svein and his goons to gang up on him alone. If Svein was willing to face him one-on-one, then so was Tem. If that's what it took to talk to Saga, so be it. He would not let his fear control him.

And if he was being truthful with himself, it would feel good to sink Squid Cutter into Svein's flesh. He wasn't proud of that desire, but it lingered in his heart like a cold black fire.

A tall old man emerged from behind a storage shed at a full sprint, nearly colliding with them.

"What's the hurry, whiskers?" Sigurd said. The man's long white beard was braided into two forks.

The old man whirled on his heel and swung a heavy oaken cudgel, just missing Sigurd's face. "*Whiskers?* You shall address me by my name."

Tem released Squid Cutter's hilt and opened his arms. "Egil! It's been a long time. Sigurd, do you remember the poet Egil? Surely you've heard his name."

Egil squinted. "Tem Espersson? And you –" he pointed his cudgel at Sigurd, who stepped back, "– you are a son of Trond, aren't you? With those arms, you must be."

"Yes, I am Sigurd Trondsson. I meant no offense."

Egil laughed. "None taken! I wasn't truly angry. I just wanted to see if you would piss yourself if an old man yelled at you. Did you?"

Sigurd frowned. "No."

"Come, walk with me back to the party. I only stepped away to have a piss myself, but there is much *öl* left to be drunk."

The three men walked astride. "What's the cause for celebration?" Tem asked Egil.

"Völund's birthday. Jarl Saga hosts a celebration every year, even though her uncle is long dead and gone."

"Völund," Sigurd said. "Wasn't he the smith that held you captive?"

"And my father killed him for that." *Murdered him*, he thought.

"Yet another reason it's dangerous for you to set foot in Kaldbrek today," Sigurd observed.

"What's the other reason?" Egil asked.

"Svein, of course," Sigurd said. "Svein demanded hólmganga, and Saga decreed that if Tem were to set foot in Kaldbrek then Svein would get his wish. And here we are."

Egil twirled his beard. "I see that news of Svein's death has not yet reached Happdal. He was killed by a trio of horse-riding sky people."

Tem's jaw dropped. "Svein is dead? Killed by people from the ringstations? How did you know they were sky people?"

"They told me so themselves. And after they passed, I followed the hoof prints and saw their craft with my own eyes."

"Who were they?" Tem asked.

Sigurd scratched his head. "What's a horse?"

"They said they were from a ship called the *Michelangelo*," Egil said in his rough, melodious voice. "They offered gold and other gifts, so I didn't trust them. But I warned them to turn back, as I had just seen Svein and his men on the same road. I knew that meeting would not go well, and I was correct. Though not in the way that I expected."

"What happened?" Tem and Sigurd asked in unison.

"The sky people fought Svein and killed both him and Geir. Keld was injured in the fight but survived. He said one of them shot lightning from her weapon, like the Red Bearded Brother."

"So Svein is truly dead." Tem felt frozen, absorbing the news.

"I don't imagine you'll shed a tear for him. Nor will I. But it's better that an outsider killed him than one of us."

"Egil!" someone cried out. "You have brought guests. Introduce them!" And then a sheep's horn of *öl* was in Tem's hand, and the next hour passed in a blur. Several times he saw Saga from a distance, but always surrounded by a crowd, and when he tried to catch the jarl's eye she looked away.

"I guess you can go if you want, Sigurd," Tem said. "Thank you for accompanying me."

"Of course, cousin. I love you like a brother. But I'm not going anywhere as long as they keep filling my horn."

Sigurd slapped Tem's shoulder and pushed his away through the crowd, in search of more *öl*. Someone grabbed Tem's ass. He turned to see Saga regarding him skeptically.

"So you dared set foot in Kaldbrek again. Did you know Svein was dead?"

"Egil told me just now."

"So you were feeling brave. Did you come to celebrate Völund's birthday? Or are you here to pay your respects to Kaldbrek's jarl?"

"I wanted to talk to you."

"Then talk."

"Could we speak alone for a few minutes?"

Saga raised an eyebrow, and Tem feared he would be forced to say his piece in front of the whole village (and he was sure every ear was turned toward them). But Saga nodded and walked away. Relieved, Tem followed, watching her closely. Was there a slight bulge to her abdomen beneath her baggy clothing? They walked in silence to a large flat rock on the edge of town. Saga sat and gestured for Tem to join her.

"You have your privacy. Now speak."

"Are you pregnant with my child?"

"It's possible. I am with child."

"You really have no idea who the father is?"

"There's a good chance it's you. And if it is, I would not be unhappy. I like your face and the color of your skin, and as a man you are both brave and kind. But even if you are the father, it will be *my* child. You need not concern yourself."

"Of course I'm going to concern myself, if it's mine."

"You live in the sky. You have another woman."

"I would find a way."

Saga laughed. "You sky people think you can do anything. But even you can't be in two places at once."

"I could live in Happdal."

"What about your woman?"

"Maggie gets along better with Elke than I thought possible."

"That's because Elke wants you back home. She's playing nice."

"Perhaps, but it's not out of the question that Maggie would live in Happdal with me. If I'm to be a father, I want to be close to my child."

"What if your woman refuses?"

"That's none of your concern."

Saga snorted appreciatively. "Fine, then. Come back in a couple years. If the child resembles you, we'll talk again."

Short of somehow convincing Saga to submit to a medical test, this was the best Tem could hope for. No certainty and no promises, but at least Saga wasn't entirely shutting him out.

"So tell me, Tem Espersson, what has happened in the sky since I last saw you? Can you explain to me why Svein and Geir are dead?"

Tem told Saga all that he knew of Maro and the *Michelangelo*, though there were many gaps in his own knowledge. Saga listened carefully and asked many questions, and Tem was reminded that she was a good jarl and would do whatever she could to protect Kaldbrek.

Saga sighed. "There are those who want me to seek revenge for the murder of Svein and Geir, but how do you fight the gods?"

"They're just men and women."

"But they might as well be gods, for all I can do against them."

Tem thought of his struggle against Manning, who had nearly killed both him and his mother. "When your enemy is more powerful, all you can do is be patient and clever. But I don't think you have enemies on the *Michelangelo* anymore. Maro has been defeated."

Saga rose from her seat. "It's good to see you, Tem, but a jarl's absence will be noticed."

Tem nodded. "I think I've had enough *öl* – will you tell Sigurd I've returned to Happdal?"

Saga clasped his forearm and bid him goodbye. Tem watched her until she was out of sight. Not once did she look back.

He did not look forward to his next conversation with Maggie.

CHAPTER FORTY-ONE

Jana felt nervous as the shuttle approached the *Stanford*'s inner hub. How would Katja react to her appearance?

"Are you feeling well?" Ekon asked. The pilot was absurdly handsome, even better looking than Maro, with a chiseled jawline and exquisite musculature. His olive skin glowed with a healthy sheen that belied his true nature.

"I feel okay. I prefer walking to spaceflight."

"Humans are not well-adapted to weightlessness," Ekon replied, stating the obvious. "But cybrids such as myself are well-suited to a wide range of environmental conditions. Now that we are citizens, a group of us have petitioned the Senate to include us in the next phase of interstellar exploration."

"I thought the *Iarudi* was returned to the *Liu Hui*."

"It was. But not before our Engineers had a very close look at it. Though you didn't hear it from me."

Ekon spoke in Italian for Jana's benefit. She still understood English – an echo of knowledge from her time as a Crucible host – but was less fluent. That skill had only partially integrated into her own brain.

"I won't mention it. It's none of my business."

"What are your plans? Will you return to Sardinia? My friend Aina is there. I believe she intends to stay."

"I will visit – my father is there. But no, I don't think I'll return for good."

"Why not, if you don't mind me asking?"

"Because I don't think my partner wants to live there. And right now, she's the most important person in my life."

Jana thanked Ekon for the ride and wished him luck on his Senate petition. Maybe cybrids would be the ones to colonize other worlds, not humans. She asked him to send her greetings to Aina as well, as Ekon had explained how some cybrids could communicate via their thoughts, and he spoke with Aina frequently that way. Jana was familiar with that ability herself, but felt it now only as a void. The voices of Sperancia, Itria, Agatha, and Giuseppina were gone from her mind forever.

She cleared the *Stanford* bioscans relatively quickly, not having returned to Earth since her last visit. She wondered if Katja would be there to greet her once she descended the hub spoke. Ekon's shuttle had received permission to approach and dock; her arrival was no secret. But she had no idea how far that information had been disseminated. Was Katja even aware of her arrival?

Jana felt the weight of her own body with some relief as the spoke elevator arrived and opened into the lobby, a spacious room decorated in oranges and reds, with many cushioned couches and chairs, and an entire wall dedicated to a viewing screen showing magnificent scenes of Earth vistas. A group was there to meet her: Katja, Regis Foster, a middle-aged couple who Jana guessed were Tem's parents, and a slight, older man with close-cropped white hair.

"Look at you!" Katja said. "What have they done to you?"

"What do you think?" Jana asked. "Do I still seem like the same person?"

Katja pursed her lips, giving Jana a thorough up-and-down. "Of course you're the same person. And I think I like the changes. Let me touch you." She moved in for an embrace, which Jana gladly accepted. "Oh! You're stronger now. Much stronger."

Jana had taken Cassia up on her offer of physical modifications. She'd worked with a *Michelangelo* biodesigner for hours, experimenting in simulations with possible permutations of her new appearance. Eventually she'd settled on changes that were not dramatically different than her original appearance – she still wanted her friends and family to recognize her – but that more closely matched the way she'd always *felt* she should look.

The surgeries and genetic reprogramming treatments had each taken many hours, but Jana had been unconscious for all of it. Whatever drugs they'd given her had controlled the pain effectively, and her recovery had been quick. Learning how to walk and otherwise navigate the world in her new form had taken weeks. But she had the hang of it now. Her new body felt more natural than the old one.

Mostly, she was heavier and stronger, with thicker bones and stronger muscles. Facially she still looked like a woman, but more masculine, with a heavier jawline. Her features were more in proportion and geometrically pleasing.

Post-modifications, her feelings of bodily dysmorphia were not entirely gone, but much lessened. This body was Jana more than ever. Not perfect, but close enough to feel comfortable in her own skin.

"Welcome back, Jana," said Regis. "From what I hear we have you to thank for avoiding a war."

"Thank you," Jana said, realizing she no longer felt any suspicion or animosity toward Regis. What she'd felt had been misplaced resentment for his obvious ease in his own body. More than anyone she'd met, Regis seemed physically comfortable, always relaxed but also strong and capable. She'd envied him, plain and simple. But that feeling had entirely dissipated.

A short woman with a pleasing face stepped forward. "My name is Car-En – I'm Tem's mother. This is Esper, his father," she said, gesturing to a tall, handsome man with long hair. Jana guessed that Tem's parents were about the age of her own father, but looked much younger. "And this is my father, Shol."

The old man nodded. "Nice to finally meet you. I was disappointed we didn't get a chance during your first visit. I want to hear all about the *Michelangelo*, when you feel up to telling stories."

"It's the strangest place I've ever visited." But even as she said the words she second-guessed herself, thinking of Itria's version of Bosa with its bizarre mythical creatures. "Where is Tem?"

"Back in the Five Valleys," Katja said. "And then to Ilium, to reunite with Maggie."

"And is there any news from Bosa?"

"Yes. Pietro and his father are home again. After treatment in Ilium, the boy is walking. Filumena and Cristo have returned as well."

Jana began to cry, a combination of happiness and relief. Katja embraced her again, not questioning her tears, and everyone else appeared to understand as well.

"Let's get you home," Shol said. "I'll cook you a meal, and when you're ready you can tell me about the new Roman Empire. I'm insanely curious."

"Take it easy, Dad," said Car-En. "She just got here."

"It's okay – it will feel good to tell you about it." Jana felt lighter than she had in a long time. War had been averted. Filumena and Cristo were home safe. And Bosa was doing just fine without her, without the

Crucible, without a maghiarja. Finally, she could live her own life without the burdens of an entire community depending on her.

★ ★ ★

Over a long family meal at Car-En and Esper's apartment, Jana entertained Shol and the others with tales of awe-inspiring museums, reconstructions of Roman architecture, and the strange people she had met on the *Michelangelo*. Jana enjoyed the rapt attention but eventually tired of their endless questions. Katja, sensing this, suggested they take an evening walk in a Starside park she had discovered, just the two of them.

The park was situated on Slope-4, the narrowest shelf high above the main habitation level of the vast torus. Katja led Jana over a series of foot bridges crossing shallow ponds and creeks, passing by huge oval portholes showing the star-filled sky.

"So what's next?" Katja asked. "Where do you want to go?"

"I want to go wherever you want to go," Jana replied. After all she'd been through, she had no desire to be anything but direct.

"Of course. I meant what's next for *us*? Where should we go? Where should we live? My brother Esper and Car-En are happy living here on the *Stanford*, but I would prefer to live on Earth."

"I don't think I'm ready to return to Bosa." Jana realized that she had inadvertently lied to Ekon; it was *her* who was not ready to return to Sardinia, even if Katja was willing. "I'll want to go back eventually to see my father and my friends, but...."

"No need to explain. It can be hard to return home. I don't think I'm ready to return to Happdal either. People see me in a certain way there, and expect me to behave the way they are used to. But I've changed. And I don't want to spend my life making other people comfortable: my mother, my brother Trond and *his* family, Jense and the other town elders."

"Would they be upset that you're in a relationship with a woman?"

"No, they wouldn't care about that. Elke has enough grandchildren already. But still, they would want to know everything about you. In a village as small as Happdal, everyone knows everything about everybody."

"I know exactly what you mean. Bosa is the same way. And even more so within the Crucible, when I was maghiarja. I never had a moment when I was truly alone."

"So, where should we go? Earth is a vast planet. We could explore."

"The *Liu Hui* has a settlement near what used to be China – we could visit there."

"Or we could borrow a hovershuttle and camping gear – and just explore anywhere we wanted. A great adventure. The scientists on the *Stanford* are always eager for more researchers – I'm sure they would be happy to supply us with whatever we need. Car-En could help us get started."

Jana silently considered Katja's proposal. What would it be like to be so far away from people for so long a time? To see places that no one else had seen for centuries?

She took Katja's hand. "I like that idea very much."

CHAPTER FORTY-TWO

Jana relaxed in the private bath in Maro's *domus*, luxuriating not only in her surroundings, but in the tanned, toned limbs of Maro's body. It was a fine body, though having male genitalia was a new experience. Her cock appeared to have a mind of its own, not always related to her thoughts. Was that universally a part of the male experience? Or was it an artifact of her strange architecture, being part Jana, part Maro, part Crucible? Maro was still using his own brain, after all, albeit trapped in Itria's virtual recreation of the *Michelangelo*. But that brain was just as connected to Maro's actual cock as was the Crucible that contained the operating facsimile of Jana's mind. And Jana *was* using at least part of Maro's actual brain to understand and speak Latin, thanks to some creative programming from Itria. It was all quite confusing.

Jana wondered what the other Jana was doing. Had her original self returned to Bosa? Had she reunited with Katja? She missed the Happdal woman sorely, and in a way it was even worse that Katja was not missing her at all. She longed to see her father was well, and Filumena, and Antonio, and even Cristo.

Perhaps she would return one day. She was, after all, a powerful senator. She could commandeer a shuttle, visit Bosa, and make peace with the townsfolk. Perhaps she could even befriend her father as Maro, though she would not reveal her secret. That would unnecessarily complicate the life of the other Jana.

She had her own life to live now, as the new Maro. It would be complicated, no doubt, but she had both Cassia and her consorteria to guide her. Cassia was becoming a friend as well; the large woman told her outrageous stories and shared her encyclopedic knowledge of Earth history. And within the Crucible she was becoming friends with the other women, who had actually lived through some of that history, and each had their own unique perspective.

Jana received a message in her optic feed. With some difficulty, focussing on icons within her field of vision, she managed to open and read it. The Engineers had successfully managed to scan the brain of the frozen ferret Cassia had discovered in the wine cellar. They had recreated it as a cybrid. Would Maro like to have the new Faustus delivered to his *domus*?

"Yes," Jana replied, and to her relief the message transcribed automatically. "As soon as possible." Hopefully the pet would not realize Maro had changed. It would be nice to have an affectionate friend that did not question or care about her identity.

Jana closed her eyes and shifted her consciousness to Crucible Bosa. As she walked along a cobblestone street in the early morning, several human-faced *squasc* chirped at her, swishing their bushy tails, before scurrying off into an alley.

"There you are," she said, spotting Itria at an outdoor table with a mug of hot tea. "I've been looking for you."

"I've been resting," Itria said. "Recreating the *Michelangelo* was no small feat."

"Has Maro figured it out yet?"

"I think he's suspicious, but his hubris blinds him. To him it's perfectly probable that he would become emperor, that the world would bend to his every whim."

"But he's intelligent – surely he'll realize what has happened?"

"Eventually, yes. There are limits to the simulation."

Jana sat in the empty chair across from Itria, who met Jana's eyes with a direct stare. Those dark eyes, with large irises and almost no visible whites, had seen the fall of civilization. Itria, as a physical host, had helped evacuate hundreds of people from Naples and surrounding areas before the eruption of Campi Flegrei. Thousands had died in the cauldron's multiple massive eruptions, millions in the global winter that had followed, hundreds of millions with the collapse of global infrastructure and trade that had destroyed agricultural and industrial systems in the decades following. Itria had witnessed it all.

"Is there any hope for Maro?" Jana asked. "Sperancia thinks he can be rehabilitated. But I don't see how he's ever going to change."

Itria shrugged. "Perhaps. Eventually the Crucible will copy every cell and connection in his brain. Once his neurological architecture is fully replicated, we can tweak it."

"Tweak it how? Make him more empathetic?"

"We could modulate the expression of certain genes. We could increase the neuroplasticity of his virtual brain. There are many options."

"Would that be ethical?"

"We'll have to discuss it as a group. But if we were to permit Maro to host without altering his personality significantly, to grant him power within our shared simulation—"

"That would be suicidal."

Itria nodded. "Do you feel bad for him? Are you regretting our decision to trap him?"

Jana considered the question before answering. Maybe part of her did feel guilty. But when she weighed what Maro had done to Filumena and Cristo, and all the other people he might have violated or trampled, the decision still made sense.

"I can live with the guilt," she finally answered.

"So can I," Itria agreed.

★ ★ ★

Jana dressed Maro's body in a simple white tunic and prepared a meal from the pantry: dried fruits, cured meats (though she doubted the meat came from animals), and a loaf of fresh bread that a spiderlike robot had delivered to her door.

Livia arrived only a few minutes late, wearing a low-cut tunic that revealed both cleavage and strong shoulder muscles. Maro's lover moved like a cat, gliding toward Jana, head level with predatory intensity. Had Livia come to kill her? She was certainly capable of it. Cassia had warned her that Livia was dangerous.

Jana managed to resist the urge to flinch. Livia kissed her lightly on both cheeks.

"You look well, Maro. I see that you managed to dress yourself without Aina's help. And prepare a meal, no less. I'm surprised you let her leave."

"Cybrids are citizens now. Her decisions are her own."

"I hear you didn't put up much of a fight in the Senate. Some are saying that you've switched sides. Your fellow *optimates* are furious."

"The Bohm upgrade is more significant than I initially understood."

Livia smiled and popped a small date into her mouth. Jana filled a cup with wine and reclined on a *triclinium*, doing her best to appear relaxed and unbothered.

"So what's your agenda?" Livia asked. "How will this new Maro influence the Senate, if not as emperor? Are we really joining that stupid Coalition?"

"It only strengthens us. We've been isolationists for long enough. And as the discovery of the *Iarudi* proved, we fell behind in certain areas." Cassia had coached her on such matters: the political landscape, Maro's new philosophy, how to approach the repopulation of Earth.

Livia gave her a bemused look. "You needn't pretend with me."

"What?"

Livia stood, and with a single smooth motion lifted her tunic and drew a gleaming gold blade from a scabbard strapped to her thigh. "I should have killed you when I had the chance, the same night you killed Felix. I loved him, you know."

"I don't know what you're talking about. I miss Felix too."

Livia straddled her and pushed the flat of the blade against her throat. Jana's neck and chest tingled with a sensation that was close to pain.

"I know who you are," Livia said through clenched teeth. "Did you think I wouldn't notice that Cassia is playing nice with you, despite the fact that Maro tried to kill her? The question is, what are you worth to me? I pretended to love Maro because it was convenient for me to be close to a senator. His power rubbed off on me in a way that I enjoyed. But what use are you?"

It made no sense to continue bluffing. With a flick of Livia's wrist she would be dead.

"I'm still a senator. And you needn't pretend to love me."

Slowly, Livia pulled the blade away from Jana's neck, and with her fingertips stroked Jana's cheek. With horror she realized that Maro's body was responding to being straddled.

Livia cocked her head. "You like this, then? You *are* just as handsome as ever."

She kissed Jana, gently at first, and then more passionately, using her tongue and teeth.

"How did you know?" Jana whispered.

Livia sat up, still straddling Jana. "Maro told me what he was planning.

He explained how the Crucible works. He was so confident he would be able to dominate you all. But he failed, didn't he? Did you kill him?"

"No. Maro is still alive. He's trapped in a world that he believes is real. He'll be there for a long time, I think."

"I knew something had gone wrong after the Senate vote. Joining the Coalition? Cybrids as citizens? That isn't the Maro I know."

"I'm sorry about Felix," Jana said. "That was Sperancia's decision, not mine."

"But you are part Sperancia, aren't you? Isn't that how the Crucible works?"

"Not right now. Sperancia can hear us. But you were right, I'm Jana."

Livia smiled wryly. "Jana the body thief. I would never have guessed you were capable of it, that first day I met you in Bosa."

They stared at each other. Jana guessed there was still a possibility that Livia would murder her, but she didn't feel scared. Maro's life was also at stake, and Livia appeared to understand that.

"Hmm, you're braver than Maro, aren't you? Interesting."

"Maybe we can get to know one another," Jana suggested. "Maybe we can help each other."

Livia kissed her again, and though Maro's body continued to respond, Jana pushed her away. Livia wasn't trustworthy. Most likely she was sociopathic.

"I am not your lover," Jana said. "I'm willing to get to know you, but not like this."

Livia shrugged, looking not at all surprised. "It was worth a try. You can't blame me for still wanting him."

"But I'm not him, as you've just pointed out."

Livia's face hardened. "You'll want me as an ally. I can make your life – whatever is left of it – extremely difficult. Or I can help you get what you want." Livia took a cup from the serving table and filled it with wine. "What *is* it that you want, *Jana*?"

What did she want? She'd rescued Filumena and Cristo. With the help of her consorteria, she'd outwitted Maro and effectively imprisoned him. She'd possibly prevented a war.

And it had felt good to do those things. To fight for what she believed in, and succeed.

"I want to bring the *Michelangelo* closer to the other ringstations. I want our artistic and historical treasures to be shared with everyone, as was originally promised."

Livia sipped her wine. "Ambitious. But not impossible. You are an influential senator, after all."

Life on the *Michelangelo* was going to be exciting. And possibly quite dangerous; she did not trust Livia, and Maro had many enemies. But she had an entire life ahead of her. She had wealth and power to wield.

She thought of the other Jana, living out her life in Bosa or wherever she was. That was no longer *her* now, but just another person who shared her name and most of her memories. She wished the best for that person, and would help her in any way she could if their paths ever crossed. But their lives had completely diverged.

She lifted her own cup and raised it to Livia. "To the *Michelangelo*, and what we may accomplish."

Livia, looking vaguely surprised, raised her cup in return. "To the *Michelangelo*, and its fine senator Maro Decimus. Whoever that may now be."

CHAPTER FORTY-THREE

Tem was filthy, and his back ached. The rich soil around Ilium yielded to his shovel, but the trench he and Shane had been tasked with digging was intended to be a meter deep and ten meters long. So far all they had for their efforts was a shallow hole.

"I thought the Hair Lab on the *Stanford* built a digging machine," Shane said, wiping his brow. "Some kind of excavator?"

"They did," said Tem, "but it keeps breaking down. And so do the replacement parts we keep printing."

"Is there any iron ore around here? Maybe you need to set up a good old-fashioned smithy and forge the parts."

Tem looked at the titanium head of his shovel. The tool had been manufactured on the *Stanford*, as had so many of the objects they depended on for daily life. Ilium was legally independent, but not functionally. If the ringships were ever to cut them off entirely, their quality of life would degrade within weeks.

"There isn't, as far as I know. But even if there was, building my own forge wouldn't be very efficient. It would make more sense to take a hovershuttle to Happdal and work at my uncle's smithy, or my grandfather's." Or even go to Kaldbrek, he thought, and work in Saga's smithy. It would be an excuse to visit his ex-lover, and eventually to meet the baby that might be his son or daughter.

"I would happily go with you," Shane said. "I once had a mission in the Harz mountains with Lydia. She recognized Car-En when your mother was a prisoner in Kaldbrek, and helped her escape. Did Car-En ever tell you that story?"

"I was there – a prisoner in Völund's basement. But no, I didn't know that Lydia helped my mother. Neither of them ever told me that." What he did remember from that night was Esper slitting Völund's throat, and the look on Saga's face as she watched her uncle bleed out. That image would forever haunt him. And how would he tell his father, if Saga did turn out to be carrying his child? Once Saga had attacked Esper in a vengeful rage, stopped only by Car-En intervening. Not exactly a good start to a harmonious family relationship.

"Back to work," Shane said. "This trench isn't going to dig itself."

Shane was recovering quickly from his time in stasis. He'd regained most of the weight he'd lost and had a tan from working outside. He still took frequent breaks and couldn't walk very far without sitting down, but Maggie said he was making great strides in his rehabilitation.

The trench grew, slowly but surely, but Tem was relieved when he heard a commotion from the common area.

Shane tossed his shovel aside, grinning. "Sounds like they're back. Let's go say hello."

"Should we wash up first?"

"Probably a good idea. You look like some kind of mud monster."

"So do you."

By the time both men had showered and dressed, Lydia and Maggie were already telling stories of their time in Ilium. Someone had made a huge pitcher of fresh lemonade, and snacks were set out on the outdoor communal tables.

"Pietro is doing great," Lydia said. "He still trips a lot, but only because he runs everywhere. He refuses to slow down." She was sitting on a bench next to Shane at one of the long tables, facing a small group that had gathered to hear stories and news. Shane held her hand, grinning with shameless delight. The two had reunited with intense joy that had almost immediately sparked into a relationship, Shane flirting even before he could properly walk. Neither seemed to care about the age difference. Lydia, though she appeared older, was more physically fit and mobile than Shane, at least at this stage of his recovery.

"Cristo and Filumena are both recovering as well," said Maggie. "They've struck up a close friendship. We're treating them both for PTSD."

"What about Aina?" Tem asked. Katja and Jana had told him about the cybrid before leaving on their exploration adventure. "Is she still there?"

"She is," Maggie said. "The Bosa townsfolk have accepted her as one of their own. In some ways she has become their new maghiarja – I've heard some of them refer to her that way. Aina has enormous physical strength and access to all the knowledge and information resources of the *Michelangelo*. She even assisted us with some of the medical procedures we performed. Honestly I don't know if they're going to need our help in the long term."

The lemonade and snacks were all consumed, replaced with platters of grilled vegetables and bottles of Ilium wine – an outdoor dinner for whoever wanted to join. Food was plentiful in Ilium; it was easy to grow a wide variety of crops in the volcanically enriched soil. And the wine from Xenus's vineyard was getting better every year.

"Want to take a walk with me?" Tem asked Maggie after he'd helped clear the table. "I've completed my work shifts for the day – I'm all yours unless you have other plans."

"How's that trench coming along?"

"Very slowly."

"A walk sounds nice. Let's take a stroll through the olive orchard."

He and Maggie were still together. To Tem's relief the botanist Roland – Maggie's 'other man' – was by all appearances in a committed relationship with another Ilium woman. And yet Tem still sometimes felt awkward around Maggie, as if he were walking on eggshells.

Maggie told him more about Bosa, including the drama around Aina, who was more sexually active and free than anyone in the town was accustomed to. One of the men she had slept with had gotten so jealous of her other partners that he'd attempted to assault her, perhaps not realizing her strength. That had not gone well for him, but Aina had been gentle, merely immobilizing the man for a humiliating half hour.

As Shane had recommended months ago, Tem had confessed his love to Maggie. She'd told him she loved him too, though her response had seemed lukewarm to him, filled with ambivalence. But she hadn't left him, and she didn't appear to be angry about what had happened with Saga.

The first stars appeared in the clear sky as they walked along the edge of the olive orchard. Tem shared his feelings, that he'd sensed some distance between them. Maggie heard him out without interrupting, and was silent for what felt like an eternity before finally responding.

"Tem, please don't take this the wrong way, but it sounds like you're asking for stability and reassurance. But you're the one who hasn't put down roots. I was born in Ilium and I'm happy to live here my whole life. This is my home."

"It's my home too."

"For now. But for how long? You're still a member of the Repopulation

Council. I don't want to live on the *Stanford*, or in a village in the Harz mountains, or anywhere but here. I like visiting other places, but I know where I belong. And that's in Ilium."

"I never asked you to leave."

"No, but you've brought it up, the possibility of us living in Happdal. You've told me how much your grandmother liked me. And you might have a child in the neighboring village."

Tem kicked a small rock, sending it skittering up the trail. Everything Maggie was saying was true.

"If you've sensed any ambivalence on my part, it's not because I don't love you. It's because I don't know if you're going to stick around. In your heart, I don't know if you're ready to settle down. I don't know if you'll ever be ready."

"You think I'm a permanent nomad?"

"Maybe? You like to seek out adventure."

"When I was little, all I dreamed of was working in my uncle's smithy and living in Happdal for the rest of my life. But everyone said my arms were like twigs."

"Well, you're a halfway decent smith now, from the pieces you've shown me."

"Thanks. I might take a stab at forging a replacement part for the excavator."

"Don't want to spend your day digging ditches by hand?"

"Not really."

Maggie was right – he'd been seeking reassurance. And he'd received it, in a way. It made sense why she felt the way she did, and was holding a part of herself back. Tem was committed to Maggie, but not necessarily to Ilium.

"Tem, if you need to explore the world and figure out what you want to do with your life, I won't hold it against you. Same goes if you need to move to Kaldbrek to be close to your child. I won't make any promises, but we can take it day by day."

The sky was bright with stars, the crescent moon, and the faintly glowing ringships. Now that he'd visited the *Liu Hui*, Tem wondered what life was like on the *Alhazen* and the *Hedonark*. And what about the new ringship settlements on Earth? Some of them dwarfed Ilium in scope and ambition.

Tem sighed. "I get it – Ilium is your home. But will you travel with me? There are so many places to see."

She took his hand. "Of course I will. But not for months at a time. There are people here that depend on me."

"Weeks, then? Lydia can handle Ilium's medical needs for a few weeks, can't she?"

"Maybe. She's pretty distracted by Shane these days."

Slowly they strolled back home. Maggie had held up a mirror to his psyche, and he was still getting used to the reflection. Why was it so hard to understand the most basic things about oneself that were so obvious to everyone else?

Maybe that was just part of growing up.

CHAPTER FORTY-FOUR

Jana and Katja flew the hovershuttle, heavy with provisions, east across the Po Valley, following the Ligurian Apennines. They passed through the ruins of ancient Italian towns that had resisted the ravages of time, many of their stone buildings and walls still standing. Why had Bosa survived, while these places were inhabited only by rodents, bats, and packs of wild dogs? They saw wolves and bears as well, who regarded them with wary curiosity, but only the packs of dogs scared them. The dogs approached them fearlessly, tongues hanging out, brazenly considering them as a possible meal.

They soon reached the Adriatic coast, and turned north, toward an area the hovershuttle map indicated had once been the city of Venice. Katja, reading from the display, explained that the city had once featured a network of canals. But when they reached the place, they found that many of the channels were dry. The Venetian Lagoon had been partially drained by the falling sea levels, the water sucked up into the glacial fields that covered the far north and far south of the planet, just as Sperancia had explained to her so long ago. Though in the deeper canals they were greeted by dolphins, who followed the hovershuttle, chirping with curiosity.

Katja wanted to explore the snow-capped Alps. She reasoned that groups of people might be inhabiting the many valleys of the great mountain range, just as her own ancestors had settled in the Harz mountains. To Jana it made more sense that people would live by the sea where fish were plentiful, but that was her own bias. Ultimately she agreed to Katja's suggestion; the craggy peaks beckoned to her for reasons she could not explain.

They headed north-east, crossing into what had once been the nation of Slovenia, according to the hovershuttle's historical map. The weather cooled as they navigated a maze of ancient overgrown roads weaving through valleys, but the lightweight clothing Car-En had provided kept them warm and dry. They ate travel rations, sweet dense bars that tasted vaguely like fruitcake, and drank water from streams after filtering it. They slept on the folded-down bench seats of the hovershuttle, spooning each other for warmth and comfort. Jana awoke each day feeling sore but happy, and excited to continue their explorations.

They climbed north, easily fueling the hovershuttle with plant biomass, dead leaves, and fallen fruit. As the peaks loomed higher, Jana pointed to a large alpine lake on the map. "Let's go there. If nothing else it will be beautiful to look at. And here – the map says it was once a pilgrimage site." She could not read as well as Katja but the map tried to help her, switching to Italian text when she looked at it.

Katja piloted the hovershuttle with fearless confidence, and Jana had become accustomed to the breakneck speeds with which Katja flew the craft through valleys, over forests, and across rivers. But her jaw dropped when she saw the lake, a smooth turquoise expanse surrounded by trees, with high white cliffs rising above the northern bank. In the middle of the lake was an island. A lone stone spire rose out of the trees.

"That's the pilgrimage site," Jana said. "The Assumption of Maria."

"I don't know who that is," said Katja, squinting in the noon light. "But look, across the lake." She pointed. "Atop the cliff."

Katja's vision was sharper, but Jana was already reaching for the binoculars Car-En had given them. Perched on the cliff was a castle of white stone walls and remnants of what had once been a red tile roof. Sections of the roof had been repaired with raw timber. Zooming in, Jana noted that the level of craftsmanship was respectable, and that the repairs were relatively recent. As she panned across the roofline something caught her eye, nearly causing her to drop the binoculars. Refocussing, she confirmed that she had really seen what she'd thought she'd seen.

"What is it?" Katja asked.

"Look for yourself."

There was a thin column of smoke rising from somewhere inside the castle, perhaps the interior courtyard.

"Well, shall we go meet them?" Katja asked.

"How will we communicate?"

"We speak three languages between the two of us. They're bound to speak at least one of those, whoever they are."

Jana was fairly sure Katja was incorrect, but she smiled. Katja's confidence was contagious.

"Okay, let's go meet them. If this lake is full of fish, they're well-fed and won't try to eat us."

Katja tilted the hovershuttle forward and revved the main rotor. Jana's heart pounded in her chest.

FLAME TREE PRESS
FICTION WITHOUT FRONTIERS
Award-Winning Authors & Original Voices

Flame Tree Press is the trade fiction imprint of Flame Tree Publishing, focusing on excellent writing in horror and the supernatural, crime and mystery, science fiction and fantasy. Our aim is to explore beyond the boundaries of the everyday, with tales from both award-winning authors and original voices.

•

Other titles in J.D. Moyer's *Reclaimed Earth* series:
The Sky Woman
The Guardian

You may also enjoy:
The Sentient by Nadia Afifi
Junction by Daniel M. Bensen
Interchange by Daniel M. Bensen
American Dreams by Kenneth Bromberg
Second Lives by P.D. Cacek
The City Among the Stars by Francis Carsac
Vulcan's Forge by Robert Mitchell Evans
The Widening Gyre by Michael R. Johnston
The Blood-Dimmed Tide by Michael R. Johnston
The Goblets Immortal by Beth Overmyer
The Apocalypse Strain by Jason Parent
The Gemini Experiment by Brian Pinkerton
The Nirvana Effect by Brian Pinkerton
A Killing Fire by Faye Snowden
Fearless by Allen Stroud
The Bad Neighbor by David Tallerman
A Savage Generation by David Tallerman
Screams from the Void by Anne Tibbets
Ten Thousand Thunders by Brian Trent
Two Lives: Tales of Life, Love & Crime by A Yi

•

Join our mailing list for free short stories, new release details, news about our authors and special promotions:

flametreepress.com